The Cheese Makers Actuary

Hawker, J. C. [from old catalog]

THE
Cheese
Makers
ACTUARY.

A Rapid Calculator adapted
especially to the wants of the
Cheesemaker.

BY J. C. HAWKER.

FIRST EDITION.

J. C. HAWKER, Publisher.
FOREST JCT., WIS.

INTRODUCTION.

In presenting this book to the trade, will say that we consider it to be the most practical work of its kind ever published, and therefor it will be found to be of great convenience and vast benefit to every cheesemaker and to all those upon whom devolves the computation of the patrons accounts.

It shows at a glance the value of from 1 to 4000 pounds of milk, at from 30 cents up to $1,30, by steps of ¼ of a cent, thus giving the value of any given number of pound of milk in four hundred diffirent prices.

No mathematical calculation is necessary, as the tables are so arranged that any person, by looking at the head of page to find the given price, and at the side for the number of pounds wanted, can tell the value of same at once.

These tables are accurate and can be relied upon, and will give universal satisfaction as they preclude all possibility of mistakes, besides doing away with the necessity of computing the value of the same number of pounds of milk a dozen or a hundred times in each season as is very often the case under the old process.

30 cts.		30¼ cts.		30½ cts.		30¾ cts.	
Lbs.	Amt.	Lbs.	Amt.	Lbs.	Amt.	Lbs.	Amt.
1	$ .00	1	$ .00	1	$ .00	1	$ .00
2	.00	2	.00	2	.00	2	.00
3	.00	3	.00	3	.00	3	.00
4	.01	4	.01	4	.01	4	.01
5	.01	5	.01	5	.01	5	.01
6	.01	6	.01	6	.01	6	.01
7	.02	7	.02	7	.02	7	.02
8	.02	8	.02	8	.02	8	.02
9	.02	9	.02	9	.02	9	.02
10	.03	10	.03	10	.03	10	.03
20	.06	20	.05	20	.06	20	.06
30	.09	30	.09	30	.09	30	.09
40	.12	40	.12	40	.12	40	.12
50	.15	50	.15	50	.15	50	.15
60	.18	60	.18	60	.18	60	.18
70	.21	70	.21	70	.21	70	.21
80	.24	80	.24	80	.24	80	.24
90	.27	90	.27	90	.27	90	.27
100	.30	100	.30	100	.30	100	.30
200	.60	200	.60	200	.61	200	.61
300	.90	300	.90	300	.91	300	.92
400	1.20	400	1.21	400	1.22	400	1.23
500	1.50	500	1.51	500	1.52	500	1.53
600	1.80	600	1.81	600	1.83	600	1.84
700	2.10	700	2.11	700	2.13	700	2.15
800	2.40	800	2.42	800	2.44	800	2.46
900	2.70	900	2.72	900	2.74	900	2.76
1000	3.00	1000	3.02	1000	3.05	1000	3.07
1100	3.30	1100	3.32	1100	3.35	1100	3.38
1200	3.60	1200	3.63	1200	3.66	1200	3.69
1300	3.90	1300	3.93	1300	3.96	1300	3.99
1400	4.20	1400	4.23	1400	4.27	1400	4.30
1500	4.50	1500	4.53	1500	4.57	1500	4.61
1600	4.80	1600	4.84	1600	4.88	1600	4.92
1700	5.10	1700	5.14	1700	5.18	1700	5.22
1800	5.40	1800	5.44	1800	5.49	1800	5.53
1900	5.70	1900	5.74	1900	5.79	1900	5.84
2000	6.00	2000	6.05	2000	6.10	2000	6.15
2100	6.30	2100	6.35	2100	6.40	2100	6.45
2200	6.60	2200	6.65	2200	6.71	2200	6.76
2300	6.90	2300	6.95	2300	7.01	2300	7.07
2400	7.20	2400	7.26	2400	7.32	2400	7.38
2500	7.50	2500	7.56	2500	7.62	2500	7.68
2600	7.80	2600	7.86	2600	7.93	2600	7.99
2700	8.10	2700	8.16	2700	8.23	2700	8.30
2800	8.40	2800	8.47	2800	8.54	2800	8.61
2900	8.70	2900	8.77	2900	8.84	2900	8.91
3000	9.00	3000	9.07	3000	9.15	3000	9.22
3100	9.30	3100	9.37	3100	9.45	3100	9.53
3200	9.60	3200	9.68	3200	9.76	3200	9.84
3300	9.90	3300	9.98	3300	10.06	3300	10.14
3400	10.20	3400	10.28	3400	10.37	3400	10.45
3500	10.50	3500	10.58	3500	10.67	3500	10.76
3600	10.80	3600	10.89	3600	10.98	3600	11.07
3700	11.10	3700	11.19	3700	11.28	3700	11.37
3800	11.40	3800	11.49	3800	11.58	3800	11.68
3900	11.70	3900	11.79	3900	11.89	3900	11.99
4000	12.00	4000	12.10	4000	12.20	4000	12.30

31 cts.		31¼ cts.		31½ cts.		31¾ cts.	
Lbs.	Amt.	Lbs.	Amt.	Lbs.	Amt.	Lbs.	Amt.
1	$ .00	1	$ .00	1	$ .00	1	$ .00
2	.00	2	.00	2	.00	2	.00
3	.00	3	.00	3	.00	3	.00
4	.01	4	.01	4	.01	4	.01
5	.01	5	.01	5	.01	5	.01
6	.01	6	.01	6	.01	6	.01
7	.02	7	.02	7	.02	7	.02
8	.02	8	.02	8	.02	8	.02
9	.02	9	.02	9	.02	9	.02
10	.03	10	.03	10	.03	10	.03
20	.06	20	.06	20	.06	20	.06
30	.09	30	.09	30	.09	30	.09
40	.12	40	.12	40	.12	40	.12
50	.15	50	.15	50	.15	50	.15
60	.18	60	.18	60	.18	60	.19
70	.21	70	.21	70	.22	70	.22
80	.24	80	.25	80	.25	80	.25
90	.27	90	.28	90	.28	90	.28
100	.31	100	.31	100	.31	100	.31
200	.62	200	.62	200	.63	200	.63
300	.93	300	.93	300	.94	300	.95
400	1.24	400	1.25	400	1.26	400	1.27
500	1.55	500	1.56	500	1.57	500	1.58
600	1.86	600	1.87	600	1.89	600	1.90
700	2.17	700	2.18	700	2.20	700	2.22
800	2.48	800	2.50	800	2.52	800	2.54
900	2.79	900	2.81	900	2.83	900	2.85
1000	3.10	1000	3.12	1000	3.15	1000	3.17
1100	3.41	1100	3.43	1100	3.46	1100	3.49
1200	3.72	1200	3.75	1200	3.78	1200	3.81
1300	4.03	1300	4.06	1300	4.09	1300	4.12
1400	4.34	1400	4.37	1400	4.41	1400	4.44
1500	4.65	1500	4.68	1500	4.72	1500	4.76
1600	4.96	1600	5.00	1600	5.04	1600	5.08
1700	5.27	1700	5.31	1700	5.35	1700	5.39
1800	5.58	1800	5.62	1800	5.67	1800	5.71
1900	5.89	1900	5.93	1900	5.98	1900	6.03
2000	6.20	2000	6.25	2000	6.30	2000	6.35
2100	6.51	2100	6.56	2100	6.61	2100	6.66
2200	6.82	2200	6.87	2200	6.93	2200	6.98
2300	7.13	2300	7.18	2300	7.24	2300	7.30
2400	7.44	2400	7.50	2400	7.56	2400	7.62
2500	7.75	2500	7.81	2500	7.87	2500	7.93
2600	8.06	2600	8.12	2600	8.19	2600	8.25
2700	8.37	2700	8.43	2700	8.50	2700	8.57
2800	8.68	2800	8.75	2800	8.82	2800	8.89
2900	8.99	2900	9.06	2900	9.13	2900	9.20
3000	9.30	3000	9.37	3000	9.45	3000	9.52
3100	9.61	3100	9.68	3100	9.76	3100	9.84
3200	9.92	3200	10.00	3200	10.08	3200	10.16
3300	10.23	3300	10.31	3300	10.39	3300	10.47
3400	10.54	3400	10.62	3400	10.71	3400	10.79
3500	10.85	3500	10.93	3500	11.02	3500	11.11
3600	11.16	3600	11.25	3600	11.34	3600	11.43
3700	11.47	3700	11.56	3700	11.65	3700	11.74
3800	11.78	3800	11.87	3800	11.97	3800	12.06
3900	12.09	3900	12.18	3900	12.28	3900	12.38
4000	12.40	4000	12.50	4000	12.60	4000	12.70

32 cts.		32¼ cts.		32½ cts.		32¾ cts.	
Lbs.	Amt.	Lbs.	Amt.	Lbs.	Amt.	Lbs.	Amt.
1	$ .00	1	$ .00	1	$ .00	1	$ .00
2	.00	2	.00	2	.00	2	.00
3	.00	3	.00	3	.00	3	.00
4	.01	4	.01	4	.01	4	.01
5	.01	5	.01	5	.01	5	.01
6	.01	6	.01	6	.01	6	.01
7	.02	7	.02	7	.02	7	.02
8	.02	8	.02	8	.02	8	.02
9	.02	9	.02	9	.02	9	.02
10	.03	10	.03	10	.03	10	.03
20	.06	20	.06	20	.06	20	.06
30	.09	30	.09	30	.09	30	.09
40	.12	40	.12	40	.13	40	.13
50	.16	50	.16	50	.16	50	.16
60	.19	60	.19	60	.19	60	.19
70	.22	70	.22	70	.22	70	.22
80	.25	80	.25	80	.26	80	.26
90	.28	90	.29	90	.29	90	.29
100	.32	100	.32	100	.32	100	.32
200	.64	200	.64	200	.65	200	.65
300	.96	300	.96	300	.97	300	.98
400	1.28	400	1.29	400	1.30	400	1.31
500	1.60	500	1.61	500	1.62	500	1.63
600	1.92	600	1.93	600	1.95	600	1.96
700	2.24	700	2.25	700	2.27	700	2.29
800	2.56	800	2.58	800	2.60	800	2.62
900	2.88	900	2.90	900	2.92	900	2.94
1000	3.20	1000	3.22	1000	3.25	1000	3.47
1100	3.52	1100	3.54	1100	3.57	1100	3.60
1200	3.84	1200	3.87	1200	3.90	1200	3.93
1300	4.16	1300	4.19	1300	4.22	1300	4.25
1400	4.48	1400	4.51	1400	4.55	1400	4.58
1500	4.80	1500	4.83	1500	4.87	1500	4.91
1600	5.12	1600	5.16	1600	5.20	1600	5.24
1700	5.44	1700	5.48	1700	5.52	1700	5.56
1800	5.76	1800	5.80	1800	5.85	1800	5.89
1900	6.08	1900	6.12	1900	6.17	1900	6.22
2000	6.40	2000	6.45	2000	6.50	2000	6.55
2100	6.72	2100	6.77	2100	6.82	2100	6.87
2200	7.04	2200	7.09	2200	7.15	2200	7.20
2300	7.36	2300	7.41	2300	7.47	2300	7.53
2400	7.68	2400	7.74	2400	7.80	2400	7.86
2500	8.00	2500	8.06	2500	8.12	2500	8.18
2600	8.32	2600	8.38	2600	8.45	2600	8·51
2700	8.64	2700	8.70	2700	8.77	2700	8.84
2800	8.96	2800	9.03	2800	9.10	2800	9.17
2900	9.28	2900	9.35	2900	9.42	2900	9.49
3000	9.60	3000	9.67	3000	9.75	3000	9.82
3100	9.92	3100	9.99	3100	10.07	3100	10.15
3200	10.24	3200	10.32	3200	10.40	3200	10.48
3300	10.56	3300	10.64	3300	10.72	3300	10.80
3400	10.88	3400	10.96	3400	11.05	3400	11.13
3500	11.20	3500	11.28	3500	11.37	3500	11.46
3600	11.52	3600	11.61	3600	11.70	3600	11.79
3700	11.84	3700	11.93	3700	12.02	3700	12.11
3800	12.16	3800	12.25	3800	12.35	3800	12.44
3900	12.48	3900	12.57	3900	12.67	3900	12.77
4000	12.80	4000	12.90	4000	13.00	4000	13.10

33 cts.		33¼ cts.		33½ cts.		33¾ cts.	
Lbs.	Amt.	Lbs.	Amt.	Lbs.	Amt.	Lbs.	Amt.
1	$ .00	1	$ .00	1	$,00	1	$ .00
2	.00	2	.00	2	,00	2	.00
3	.00	3	.00	3	,00	3	.00
4	.01	4	.01	4	,01	4	.01
5	.01	5	.01	5	,01	5	.01
6	.01	6	.01	6	,01	6	.02
7	.02	7	.02	7	,02	7	.02
8	.02	8	.02	8	,02	8	.02
9	.02	9	.02	9	,02	9	.03
10	.03	10	.03	10	,03	10	.03
20	.06	20	.06	20	,06	20	.06
30	.09	30	.09	30	,10	30	.10
40	.13	40	.13	40	,13	40	.13
50	.16	50	.16	50	,16	50	.16
60	.19	60	.19	60	,20	60	.20
70	.23	70	.23	70	,23	70	.23
80	.26	80	.26	80	,26	80	.27
90	.29	90	.29	90	,30	90	.30
100	.33	100	.33	100	,33	100	.33
200	.66	200	.66	200	,67	200	.67
300	.99	300	.99	300	1,00	300	1.01
400	1.32	400	1.33	400	1,34	400	1.35
500	1.65	500	1.66	500	1,67	500	1.68
600	1.98	600	1.99	600	2,01	600	2.02
700	2.31	700	2.32	700	2,34	700	2.36
800	2.64	800	2.66	800	2,68	800	2.70
900	2.97	900	2.99	900	3,01	900	3.03
1000	3.30	1000	3.32	1000	3,35	1000	3.37
1100	3.63	1100	3.65	1100	3,68	1100	3.71
1200	3.96	1200	3.99	1200	4,02	1200	4.05
1300	4.29	1300	4.32	1300	4,35	1300	4.38
1400	4.62	1400	4.65	1400	4,69	1400	4.72
1500	4.95	1500	4.98	1500	5,02	1500	5.06
1600	5.28	1600	5.32	1600	5,36	1600	5.40
1700	5.61	1700	5.65	1700	5,69	1700	5.73
1800	5.94	1800	5.98	1800	6,03	1800	6.07
1900	6.27	1900	6.31	1900	6,36	1900	6.41
2000	6.60	2000	6.65	2000	6,70	2000	6.75
2100	6.93	2100	6.98	2100	7,03	2100	7.08
2200	7.26	2200	7.31	2200	7,37	2200	7.42
2300	7.59	2300	7.64	2300	7,70	2300	7.76
2400	7.92	2400	7.98	2400	8,04	2400	8.10
2500	8.25	2500	8.31	2500	8,37	2500	8.43
2600	8.58	2600	8.64	2600	8,71	2600	8.77
2700	8.91	2700	8.97	2700	9,04	2700	9.11
2800	9.24	2800	9.31	2800	9,38	2800	9.45
2900	9.57	2900	9.64	2900	9,71	2900	9.78
3000	9.90	3000	9.97	3000	10,05	3000	10.12
3100	10.23	3100	10.30	3100	10,38	3100	10.46
3200	10.56	3200	10.64	3200	10,72	3200	10.80
3300	10.89	3300	10.97	3300	11,05	3300	11.13
3400	11.22	3400	11.30	3400	11,39	3400	11.47
3500	11.55	3500	11.63	3500	11,72	3500	11.81
3600	11.88	3600	11.97	3600	12,05	3600	12.15
3700	12.21	3700	12.30	3700	12,39	3700	12.48
3800	12.54	3800	12.63	3800	12,73	3800	12.82
3900	12.87	3900	12.96	3900	13,06	3900	13.16
4000	13.20	4000	13.30	4000	13,40	4000	13.50

34 cts.		34¼ cts.		34½ cts.		34¾ cts.	
Lbs.	Amt.	Lbs.	Amt.	Lbs.	Amt.	Lbs.	Amt.
1	$ .00	1	$ .00	1	$ .00	1	$ .00
2	.00	2	.00	2	.00	2	.00
3	.01	3	.01	3	.01	3	.01
4	.01	4	.01	4	.01	4	.01
5	.01	5	.01	5	.01	5	.01
6	.02	6	.02	6	.02	6	.02
7	.02	7	.02	7	.02	7	.02
8	.02	8	.02	8	.02	8	.02
9	.03	9	.03	9	.03	9	.03
10	.03	10	.03	10	.03	10	.03
20	.06	20	.06	20	.06	20	.06
30	.10	30	.10	30	.10	30	.10
40	.13	40	.13	40	.13	40	.13
50	.17	50	.17	50	.17	50	.17
60	.20	60	.20	60	.20	60	.20
70	.23	70	.23	70	.24	70	.24
80	.27	80	.27	80	.27	80	.27
90	.30	90	.30	90	.31	90	.31
100	.34	100	.34	100	.34	100	.34
200	.68	200	.68	200	.69	200	.69
300	1.02	300	1.02	300	1.03	300	1.04
400	1.36	400	1.37	400	1.38	400	1.39
500	1.70	500	1.71	500	1.72	500	1.73
600	2.04	600	2.05	600	2.07	600	2.08
700	2.38	700	2.39	700	2.41	700	2.43
800	2.72	800	2.74	800	2.76	800	2.78
900	3.06	900	3.08	900	3.10	900	3.12
1000	3.40	1000	3.42	1000	3.45	1000	3.47
1100	3.74	1100	3.76	1100	3.79	1100	3.82
1200	4.08	1200	4.11	1200	4.14	1200	4.17
1300	4.42	1300	4.45	1300	4.48	1300	4.51
1400	4.76	1400	4.79	1400	4.83	1400	4.86
1500	5.10	1500	5.13	1500	5.17	1500	5.21
1600	5.44	1600	5.48	1600	5.52	1600	5.56
1700	5.78	1700	5.82	1700	5.86	1700	5.90
1800	6.12	1800	6.16	1800	6.21	1800	6.25
1900	6.46	1900	6.50	1900	6.55	1900	6.60
2000	6.80	2000	6.85	2000	6.90	2000	6.95
2100	7.14	2100	7.19	2100	7.24	2100	7.29
2200	7.48	2200	7.53	2200	7.59	2200	7.64
2300	7.82	2300	7.87	2300	7.93	2300	7.99
2400	8.16	2400	8.22	2400	8.28	2400	8.34
2500	8.50	2500	8·56	2500	8.62	2500	8.68
2600	8.84	2600	8.90	2600	8.97	2600	9.03
2700	9.18	2700	9.24	2700	9.31	2700	9.38
2800	9.52	2800	9.59	2800	9.66	2800	9.73
2900	9.86	2900	9.93	2900	10.00	2900	10.07
3000	10.20	3000	10.27	3000	10.35	3000	10.42
3100	10.54	3100	10.61	3100	10.69	3100	10.77
3200	10.88	3200	10.96	3200	11.04	3200	11.02
3300	11.22	3300	11.30	3300	11.38	3300	11.46
3400	11.56	3400	11.64	3400	11.73	3400	11.81
3500	11.90	3500	11.98	3500	12.07	3500	12.16
3600	12.24	3600	12.33	3600	12.42	3600	12.51
3700	12.58	3700	12.67	3700	12.76	3700	12.85
3800	12.92	3800	13.01	3800	13.11	3800	13.20
3900	13.26	3900	13.35	3900	13.45	3900	13.55
4000	13.60	4000	13.70	4000	13.80	4000	13.90

35 cts.		35¼ cts.		35½ cts.		35¾ cts.	
Lbs.	Amt.	Lbs.	Amt.	Lbs.	Amt.	Lbs.	Amt.
1	$ .00	1	$ .00	1	$ .00	1	$ .00
2	.00	2	.00	2	.00	2	.00
3	.01	3	.01	3	.01	3	.01
4	.01	4	.01	4	.01	4	.01
5	.01	5	.01	5	.01	5	.01
6	.02	6	.02	6	.02	6	.02
7	.02	7	.02	7	.02	7	.02
8	.02	8	.02	8	.02	8	.02
9	.03	9	.03	9	.03	9	.03
10	.03	10	.03	10	.03	10	.03
20	.07	20	.07	20	.07	20	.07
30	.10	30	.10	30	.10	30	.10
40	.14	40	.14	40	.14	40	.14
50	.17	50	.17	50	.17	50	.17
60	.21	60	.21	60	.21	60	.21
70	.24	70	.24	70	.24	70	.25
80	.28	80	.28	80	.28	80	.28
90	.31	90	.31	90	.31	90	.32
100	.35	100	.35	100	.35	100	.35
200	.70	200	.70	200	.71	200	.71
300	1.05	300	1.05	300	1.06	300	1.07
400	1.40	400	1.41	400	1.42	400	1.43
500	1.75	500	1.76	500	1.77	500	1.78
600	2.10	600	2.11	600	2.13	600	2.14
700	2.45	700	2.46	700	2.48	700	2.50
800	2.80	800	2.82	800	2.84	800	2.86
900	3.15	900	3.17	900	3.19	900	3.21
1000	3.50	1000	3.52	1000	3.55	1000	3.57
1100	3.85	1100	3.87	1100	3.90	1100	3.93
1200	4.20	1200	4.23	1200	4.26	1200	4.29
1300	4.55	1300	4.58	1300	4.61	1300	4.64
1400	4.90	1400	4.93	1400	4.97	1400	5.00
1500	5.25	1500	5.28	1500	5.32	1500	5.36
1600	5.60	1600	5.64	1600	5.68	1600	5.72
1700	5.95	1700	5.99	1700	6.03	1700	6.07
1800	6.30	1800	6.34	1800	6.39	1800	6.43
1900	6.65	1900	6.69	1900	6.74	1900	6.79
2000	7.00	2000	7.05	2000	7.10	2000	7.15
2100	7.35	2100	7.40	2100	7.45	2100	7.50
2200	7.70	2200	7.75	2200	7.81	2200	7.86
2300	8.05	2300	8.10	2300	8.16	2300	8.22
2400	8.40	2400	8.46	2400	8.52	2400	8.58
2500	8.75	2500	8.81	2500	8.87	2500	8.93
2600	9.10	2600	9.16	2600	9.23	2600	9.29
2700	9.45	2700	9.51	2700	9.58	2700	9.65
2800	9.80	2800	9.87	2800	9.94	2800	10.01
2900	10.15	2900	10.22	2900	10.29	2900	10.36
3000	10.50	3000	10.57	3000	10.65	3000	10.72
3100	10.85	3100	10.92	3100	11.00	3100	11.08
3200	11.20	3200	11.28	3200	11.36	3200	11.44
3300	11.55	3300	11.63	3300	11.71	3300	11.79
3400	11.90	3400	11.98	3400	12.07	3400	12.15
3500	12.25	3500	12.33	3500	12.42	3500	12.51
3600	12.60	3600	12.69	3600	12.78	3600	12.87
3700	12.95	3700	13.04	3700	13.13	3700	13.22
3800	13.30	3800	13.39	3800	13.49	3800	13.58
3900	13.65	3900	13.74	3900	13.84	3900	13.93
4000	14.00	4000	14.10	4000	14.20	4000	14.30

36 cts.		36¼ cts.		36½ cts.		36¾ cts.	
Lbs.	Amt.	Lbs.	Amt.	Lbs.	Amt.	Lbs.	Amt.
1	$ .00	1	$ .00	1	$ .00	1	$ .00
2	.00	2	.00	2	.00	2	.00
3	.01	3	.01	3	.01	3	.01
4	.01	4	.01	4	.01	4	.01
5	.01	5	.01	5	.01	5	.01
6	.02	6	.02	6	.02	6	.02
7	.02	7	.02	7	.02	7	.02
8	.02	8	.02	8	.02	8	.02
9	.03	9	.03	9	.03	9	.03
10	.03	10	.03	10	.03	10	.03
20	.07	20	.07	20	.07	20	.07
30	.10	30	.10	30	.10	30	.11
40	.14	40	.14	40	.14	40	.14
50	.18	50	.18	50	.18	50	.18
60	.21	60	.21	60	.21	60	.22
70	.25	70	.25	70	.25	70	.25
80	.28	80	.29	80	.29	80	.29
90	.32	90	.32	90	.32	90	.33
100	.36	100	.36	100	.36	100	.36
200	.72	200	.72	200	.73	200	.73
300	1.08	300	1.08	300	1.09	300	1.10
400	1.44	400	1.45	400	1.46	400	1.47
500	1.80	500	1.81	500	1.82	500	1.83
600	2.16	600	2.17	600	2.19	600	2.20
700	2.52	700	2.53	700	2.55	700	2.57
800	2.88	800	2.90	800	2.92	800	2.94
900	3.24	900	3.26	900	3.28	900	3.30
1000	3.60	1000	3.62	1000	3.65	1000	3.67
1100	3.96	1100	3.98	1100	4.01	1100	4.04
1200	4.32	1200	4.35	1200	4.38	1200	4.41
1300	4.68	1300	4.71	1300	4.74	1300	4.77
1400	5.04	1400	5.07	1400	5.11	1400	5.14
1500	5.40	1500	5.43	1500	5.47	1500	5.51
1600	5.76	1600	5.80	1600	5.84	1600	5.88
1700	6.12	1700	6.16	1700	6.20	1700	6.24
1800	6.48	1800	6.52	1800	6.57	1800	6.61
1900	6.84	1900	6.88	1900	6.93	1900	6.98
2000	7.20	2000	7.25	2000	7.30	2000	7.35
2100	7.56	2100	7.61	2100	7.66	2100	7.71
2200	7.92	2200	7.97	2200	8.03	2200	8.08
2300	8.28	2300	8.33	2300	8.39	2300	8.45
2400	8.64	2400	8.70	2400	8.76	2400	8.82
2500	9.00	2500	9.06	2500	9.12	2500	9.18
2600	9.36	2600	9.42	2600	9.49	2600	9.55
2700	9.72	2700	9.78	2700	9.85	2700	9.92
2800	10.08	2800	10.15	2800	10.22	2800	10.29
2900	10.44	2900	10.51	2900	10.58	2900	10.65
3000	10.80	3000	10.87	3000	10.95	3000	11.02
3100	11.16	3100	11.23	3100	11.31	3100	11.39
3200	11.52	3200	11.60	3200	11.68	3200	11.76
3300	11.88	3300	11.96	3300	12.04	3300	12.12
3400	12.24	3400	12.32	3400	12.41	3400	12.49
3500	12.60	3500	12.68	3500	12.77	3500	12.86
3600	12.96	3600	13.05	3600	13.14	3600	13.23
3700	13.32	3700	13.41	3700	13.50	3700	13.59
3800	13.68	3800	13.77	3800	13.87	3800	13.96
3900	14.04	3900	14.13	3900	14.23	3900	14.33
4000	14.40	4000	14.50	4000	14.60	4000	14.70

37 cts.		37¼ cts.		37½ cts.		37¾ cts.	
Lbs.	Amt.	Lbs.	Amt.	Lbs.	Amt.	Lbs.	Amt.
1	$ .00	1	$ .00	1	$ .00	1	$ .00
2	.00	2	.00	2	.00	2	.00
3	.01	3	.01	3	.01	3	.01
4	.01	4	.01	4	.01	4	.01
5	.01	5	.01	5	.01	5	.01
6	.02	6	.02	6	.02	6	.02
7	.02	7	.02	7	.02	7	.02
8	.02	8	.02	8	.02	8	.02
9	.03	9	.03	9	.03	9	.03
10	.03	10	.03	10	.03	10	.03
20	.07	20	.07	20	.07	20	.07
30	.11	30	.11	30	.11	30	.11
40	.14	40	.14	40	.15	40	.15
50	.18	50	.18	50	.18	50	.18
60	.22	60	.22	60	.22	60	.22
70	.25	70	.26	70	.26	70	.26
80	.29	80	.29	80	.30	80	.30
90	.33	90	.33	90	.33	90	.33
100	.37	100	.37	100	.37	100	.37
200	.74	200	.74	200	.75	200	.75
300	1.11	300	1.11	300	1.12	300	1.13
400	1.48	400	1.49	400	1.50	400	1.51
500	1.85	500	1.86	500	1.87	500	1.88
600	2.22	600	2.23	600	2.25	600	2.26
700	2.59	700	2.60	700	2.62	700	2.64
800	2.96	800	2.98	800	3.00	800	3.02
900	3.33	900	3.35	900	3.37	900	3.39
1000	3.70	1000	3.72	1000	3.75	1000	3.77
1100	4.07	1100	4.09	1100	4.12	1100	4.15
1200	4.44	1200	4.47	1200	4.50	1200	4.53
1300	4.81	1300	4.84	1300	4.87	1300	4.90
1400	5.18	1400	5.21	1400	5.25	1400	5.28
1500	5.55	1500	5.58	1500	5.62	1500	5.66
1600	5.92	1600	5.96	1600	6.00	1600	6.04
1700	6.29	1700	6.33	1700	6.37	1700	6.41
1800	6.66	1800	6.70	1800	6.75	1800	6.79
1900	7.03	1900	7.07	1900	7.12	1900	7.17
2000	7.40	2000	7.45	2000	7.50	2000	7.55
2100	7.77	2100	7.82	2100	7.87	2100	7.92
2200	8.14	2200	8.19	2200	8.25	2200	8.30
2300	8.51	2300	8.56	2300	8.62	2300	8.68
2400	8.88	2400	8.94	2400	9.00	2400	9.06
2500	9.25	2500	9.31	2500	9.37	2500	9.43
2600	9.62	2600	9.68	2600	9.75	2600	9.81
2700	9.99	2700	10.05	2700	10.12	2700	10.19
2800	10.36	2800	10.43	2800	10.50	2800	10.57
2900	10.73	2900	10.80	2900	10.87	2900	10.94
3000	11.10	3000	11.17	3000	11.25	3000	11.32
3100	11.47	3100	11.54	3100	11.62	3100	11.70
3200	11.84	3200	11.92	3200	12.00	3200	12.08
3300	12.21	3300	12.29	3300	12.37	3300	12.45
3400	12.58	3400	12.66	3400	12.75	3400	12.83
3500	12.95	3500	13.03	3500	13.12	3500	13.21
3600	13.32	3600	13.41	3600	13.50	3600	13.59
3700	13.69	3700	13.78	3700	13.87	3700	13.96
3800	14.06	3800	14.15	3800	14.25	3800	14.34
3900	14.43	3900	14.52	3900	14.62	3900	14.72
4000	14.80	4000	14.90	4000	15.00	4000	15.10

38 cts.		38¼ cts.		38½ cts.		38¾ cts.	
Lbs.	Amt.	Lbs.	Amt.	Lbs.	Amt.	Lbs.	Amt.
1	$ .00	1	$ .00	1	$ .00	1	$ .00
2	.00	2	.00	2	.00	2	.00
3	.01	3	.01	3	.01	3	.01
4	.01	4	.01	4	.01	4	.01
5	.01	5	.01	5	.01	5	.01
6	.02	6	.02	6	.02	6	.02
7	.02	7	.02	7	.02	7	.02
8	.03	8	.03	8	.03	8	.03
9	.03	9	.03	9	.03	9	.03
10	.03	10	.03	10	.03	10	.03
20	.07	20	.07	20	.07	20	.07
30	.11	30	.11	30	.11	30	.11
40	.15	40	.15	40	.15	40	.15
50	.19	50	.19	50	.19	50	.19
60	.22	60	.22	60	.23	60	.23
70	.26	70	.26	70	.26	70	.27
80	.30	80	.30	80	.30	80	.31
90	.34	90	.34	90	.34	90	.34
100	.38	100	.38	100	.38	100	.38
200	.76	200	.76	200	.77	200	.77
300	1.14	300	1.14	300	1.15	300	1.16
400	1.52	400	1.53	400	1.54	400	1.55
500	1.90	500	1.91	500	1.92	500	1.93
600	2.28	600	2.29	600	2.31	600	2.32
700	2.66	700	2.67	700	2.69	700	2.71
800	3.04	800	3.06	800	3.08	800	3.10
900	3.42	900	3.44	900	3.46	900	3.48
1000	3.80	1000	3.82	1000	3.85	1000	3.87
1100	4.18	1100	4.20	1100	4.23	1100	4.26
1200	4.56	1200	4.59	1200	4.62	1200	4.65
1300	4.94	1300	4.97	1300	5.00	1300	5.03
1400	5.32	1400	5.35	1400	5.39	1400	5.42
1500	5.70	1500	5.73	1500	5.77	1500	5.81
1600	6.08	1600	6.12	1600	6.16	1600	6.20
1700	6.46	1700	6.50	1700	6.54	1700	6.58
1800	6.84	1800	6.88	1800	6.93	1800	6.97
1900	7.22	1900	7.26	1900	7.31	1900	7.36
2000	7.60	2000	7.65	2000	7.70	2000	7.75
2100	7.98	2100	8.03	2100	8.08	2100	8.13
2200	8.36	2200	8.41	2200	8.47	2200	8.52
2300	8.74	2300	8.79	2300	8.85	2300	8.91
2400	9.12	2400	9.18	2400	9.24	2400	9.30
2500	9.50	2500	9.56	2500	9.62	2500	9.68
2600	9.88	2600	9.94	2600	10.01	2600	10.07
2700	10.26	2700	10.32	2700	10.39	2700	10.46
2800	10.64	2800	10.71	2800	10.78	2800	10.85
2900	11.02	2900	11.09	2900	11.16	2900	11.23
3000	11.40	3000	11.47	3000	11.55	3000	11.62
3100	11.78	3100	11.85	3100	11.93	3100	12.01
3200	12.16	3200	12.24	3200	12.32	3200	12.40
3300	12.54	3300	12.62	3300	12.70	3300	12.78
3400	12.92	3400	13.00	3400	13.09	3400	13.17
3500	13.30	3500	13.38	3500	13.47	3500	13.56
3600	13.68	3600	13.77	3600	13.86	3600	13.95
3700	14.06	3700	14.15	3700	14.24	3700	14.33
3800	14.44	3800	14.53	3800	14.63	3800	14.72
3900	14.82	3900	14.91	3900	15.01	3900	15.11
4000	15.20	4000	15.30	4000	15.40	4000	15.50

39 cts.		39¼ cts.		39½ cts.		39¾ cts.	
Lbs.	Amt.	Lbs.	Amt.	Lbs.	Amt.	Lbs.	Amt.
1	$ .00	1	$ .00	1	$ .00	1	$ .00
2	.00	2	.00	2	.00	2	.00
3	.01	3	.01	3	.01	3	.01
4	.01	4	.01	4	.01	4	.01
5	.01	5	.01	5	.01	5	.01
6	.02	6	.02	6	.02	6	.02
7	.02	7	.02	7	.02	7	.02
8	.03	8	.03	8	.03	8	.03
9	.03	9	.03	9	.03	9	.03
10	.03	10	.03	10	.03	10	.03
20	.07	20	.07	20	.07	20	.07
30	.11	30	.11	30	.11	30	.11
40	.15	40	.15	40	.15	40	.15
50	.19	50	.19	50	.19	50	.19
60	.23	60	.23	60	.23	60	.23
70	.27	70	.27	70	.27	70	.27
80	.31	80	.31	80	.31	80	.31
90	.35	90	.35	90	.35	90	.35
100	.39	100	.39	100	.39	100	.39
200	.78	200	.78	200	.79	200	.79
300	1.17	300	1.17	300	1.18	300	1.19
400	1.56	400	1.57	400	1.58	400	1.59
500	1.95	500	1.96	500	1.97	500	1.98
600	2.34	600	2.35	600	2.37	600	2.38
700	2.73	700	2.74	700	2.76	700	2.78
800	3.12	800	3.14	800	3.16	800	3.18
900	3.51	900	3.53	900	3.55	900	3.57
1000	3.90	1000	3.92	1000	3.95	1000	3.97
1100	4.29	1100	4.31	1100	4.34	1100	4.37
1200	4.68	1200	4.71	1200	4.74	1200	4.77
1300	5.07	1300	5.10	1300	5.13	1300	5.16
1400	5.46	1400	5.49	1400	5.53	1400	5.56
1500	5.85	1500	5.88	1500	5.92	1500	5.96
1600	6.24	1600	6.28	1600	6.32	1600	6.36
1700	6.63	1700	6.67	1700	6.71	1700	6.75
1800	7.02	1800	7.06	1800	7.11	1800	7.15
1900	7.41	1900	7.45	1900	7.50	1900	7.55
2000	7.80	2000	7.85	2000	7.90	2000	7.95
2100	8.19	2100	8.24	2100	8.29	2100	8.34
2200	8.58	2200	8.63	2200	8.69	2200	8.74
2300	8.97	2300	9.02	2300	9.08	2300	9.14
2400	9.36	2400	9.42	2400	9.48	2400	9.54
2500	9.75	2500	9.81	2500	9.87	2500	9.93
2600	10.14	2600	10.20	2600	10.27	2600	10.33
2700	10.53	2700	10.59	2700	10.66	2700	10.73
2800	10.92	2800	10.99	2800	11.06	2800	11.13
2900	11.31	2900	11.38	2900	11.45	2900	11.52
3000	11.70	3000	11.77	3000	11.85	3000	11.92
3100	12.09	3100	12.16	3100	12.24	3100	12.32
3200	12.48	3200	12.56	3200	12.64	3200	12.72
3300	12.87	3300	12.95	3300	13.03	3300	13.11
3400	13.26	3400	13.34	3400	13.43	3400	13.51
3500	13.65	3500	13.73	3500	13.82	3500	13.91
3600	14.04	3600	14.13	3600	14.22	3600	14.31
3700	14.43	3700	14.52	3700	14.61	3700	14.70
3800	14.82	3800	14.91	3800	15.01	3800	15.10
3900	15.21	3900	15.30	3900	15.40	3900	15.50
4000	15.60	4000	15.70	4000	15.80	4000	15.90

40 cts.		40¼ cts.		40½ cts.		40¾ cts.	
Lbs.	Amt.	Lbs.	Amt.	Lbs.	Amt.	Lbs.	Amt.
1	$ .00	1	$ .00	1	$ .00	1	$ .00
2	.00	2	.00	2	.00	2	.00
3	.01	3	.01	3	.01	3	.01
4	.01	4	.01	4	.01	4	.01
5	.02	5	.02	5	.02	5	.02
6	.02	6	.02	6	.02	6	.02
7	.02	7	.02	7	.02	7	.02
8	.03	8	.03	8	.03	8	.03
9	.03	9	.03	9	.03	9	.03
10	.04	10	.04	10	.04	10	.04
20	.08	20	.08	20	.08	20	.08
30	.12	30	.12	30	.12	30	.12
40	.16	40	.16	40	.16	40	.16
50	.20	50	.20	50	.20	50	.20
60	.24	60	.24	60	.24	60	.24
70	.28	70	.28	70	.28	70	.28
80	.32	80	.32	80	.32	80	.32
90	.36	90	.36	90	.36	90	.36
100	.40	100	.40	100	.40	100	.40
200	.80	200	.80	200	.81	200	.81
300	1.20	300	1.20	300	1.21	300	1.22
400	1.60	400	1.61	400	1.62	400	1.63
500	2.00	500	2.01	500	2.02	500	2.03
600	2.40	600	2.41	600	2.43	600	2.44
700	2.80	700	2.81	700	2.83	700	2.85
800	3.20	800	3.22	800	3.24	800	3.26
900	3.60	900	3.62	900	3.64	900	3.66
1000	4.00	1000	4.02	1000	4.05	1000	4.07
1100	4.40	1100	4.42	1100	4.45	1100	4.48
1200	4.80	1200	4.83	1200	4.86	1200	4.89
1300	5.20	1300	5.23	1300	5.26	1300	5.29
1400	5.60	1400	5.63	1400	5.67	1400	5.70
1500	6.00	1500	6.03	1500	6.07	1500	6.11
1600	6.40	1600	6.44	1600	6.48	1600	6.52
1700	6.80	1700	6.84	1700	6.88	1700	6.92
1800	7.20	1800	7.24	1800	7.29	1800	7.33
1900	7.60	1900	7.64	1900	7.69	1900	7.74
2000	8.00	2000	8.05	2000	8.10	2000	8.15
2100	8.40	2100	8.45	2100	8.50	2100	8.55
2200	8.80	2200	8.85	2200	8.91	2200	8.95
2300	9.20	2300	9.25	2300	9.31	2300	9.37
2400	9.60	2400	9.66	2400	9.72	2400	9.78
2500	10.00	2500	10.06	2500	10.12	2500	10.18
2600	10.40	2600	10.46	2600	10.53	2600	10.59
2700	10.80	2700	10.86	2700	10.93	2700	11.00
2800	11.20	2800	11.27	2800	11.34	2800	11.41
2900	11.60	2900	11.67	2900	11.74	2900	11.81
3000	12.00	3000	12.07	3000	12.15	3000	12.22
3100	12.40	3100	12.47	3100	12.55	3100	12.63
3200	12.80	3200	12.88	3200	12.96	3200	13.04
3300	13.20	3300	13.28	3300	13.36	3300	13.44
3400	13.60	3400	13.68	3400	13.77	3400	13.85
3500	14.00	3500	14.08	3500	14.17	3500	14.26
3600	14.40	3600	14.49	3600	14.58	3600	14.67
3700	14.80	3700	14.89	3700	14.98	3700	15.07
3800	15.20	3800	15.29	3800	15.39	3800	15.48
3900	15.60	3900	15.69	3900	15.79	3900	15.89
4000	16.00	4000	16.10	4000	16.20	4000	16.30

41 cts.		41¼ cts.		41½ cts.		41¾ cts.	
Lbs.	Amt.	Lbs.	Amt.	Lbs.	Amt.	Lbs.	Amt.
1	$ .00	1	$ .00	1	$ .00	1	$ .00
2	.00	2	.00	2	.00	2	.00
3	.01	3	.01	3	.01	3	.01
4	.01	4	.01	4	.01	4	.01
5	.02	5	.02	5	.02	5	.02
6	.02	6	.02	6	.02	6	.02
7	.02	7	.02	7	.02	7	.02
8	.03	8	.03	8	.03	8	.03
9	.03	9	.03	9	.03	9	.03
10	.04	10	.04	10	.04	10	.04
20	.08	20	.08	20	.08	20	.08
30	.12	30	.12	30	.12	30	.12
40	.16	40	.16	40	.16	40	.16
50	.20	50	.20	50	.20	50	.20
60	.24	60	.24	60	.24	60	.25
70	.28	70	.28	70	.29	70	.29
80	.32	80	.33	80	.33	80	.33
90	.36	90	.36	90	.37	90	.37
100	.41	100	.41	100	.41	100	.41
200	.82	200	.82	200	.83	200	.83
300	1.23	300	1.23	300	1.24	300	1.25
400	1.64	400	1.65	400	1.65	400	1.67
500	2.05	500	2.06	500	2.07	500	2.08
600	2.46	600	2.47	600	2.49	600	2.50
700	2.87	700	2.88	700	2.90	700	2.92
800	3.28	800	3.30	800	3.32	800	3.34
900	3.69	900	3.71	900	3.73	900	3.75
1000	4.10	1000	4.12	1000	4.15	1000	4.17
1100	4.51	1100	4.53	1100	4.56	1100	4.59
1200	4.92	1200	4.95	1200	4.98	1200	5.01
1300	5.33	1300	5.36	1300	5.39	1300	5.42
1400	5.74	1400	5.77	1400	5.81	1400	5.84
1500	6.15	1500	6.18	1500	6.22	1500	6.26
1600	6.56	1600	6.60	1600	6.64	1600	6.68
1700	6.97	1700	7.01	1700	7.05	1700	7.09
1800	7.38	1800	7.42	1800	7.47	1800	7.51
1900	7.79	1900	7.83	1900	7.88	1900	7.93
2000	8.20	2000	8.25	2000	8.30	2000	8.35
2100	8.61	2100	8.66	2100	8.71	2100	8.76
2200	9.02	2200	9.07	2200	9.13	2200	9.18
2300	9.43	2300	9.48	2300	9.54	2300	9.60
2400	9.84	2400	9.90	2400	9.96	2400	10.02
2500	10.25	2500	10.31	2500	10.37	2500	10.43
2600	10.66	2600	10.72	2600	10.79	2600	10.85
2700	11.07	2700	11.13	2700	11.20	2700	11.27
2800	11.48	2800	11.55	2800	11.62	2800	11.69
2900	11.89	2900	11.96	2900	12.03	2900	12.10
3000	12.30	3000	12.37	3000	12.45	3000	12.52
3100	12.71	3100	12.78	3100	12.86	3100	12.94
3200	13.12	3200	13.20	3200	13.28	3200	13.36
3300	13.53	3300	13.61	3300	13.69	3300	13.77
3400	13.94	3400	14.02	3400	14.11	3400	14.19
3500	14.35	3500	14.43	3500	14.52	3500	14.61
3600	14.76	3600	14.85	3600	14.94	3600	15.03
3700	15.17	3700	15.26	3700	15.35	3700	15.44
3800	15.58	3800	15.67	3800	15.77	3800	15.86
3900	15.99	3900	16.08	3900	16.18	3900	16.28
4000	16.40	4000	16.50	4000	16.60	4000	16.70

42 cts.		42¼ cts.		42½ cts.		42¾ cts.	
Lbs.	Amt.	Lbs.	Amt.	Lbs.	Amt.	Lbs.	Amt.
1	$ .00	1	$ .00	1	$ .00	1	$ .00
2	.00	2	.00	2	.00	2	.00
3	.01	3	.01	3	.01	3	.01
4	.01	4	.01	4	.01	4	.01
5	.02	5	.02	5	.02	5	.02
6	.02	6	.02	6	.02	6	.02
7	.02	7	.02	7	.02	7	.02
8	.03	8	.03	8	.03	8	.03
9	.03	9	.03	9	.03	9	.03
10	.04	10	.04	10	.04	10	.04
20	.08	20	.08	20	.08	20	.08
30	.12	30	.12	30	.12	30	.12
40	.16	40	.16	40	.17	40	.17
50	.21	50	.21	50	.21	50	.21
60	.25	60	.25	60	.25	60	.25
70	.29	70	.29	70	.29	70	.29
80	.33	80	.33	80	.34	80	.34
90	.38	90	.38	90	.38	90	.38
100	.42	100	.42	100	.42	100	.42
200	.84	200	.84	200	.85	200	.85
300	1.26	300	1.26	300	1.27	300	1.28
400	1.68	400	1.69	400	1.70	400	1.71
500	2.10	500	2.11	500	2.12	500	2.13
600	2.52	600	2.53	600	2.55	600	2.56
700	2.94	700	2.95	700	2.97	700	2.99
800	3.36	800	3.38	800	3.40	800	3.42
900	3.78	900	3.80	900	3.82	900	3.84
1000	4.20	1000	4.22	1000	4.25	1000	4.27
1100	4.62	1100	4.64	1100	4.67	1100	4.70
1200	5.04	1200	5.07	1200	5.10	1200	5.13
1300	5.46	1300	5.49	1300	5.52	1300	5.55
1400	5.88	1400	5.91	1400	5.95	1400	5.98
1500	6.30	1500	6.33	1500	6.37	1500	6.41
1600	6.72	1600	6.76	1600	6.80	1600	6.84
1700	7.14	1700	7.18	1700	7.22	1700	7.26
1800	7.56	1800	7.60	1800	7.65	1800	7.69
1900	7.98	1900	8.02	1900	8.07	1900	8.12
2000	8.40	2000	8.45	2000	8.50	2000	8.55
2100	8.82	2100	8.87	2100	8.92	2100	8.97
2200	9.24	2200	9.29	2200	9.35	2200	9.40
2300	9.66	2300	9.71	2300	9.77	2300	9.83
2400	10.08	2400	10.14	2400	10.20	2400	10.26
2500	10.50	2500	10.56	2500	10.62	2500	10.68
2600	10.92	2600	10.98	2600	11.05	2600	11.11
2700	11.34	2700	11.40	2700	11.47	2700	11.54
2800	11.76	2800	11.83	2800	11.90	2800	11.97
2900	12.18	2900	12.25	2900	12.32	2900	12.39
3000	12.60	3000	12.67	3000	12.75	3000	12.82
3100	13.02	3100	13.09	3100	13.17	3100	13.25
3200	13.44	3200	13.52	3200	13.60	3200	13.68
3300	13.86	3300	13.94	3300	14.02	3300	14.10
3400	14.28	3400	14.36	3400	14.45	3400	14.53
3500	14.70	3500	14.78	3500	14.87	3500	14.96
3600	15.12	3600	15.21	3600	15.30	3600	15.39
3700	15.54	3700	15.63	3700	15.72	3700	15.81
3800	15.96	3800	16.05	3800	16.15	3800	16.24
3900	16.38	3900	16.47	3900	16.57	3900	16.67
4000	16.80	4000	16.90	4000	17.00	4000	17.10

43 cts.		43¼ cts.		43½ cts.		43¾ cts.	
Lbs.	Amt.	Lbs.	Amt.	Lbs.	Amt.	Lbs.	Amt.
1	$ .00	1	$ .00	1	$ .00	1	$ .00
2	.00	2	.00	2	.00	2	.00
3	.01	3	.01	3	.01	3	.01
4	.01	4	.01	4	.01	4	.01
5	.02	5	.02	5	.02	5	.02
6	.02	6	.02	6	.02	6	.02
7	.03	7	.03	7	.03	7	.03
8	.03	8	.03	8	.03	8	.03
9	.03	9	.03	9	.03	9	.03
10	.04	10	.04	10	.04	10	.04
20	.08	20	.08	20	.08	20	.08
30	.12	30	.12	30	.13	30	.13
40	.17	40	.17	40	.17	40	.17
50	.21	50	.21	50	.21	50	.21
60	.25	60	.25	60	.26	60	.26
70	.30	70	.30	70	.30	70	.30
80	.34	80	.34	80	.34	80	.35
90	.38	90	.38	90	.39	90	.39
100	.43	100	.43	100	.43	100	.43
200	.86	200	.86	200	.87	200	.87
300	1.29	300	1.29	300	1.30	300	1.31
400	1.72	400	1.73	400	1.74	400	1.75
500	2.15	500	2.16	500	2.17	500	2.18
600	2.58	600	2.59	600	2.61	600	2.62
700	3.01	700	3.02	700	3.04	700	3.06
800	3.44	800	3.46	800	3.48	800	3.50
900	3.87	900	3.89	900	3.91	900	3.93
1000	4.30	1000	4.32	1000	4.35	1000	4.37
1100	4.73	1100	4.75	1100	4.78	1100	4.81
1200	5.16	1200	5.19	1200	5.22	1200	5.25
1300	5.59	1300	5.62	1300	5.65	1300	5.68
1400	6.02	1400	6.05	1400	6.09	1400	6.12
1500	6.45	1500	6.48	1500	6.52	1500	6.56
1600	6.88	1600	6.92	1600	6.96	1600	7.00
1700	7.31	1700	7.35	1700	7.39	1700	7.43
1800	7.74	1800	7.78	1800	7.83	1800	7.87
1900	8.17	1900	8.21	1900	8.26	1900	8.31
2000	8.60	2000	8.65	2000	8.70	2000	8.75
2100	9.03	2100	9.08	2100	9.13	2100	9.18
2200	9.46	2200	9.51	2200	9.57	2200	9.62
2300	9.89	2300	9.94	2300	10.00	2300	10.06
2400	10.32	2400	10.38	2400	10.44	2400	10.50
2500	10.75	2500	10.81	2500	10.87	2500	10.93
2600	11.18	2600	11.24	2600	11.31	2600	11.37
2700	11.61	2700	11.67	2700	11.74	2700	11.81
2800	12.04	2800	12.11	2800	12.18	2800	12.25
2900	12.47	2900	12.54	2900	12.61	2900	12.68
3000	12.90	3000	12.97	3000	13.05	3000	13.12
3100	13.33	3100	13.40	3100	13.48	3100	13.56
3200	13.76	3200	13.84	3200	13.92	3200	14.00
3300	14.19	3300	14.27	3300	14.35	3300	14.43
3400	14.62	3400	14.70	3400	14.79	3400	14.87
3500	15.05	3500	15.13	3500	15.22	3500	15.31
3600	15.48	3600	15.57	3600	15.66	3600	15.75
3700	15.91	3700	16.00	3700	16.09	3700	16.18
3800	16.34	3800	16.43	3800	16.53	3800	16.62
3900	16.77	3900	16.86	3900	16.96	3900	17.06
4000	17.20	4000	17.30	4000	17.40	4000	17.50

44 cts.		44¼ cts.		44½ cts.		44¾ cts.	
Lbs.	Amt.	Lbs.	Amt.	Lbs.	Amt.	Lbs.	Amt.
1	$ .00	1	$ .00	1	$ .00	1	$ .00
2	.00	2	.00	2	.00	2	.00
3	.01	3	.01	3	.01	3	.01
4	.01	4	.01	4	.01	4	.01
5	.02	5	.02	5	.02	5	.02
6	.02	6	.02	6	.02	6	.02
7	.03	7	.03	7	.03	7	.03
8	.03	8	.03	8	.03	8	.03
9	.03	9	.04	9	.04	9	.04
10	.04	10	.04	10	.04	10	.04
20	.08	20	.08	20	.08	20	.08
30	.13	30	.13	30	.13	30	.13
40	.17	40	.17	40	.17	40	.17
50	.22	50	.22	50	.22	50	.22
60	.26	60	.26	60	.26	60	.26
70	.30	70	.30	70	.31	70	.31
80	.35	80	.35	80	.35	80	.35
90	.39	90	.39	90	.40	90	.40
100	.44	100	.44	100	.44	100	.44
200	.88	200	.88	200	.89	200	.89
300	1.22	300	1.32	300	1.33	300	1.34
400	1.76	400	1.77	400	1.78	400	1.79
500	2.20	500	2.21	500	2.22	500	2.23
600	2.64	600	2.65	600	2.67	600	2.68
700	3.08	700	3.09	700	3.11	700	3.13
800	3.52	800	3.54	800	3.56	800	3.58
900	3.96	900	3.98	900	4.00	900	4.02
1000	4.40	1000	4.42	1000	4.45	1000	4.47
1100	4.84	1100	4.86	1100	4.89	1100	4.92
1200	5.28	1200	5.31	1200	5.34	1200	5.37
1300	5.72	1300	5.75	1300	5.78	1300	5.81
1400	6.16	1400	6.19	1400	6.23	1400	6.26
1500	6.60	1500	6.63	1500	6.67	1500	6.71
1600	7.04	1600	7.08	1600	7.12	1600	7.16
1700	7.48	1700	7.52	1700	7.56	1700	7.60
1800	7.92	1800	7.96	1800	8.01	1800	8.05
1900	8.36	1900	8.40	1900	8.45	1900	8.50
2000	8.80	2000	8.85	2000	8.90	2000	8.95
2100	9.24	2100	9.29	2100	9.34	2100	9.39
2200	9.68	2200	9.73	2200	9.79	2200	9.84
2300	10.12	2300	10.17	2300	10.23	2300	10.29
2400	10.56	2400	10.62	2400	10.68	2400	10.74
2500	11.00	2500	11.06	2500	11.12	2500	11.18
2600	11.44	2600	11.50	2600	11.57	2600	11.63
2700	11.88	2700	11.94	2700	12.01	2700	12.08
2800	12.32	2800	12.39	2800	12.46	2800	12.53
2900	12.76	2900	12.83	2900	12.90	2900	12.97
3000	13.20	3000	13.27	3000	13.35	3000	13.42
3100	13.64	3100	13.71	3100	13.79	3100	13.87
3200	14.08	3200	14.16	3200	14.24	3200	14.32
3300	14.52	3300	14.60	3300	14.68	3300	14.76
3400	14.96	3400	15.04	3400	15.13	3400	15.21
3500	15.40	3500	15.48	3500	15.57	3500	15.66
3600	15.84	3600	15.93	3600	16.02	3600	16.11
3700	16.28	3700	16.37	3700	16.46	3700	16.55
3800	16.72	3800	16.81	3800	16.91	3800	17.00
3900	17.16	3900	17.25	3900	17.35	3900	17.45
4000	17.60	4000	17.70	4000	17.80	4000	17.90

45 cts.		45¼ cts.		45½ cts.		45¾ cts.	
Lbs.	Amt.	Lbs.	Amt.	Lbs.	Amt.	Lbs.	Amt.
1	$ .00	1	$ .00	1	$ .00	1	$ .00
2	.00	2	.00	2	.00	2	.00
3	.01	3	.01	3	.01	3	.01
4	.01	4	.01	4	.01	4	.01
5	.02	5	.02	5	.02	5	.02
6	.02	6	.02	6	.02	6	.02
7	.03	7	.03	7	.03	7	.03
8	.03	8	.03	8	.03	8	.03
9	.04	9	.04	9	.04	9	.04
10	.04	10	.04	10	.04	10	.04
20	.09	20	.09	20	.09	20	.09
30	.13	30	.13	30	.13	30	.13
40	.18	40	.18	40	.18	40	.18
50	.22	50	.22	50	.22	50	.22
60	.27	60	.27	60	.27	60	.27
70	.31	70	.31	70	.31	70	.32
80	.36	80	.36	80	.36	80	.36
90	.40	90	.40	90	.40	90	.41
100	.45	100	.45	100	.45	100	.45
200	.90	200	.90	200	.91	200	.91
300	1.35	300	1.35	300	1.36	300	1.37
400	1.80	400	1.81	400	1.82	400	1.83
500	2.25	500	2.26	500	2.27	500	2.28
600	2.70	600	2.71	600	2.73	600	2.74
700	3.15	700	3.16	700	3.18	700	3.20
800	3.60	800	3.62	800	3.64	800	3.66
900	4.05	900	4.07	900	4.09	900	4.11
1000	4.50	1000	4.52	1000	4.55	1000	4.57
1100	4.95	1100	4.97	1100	5.00	1100	5.03
1200	5.40	1200	5.43	1200	5.46	1200	5.49
1300	5.85	1300	5.88	1300	5.91	1300	5.94
1400	6.30	1400	6.33	1400	6.37	1400	6.40
1500	6.75	1500	6.78	1500	6.82	1500	6.86
1600	7.20	1600	7.24	1600	7.28	1600	7.32
1700	7.65	1700	7.69	1700	7.73	1700	7.77
1800	8.10	1800	8.14	1800	8.19	1800	8.23
1900	8.55	1900	8.59	1900	8.64	1900	8.69
2000	9.00	2000	9.05	2000	9.10	2000	9.15
2100	9.45	2100	9.50	2100	9.55	2100	9.60
2200	9.90	2200	9.95	2200	10.01	2200	10.06
2300	10.35	2300	10.40	2300	10.46	2300	10.52
2400	10.80	2400	10.86	2400	10.92	2400	10.98
2500	11.25	2500	11.31	2500	11.37	2500	11.43
2600	11.70	2600	11.76	2600	11.83	2600	11.89
2700	12.15	2700	12.21	2700	12.28	2700	12.35
2800	12.60	2800	12.67	2800	12.74	2800	12.81
2900	13.05	2900	13.12	2900	13.19	2900	13.26
3000	13.50	3000	13.57	3000	13.65	3000	13.72
3100	13.95	3100	14.02	3100	14.10	3100	14.18
3200	14.40	3200	14.48	3200	14.56	3200	14.64
3300	14.85	3300	14.93	3300	15.01	3300	15.09
3400	15.30	3400	15.38	3400	15.47	3400	15.55
3500	15.75	3500	15.83	3500	15.92	3500	16.01
3600	16.20	3600	16.29	3600	16.38	3600	16.47
3700	16.65	3700	16.74	3700	16.83	3700	16.92
3800	17.10	3800	17.19	3800	17.29	3800	17.38
3900	17.55	3900	17.64	3900	17.74	3900	17.84
4000	18.00	4000	18.10	4000	18.20	4000	18.30

46 cts.		46¼ cts.		46½ cts.		46¾ cts.	
Lbs.	Amt.	Lbs.	Amt.	Lbs.	Amt.	Lbs.	Amt.
1	$ .00	1	$ .00	1	$ .00	1	$ .00
2	.00	2	.00	2	.00	2	.00
3	.01	3	.01	3	.01	3	.01
4	.01	4	.01	4	.01	4	.01
5	.02	5	.02	5	.02	5	.02
6	.02	6	.02	6	.02	6	.02
7	.03	7	.03	7	.03	7	.03
8	.03	8	.03	8	.03	8	.03
9	.04	9	.04	9	.04	9	.04
10	.04	10	.04	10	.04	10	.04
20	.09	20	.09	20	.09	20	.09
30	.13	30	.13	30	.13	30	.14
40	.18	40	.18	40	.18	40	.18
50	.23	50	.23	50	.23	50	.23
60	.27	60	.27	60	.27	60	.27
70	.32	70	.32	70	.32	70	.32
80	.36	80	.37	80	.37	80	.37
90	.41	90	.41	90	.41	90	.41
100	.46	100	.46	100	.46	100	.46
200	.92	200	.92	200	.93	200	.93
300	1.38	300	1.38	300	1.39	300	1.40
400	1.84	400	1.82	400	1.86	400	1.87
500	2.30	500	2.31	500	2.32	500	2.33
600	2.76	600	2.77	600	2.79	600	2.80
700	3.22	700	3.23	700	3.25	700	3.27
800	3.68	800	3.70	800	3.72	800	3.74
900	4.14	900	4.16	900	4.18	900	4.20
1000	4.60	1000	4.62	1000	4.65	1000	4.67
1100	5.06	1100	5.08	1100	5.11	1100	5.14
1200	5.52	1200	5.55	1200	5.58	1200	5.61
1300	5.98	1300	6.01	1300	6.04	1300	6.07
1400	6.44	1400	6.47	1400	6.51	1400	6.54
1500	6.90	1500	6.93	1500	6.97	1500	7.01
1600	7.36	1600	7.40	1600	7.44	1600	7.48
1700	7.82	1700	7.86	1700	7.90	1700	7.94
1800	8.28	1800	8.32	1800	8.37	1800	8.41
1900	8.74	1900	8.78	1900	8.83	1900	8.88
2000	9.20	2000	9.25	2000	9.30	2000	9.35
2100	9.66	2100	9.71	2100	9.76	2100	9.81
2200	10.12	2200	10.17	2200	10.23	2200	10.28
2300	10.58	2300	10.63	2300	10.69	2300	10.75
2400	11.04	2400	11.10	2400	11.16	2400	11.22
2500	11.50	2500	11.56	2500	11.62	2500	11.68
2600	11.96	2600	12.02	2600	12.09	2600	12.15
2700	12.42	2700	12.48	2700	12.55	2700	12.62
2800	12.88	2800	12.95	2800	13.02	2800	13.09
2900	13.34	2900	13.41	2900	13.48	2900	13.55
3000	13.80	3000	13.87	3000	13.95	3000	14.02
3100	14.26	3100	14.33	3100	14.41	3100	14.49
3200	14.72	3200	14.80	3200	14.88	3200	14.96
3300	15.18	3300	15.26	3300	15.34	3300	15.42
3400	15.64	3400	15.72	3400	15.81	3400	15.89
3500	16.10	3500	16.18	3500	16.27	3500	16.36
3600	16.56	3600	16.65	3600	16.74	3600	16.83
3700	17.02	3700	17.11	3700	17.20	3700	17.29
3800	17.48	3800	17.57	3800	17.67	3800	17.76
3900	17.94	3900	18.03	3900	18.13	3900	18.23
4000	18.40	4000	18.50	4000	18.60	4000	18.70

47 cts.		47¼ cts.		47½ cts.		47¾ cts.	
Lbs.	Amt.	Lbs.	Amt.	Lbs.	Amt.	Lbs.	Amt.
1	$ .00	1	$ .00	1	$ .00	1	$ .00
2	.00	2	.00	2	.00	2	.00
3	.01	3	.01	3	.01	3	.01
4	.01	4	.01	4	.01	4	.01
5	.02	5	.02	5	.02	5	.02
6	.02	6	.02	6	.02	6	.02
7	.03	7	.03	7	.03	7	.03
8	.03	8	.03	8	.03	8	.03
9	.04	9	.04	9	.04	9	.04
10	.04	10	.04	10	.04	10	.04
20	.09	20	.09	20	.09	20	.09
30	.14	30	.14	30	.14	30	.14
40	.18	40	.18	40	.18	40	.19
50	.23	50	.23	50	.23	50	.23
60	.28	60	.28	60	.28	60	.28
70	.32	70	.33	70	.33	70	.33
80	.37	80	.37	80	.38	80	.38
90	.42	90	.42	90	.42	90	.42
100	.47	100	.47	100	.47	100	.47
200	.94	200	.94	200	.95	200	.95
300	1.41	300	1.41	300	1.42	300	1.43
400	1.88	400	1.89	400	1.90	400	1.91
500	2.35	500	2.36	500	2.37	500	2.38
600	2.82	600	2.83	600	2.85	600	2.86
700	3.29	700	3.30	700	3.32	700	3.34
800	3.76	800	3.78	800	3.80	800	3.82
900	4.23	900	4.25	900	4.27	900	4.29
1000	4.70	1000	4.72	1000	4.75	1000	4.77
1100	5.17	1100	5.19	1100	5.22	1100	5.25
1200	5.64	1200	5.67	1200	5.70	1200	5.73
1300	6.11	1300	6.14	1300	6.17	1300	6.20
1400	6.58	1400	6.61	1400	6.65	1400	6.68
1500	7.05	1500	7.08	1500	7.12	1500	7.16
1600	7.52	1600	7.56	1600	7.60	1600	7.64
1700	7.99	1700	8.03	1700	8.07	1700	8.11
1800	8.46	1800	8.50	1800	8.55	1800	8.59
1900	8.93	1900	8.97	1900	9.02	1900	9.07
2000	9.40	2000	9.45	2000	9.50	2000	9.55
2100	9.87	2100	9.92	2100	9.97	2100	10.02
2200	10.34	2200	10.39	2200	10.45	2200	10.50
2300	10.81	2300	10.86	2300	10.92	2300	10.98
2400	11.28	2400	11.34	2400	11.40	2400	11.46
2500	11.75	2500	11.81	2500	11.87	2500	11.93
2600	12.22	2600	12.28	2600	12.35	2600	12.41
2700	12.69	2700	12.75	2700	12.82	2700	12.89
2800	13.16	2800	13.23	2800	13.30	2800	13.37
2900	13.63	2900	13.70	2900	13.77	2900	13.84
3000	14.10	3000	14.17	3000	14.25	3000	14.32
3100	14.57	3100	14.64	3100	14.72	3100	14.80
3200	15.04	3200	15.12	3200	15.20	3200	15.28
3300	15.51	3300	15.59	3300	15.67	3300	15.75
3400	15.98	3400	16.06	3400	16.15	3400	16.23
3500	16.45	3500	16.53	3500	16.62	3500	16.71
3600	16.92	3600	17.01	3600	17.10	3600	17.19
3700	17.39	3700	17.48	3700	17.57	3700	17.66
3800	17.86	3800	17.95	3800	18.05	3800	18.14
3900	18.33	3900	18.42	3900	18.52	3900	18.62
4000	18.80	4000	18.90	4000	19.00	4000	19.10

48 cts.		48¼ cts.		48½ cts.		48¾ cts.	
Lbs.	Amt.	Lbs.	Amt.	Lbs.	Amt.	Lbs.	Amt.
1	$ .00	1	$ .00	1	$ .00	1	$ .00
2	.00	2	.00	2	.00	2	.00
3	.01	3	.01	3	.01	3	.01
4	.01	4	.01	4	.01	4	.01
5	.02	5	.02	5	.02	5	.02
6	.02	6	.02	6	.02	6	.02
7	.03	7	.03	7	.03	7	.03
8	.03	8	.03	8	.03	8	.03
9	.04	9	.04	9	.04	9	.04
10	.04	10	.04	10	.04	10	.04
20	.09	20	.09	20	.09	20	.09
30	.14	30	.14	30	.14	30	.14
40	.19	40	.19	40	.19	40	.19
50	.24	50	.24	50	.24	50	.24
60	.28	60	.28	60	.29	60	.29
70	.33	70	.33	70	.33	70	.34
80	.38	80	.38	80	.38	80	.39
90	.43	90	.43	90	.43	90	.43
100	.48	100	.48	100	.48	100	.48
200	.96	200	.96	200	.97	200	.97
300	1.44	300	1.44	300	1.45	300	1.46
400	1.92	400	1.93	400	1.94	400	1.95
500	2.40	500	2.41	500	2.42	500	2.43
600	2.88	600	2.89	600	2.91	600	2.92
700	3.36	700	3.37	700	3.39	700	3.41
800	3.84	800	3.86	800	3.88	800	3.90
900	4.32	900	4.34	900	4.36	900	4.38
1000	4.80	1000	4.82	1000	4.85	1000	4.87
1100	5.28	1100	5.30	1100	5.33	1100	5.36
1200	5.76	1200	5.79	1200	5.82	1200	5.85
1300	6.24	1300	6.27	1300	6.30	1300	6.33
1400	6.72	1400	6.75	1400	6.79	1400	6.82
1500	7.20	1500	7.23	1500	7.27	1500	7.31
1600	7.68	1600	7.72	1600	7.76	1600	7.80
1700	8.16	1700	8.20	1700	8.24	1700	8.28
1800	8.64	1800	8.68	1800	8.73	1800	8.77
1900	9.12	1900	9.16	1900	9.21	1900	9.26
2000	9.60	2000	9.65	2000	9.70	2000	9.75
2100	10.08	2100	10.13	2100	10.18	2100	10.23
2200	10.56	2200	10.61	2200	10.67	2200	10.72
2300	11.04	2300	11.09	2300	11.15	2300	11.21
2400	11.52	2400	11.58	2400	11.64	2400	11.70
2500	12.00	2500	12.06	2500	12.12	2500	12.18
2600	12.48	2600	12.54	2600	12.61	2600	12.67
2700	12.96	2700	13.02	2700	13.09	2700	13.16
2800	13.44	2800	13.51	2800	13.58	2800	13.65
2900	13.92	2900	13.99	2900	14.06	2900	14.13
3000	14.40	3000	14.47	3000	14.55	3000	14.62
3100	14.88	3100	14.95	3100	15.03	3100	15.11
3200	15.36	3200	15.44	3200	15.52	3200	15.60
3300	15.84	3300	15.92	3300	16.00	3300	16.08
3400	16.32	3400	16.40	3400	16.49	3400	16.57
3500	16.80	3500	16.88	3500	16.97	3500	17.06
3600	17.28	3600	17.37	3600	17.46	3600	17.55
3700	17.76	3700	17.85	3700	17.94	3700	18.03
3800	18.24	3800	18.33	3800	18.43	3800	18.52
3900	18.72	3900	18.81	3900	18.91	3900	19.01
4000	19.20	4000	19.30	4000	19.40	4000	19.50

49 cts.		49¼ cts.		49½ cts.		49¾ cts.	
Lbs.	Amt.	Lbs.	Amt.	Lbs.	Amt.	Lbs.	Amt.
1	$ .00	1	$ .00	1	$ .00	1	$ .00
2	.00	2	.00	2	.00	2	.00
3	.01	3	.01	3	.01	3	.01
4	.01	4	.01	4	.01	4	.01
5	.02	5	.02	5	.02	5	.02
6	.02	6	.02	6	.02	6	.02
7	.03	7	.03	7	.03	7	.03
8	.03	8	.03	8	.03	8	.03
9	.04	9	.04	9	.04	9	.04
10	.04	10	.04	10	.04	10	.04
20	.09	20	.09	20	.09	20	.09
30	.14	30	.14	30	.14	30	.14
40	.19	40	.19	40	.19	40	.19
50	.24	50	.24	50	.24	50	.24
60	.29	60	.29	60	.29	60	.29
70	.34	70	.34	70	.34	70	.34
80	.39	80	.39	80	.39	80	.39
90	.44	90	.44	90	.44	90	.44
100	.49	100	.49	100	.49	100	.49
200	.98	200	.98	200	.99	200	.99
300	1.47	300	1.47	300	1.48	300	1.49
400	1.96	400	1.97	400	1.98	400	1.99
500	2.45	500	2.46	500	2.47	500	2.48
600	2.94	600	2.95	600	2.97	600	2.98
700	3.43	700	3.44	700	3.46	700	3.48
800	3.92	800	3.94	800	3.96	800	3.98
900	4.41	900	4.43	900	4.45	900	4.47
1000	4.90	1000	4.92	1000	4.95	1000	4.97
1100	5.39	1100	5.41	1100	5.44	1100	5.47
1200	5.88	1200	5.91	1200	5.94	1200	5.97
1300	6.37	1300	6.40	1300	6.43	1300	6.46
1400	6.86	1400	6.89	1400	6.93	1400	6.96
1500	7.35	1500	7.38	1500	7.42	1500	7.46
1600	7.84	1600	7.88	1600	7.92	1600	7.96
1700	8.33	1700	8.37	1700	8.41	1700	8.45
1800	8.82	1800	8.86	1800	8.91	1800	8.95
1900	9.31	1900	9.35	1900	9.40	1900	9.45
2000	9.80	2000	9.85	2000	9.90	2000	9.95
2100	10.29	2100	10.34	2100	10.39	2100	10.44
2200	10.78	2200	10.83	2200	10.89	2200	10.94
2300	11.27	2300	11.32	2300	11.38	2300	11.44
2400	11.76	2400	11.82	2400	11.88	2400	11.94
2500	12.25	2500	12.31	2500	12.37	2500	12.43
2600	12.74	2600	12.80	2600	12.87	2600	12.93
2700	13.23	2700	13.29	2700	13.36	2700	13.43
2800	13.72	2800	13.79	2800	13.86	2800	13.93
2900	14.21	2900	14.28	2900	14.35	2900	14.42
3000	14.70	3000	14.77	3000	14.85	3000	14.92
3100	15.19	3100	15.26	3100	15.34	3100	15.42
3200	15.68	3200	15.76	3200	15.84	3200	15.92
3300	16.17	3300	16.25	3300	16.33	3300	16.41
3400	16.66	3400	16.74	3400	16.83	3400	16.91
3500	17.15	3500	17.23	3500	17.32	3500	17.41
3600	17.64	3600	17.73	3600	17.82	3600	17.91
3700	18.13	3700	18.22	3700	18.31	3700	18.40
3800	18.62	3800	18.71	3800	18.81	3800	18.90
3900	19.11	3900	19.20	3900	19.30	3900	19.40
4000	19.60	4000	19.70	4000	19.80	4000	19.90

50 cts.		50¼ cts.		50½ cts.		50¾ cts.	
Lbs.	Amt.	Lbs.	Amt.	Lbs.	Amt.	Lbs.	Amt.
1	$ .00	1	$ .00	1	$ .00	1	$ .00
2	.01	2	.01	2	.01	2	.01
3	.01	3	.01	3	.01	3	.01
4	.02	4	.02	4	.02	4	.02
5	.02	5	.02	5	.02	5	.02
6	.03	6	.03	6	.03	6	.03
7	.03	7	.03	7	.03	7	.03
8	.04	8	.04	8	.04	8	.04
9	.04	9	.04	9	.04	9	.04
10	.05	10	.05	10	.05	10	.05
20	.10	20	.10	20	.10	20	.10
30	.15	30	.15	30	.15	30	.15
40	.20	40	.20	40	.20	40	.20
50	.25	50	.25	50	.25	50	.25
60	.30	60	.30	60	.30	60	.30
70	.35	70	.35	70	.35	70	.35
80	.40	80	.40	80	.40	80	.40
90	.45	90	.45	90	.45	90	.45
100	.50	100	.50	100	.50	100	.50
200	1.00	200	1.00	200	1.01	200	1.01
300	1.50	300	1.50	300	1.51	300	1.52
400	2.00	400	2.01	400	2.02	400	2.03
500	2.50	500	2.51	500	2.52	500	2.53
600	3.00	600	3.01	600	3.03	600	3.04
700	3.50	700	3.51	700	3.53	700	3.55
800	4.00	800	4.02	800	4.04	800	4.06
900	4.50	900	4.52	900	4.54	900	4.56
1000	5.00	1000	5.02	1000	5.05	1000	5.07
1100	5.50	1100	5.52	1100	5.55	1100	5.58
1200	6.00	1200	6.03	1200	6.06	1200	6.09
1300	6.50	1300	6.53	1300	6.56	1300	6.59
1400	7.00	1400	7.03	1400	7.07	1400	7.10
1500	7.50	1500	7.53	1500	7.57	1500	7.61
1600	8.00	1600	8.04	1600	8.08	1600	8.12
1700	8.50	1700	8.54	1700	8.58	1700	8.62
1800	9.00	1800	9.04	1800	9.09	1800	9.13
1900	9.50	1900	9.54	1900	9.59	1900	9.64
2000	10.00	2000	10.05	2000	10.10	2000	10.15
2100	10.50	2100	10.55	2100	10.60	2100	10.65
2200	11.00	2200	11.05	2200	11.11	2200	11.16
2300	11.50	2300	11.55	2300	11.61	2300	11.67
2400	12.00	2400	12.06	2400	12.12	2400	12.18
2500	12.50	2500	12.56	2500	12.62	2500	12.68
2600	13.00	2600	13.06	2600	13.13	2600	13.19
2700	13.50	2700	13.56	2700	13.63	2700	13.70
2800	14.00	2800	14.07	2800	14.14	2800	14.21
2900	14.50	2900	14.57	2900	14.64	2900	14.71
3000	15.00	3000	15.07	3000	15.15	3000	15.22
3100	15.50	3100	15.57	3100	15.65	3100	15.73
3200	16.00	3200	16.08	3200	16.16	3200	16.24
3300	16.50	3300	16.58	3300	16.66	3300	16.74
3400	17.00	3400	17.08	3400	17.17	3400	17.25
3500	17.50	3500	17.58	3500	17.67	3500	17.76
3600	18.00	3600	18.09	3600	18.18	3600	18.27
3700	18.50	3700	18.59	3700	18.68	3700	18.77
3800	19.00	3800	19.09	3800	19.19	3800	19.28
3900	19.50	3900	19.59	3900	19.69	3900	19.79
4000	20.00	4000	20.10	4000	20.20	4000	20.30

51 cts.		51¼ cts.		51½ cts.		51¾ cts.	
Lbs.	Amt.	Lbs.	Amt.	Lbs.	Amt.	Lbs.	Amt.
1	$ .00	1	$ .00	1	$ .00	1	$ .00
2	.01	2	.01	2	.01	2	.01
3	.01	3	.01	3	.01	3	.01
4	.02	4	.02	4	.02	4	.02
5	.02	5	.02	5	.02	5	.02
6	.03	6	.03	6	.03	6	.03
7	.03	7	.03	7	.03	7	.03
8	.04	8	.04	8	.04	8	.04
9	.04	9	.04	9	.04	9	.04
10	.05	10	.05	10	.05	10	.05
20	.10	20	.10	20	.10	20	.10
30	.15	30	.15	30	.15	30	.15
40	.20	40	.20	40	.20	40	.20
50	.25	50	.25	50	.25	50	.25
60	.30	60	.30	60	.30	60	.31
70	.35	70	.35	70	.36	70	.36
80	.40	80	.41	80	.41	80	.41
90	.45	90	.46	90	.46	90	.46
100	.51	100	.51	100	.51	100	.51
200	1.02	200	1.02	200	1.03	200	1.03
300	1.53	300	1.53	300	1.54	300	1.55
400	2.04	400	2.05	400	2.06	400	2.07
500	2.55	500	2.56	500	2.57	500	2.58
600	3.06	600	3.07	600	3.09	600	3.10
700	3.57	700	3.58	700	3.60	700	3.62
800	4.08	800	4.10	800	4.12	800	4.14
900	4.59	900	4.61	900	4.63	900	4.65
1000	5.10	1000	5.12	1000	5.15	1000	5.17
1100	5.61	1100	5.63	1100	5.66	1100	5.69
1200	6.12	1200	6.15	1200	6.18	1200	6.21
1300	6.63	1300	6.66	1300	6.69	1300	6.72
1400	7.14	1400	7.17	1400	7.21	1400	7.24
1500	7.65	1500	7.68	1500	7.72	1500	7.76
1600	8.16	1600	8.20	1600	8.24	1600	8.28
1700	8.67	1700	8.71	1700	8.75	1700	8.79
1800	9.18	1800	9.22	1800	9.27	1800	9.31
1900	9.69	1900	9.73	1900	9.78	1900	9.83
2000	10.20	2000	10.25	2000	10.30	2000	10.35
2100	10.71	2100	10.76	2100	10.81	2100	10.86
2200	11.22	2200	11.27	2200	11.33	2200	11.38
2300	11.73	2300	11.78	2300	11.84	2300	11.90
2400	12.24	2400	12.30	2400	12.36	2400	12.42
2500	12.75	2500	12.81	2500	12.87	2500	12.93
2600	13.26	2600	13.32	2600	13.39	2600	13.45
2700	13.77	2700	13.83	2700	13.90	2700	13.97
2800	14.28	2800	14.35	2800	14.42	2800	14.49
2900	14.79	2900	14.86	2900	14.93	2900	15.00
3000	15.30	3000	15.37	3000	15.45	3000	15.52
3100	15.81	3100	15.88	3100	15.96	3100	16.04
3200	16.32	3200	16.40	3200	16.48	3200	16.56
3300	16.83	3300	16.91	3300	16.99	3300	17.07
3400	17.34	3400	17.42	3400	17.51	3400	17.59
3500	17.85	3500	17.93	3500	18.02	3500	18.11
3600	18.36	3600	18.45	3600	18.54	3600	18.63
3700	18.87	3700	18.96	3700	19.05	3700	19.14
3800	19.38	3800	19.47	3800	19.57	3800	19.66
3900	19.89	3900	19.98	3900	20.08	3900	20.18
4000	20.40	4000	20.50	4000	20.60	4000	20.70

52 cts.		52¼ cts.		52½ cts.		52¾ cts.	
Lbs.	Amt.	Lbs.	Amt.	Lbs.	Amt.	Lbs.	Amt.
1	$ .00	1	$ .00	1	$ .00	1	$ .00
2	.01	2	.01	2	.01	2	.01
3	.01	3	.01	3	.01	3	.01
4	.02	4	.02	4	.02	4	.02
5	.02	5	.02	5	.02	5	.02
6	.03	6	.03	6	.03	6	.03
7	.03	7	.03	7	.03	7	.03
8	.04	8	.04	8	.04	8	.04
9	.04	9	.04	9	.04	9	.04
10	.05	10	.05	10	.05	10	.05
20	.10	20	.10	20	.10	20	.10
30	.15	30	.15	30	.15	30	.15
40	.20	40	.20	40	.21	40	.21
50	.26	50	.26	50	.26	50	.26
60	.31	60	.31	60	.31	60	.31
70	.36	70	.36	70	.36	70	.36
80	.41	80	.41	80	.42	80	.42
90	.46	90	.47	90	.47	90	.47
100	.52	100	.52	100	.52	100	.52
200	1.04	200	1.04	200	1.05	200	1.05
300	1.56	300	1.56	300	1.57	300	1.58
400	2.08	400	2.09	400	2.10	400	2.11
500	2.60	500	2.61	500	2.62	500	2.63
600	3.12	600	3.13	600	3.15	600	3.16
700	3.64	700	3.65	700	3.67	700	3.69
800	4.16	800	4.18	800	4.20	800	4.22
900	4.68	900	4.70	900	4.72	900	4.74
1000	5.20	1000	5.22	1000	5.25	1000	5.27
1100	5.72	1100	5.74	1100	5.77	1100	5.80
1200	6.24	1200	6.27	1200	6.30	1200	6.33
1300	6.76	1300	6.79	1300	6.82	1300	6.85
1400	7.28	1400	7.31	1400	7.35	1400	7.38
1500	7.80	1500	7.83	1500	7.87	1500	7.91
1600	8.32	1600	8.36	1600	8.40	1600	8.44
1700	8.84	1700	8.88	1700	8.92	1700	8.96
1800	9.36	1800	9.40	1800	9.45	1800	9.49
1900	9.88	1900	9.92	1900	9.97	1900	10.02
2000	10.40	2000	10.45	2000	10.50	2000	10.55
2100	10.92	2100	10.97	2100	11.02	2100	11.07
2200	11.44	2200	11.49	2200	11.55	2200	11.60
2300	11.96	2300	12.01	2300	12.07	2300	12.13
2400	12.48	2400	12.54	2400	12.60	2400	12.66
2500	13.00	2500	13.06	2500	13.12	2500	13.18
2600	13.52	2600	13.58	2600	13.65	2600	13.71
2700	14.04	2700	14.20	2700	14.27	2700	14.34
2800	14.56	2800	14.63	2800	14.70	2800	14.77
2900	15.08	2900	15.15	2900	15.22	2900	15.29
3000	15.60	3000	15.67	3000	15.75	3000	15.82
3100	16.12	3100	16.19	3100	16.27	3100	16.35
3200	16.64	3200	16.72	3200	16.80	3200	16.88
3300	17.16	3300	17.24	3300	17.32	3300	17.40
3400	17.68	3400	17.76	3400	17.85	3400	17.93
3500	18.20	3500	18.28	3500	18.27	3500	18.36
3600	18.72	3600	18.81	3600	18.90	3600	18.99
3700	19.24	3700	19.33	3700	19.42	3700	19.41
3800	19.76	3800	19.85	3800	19.95	3800	20.04
3900	20.28	3900	20.37	3900	20.47	3900	20.57
4000	20.80	4000	20.90	4000	21.00	4000	21.10

53 cts.		53¼ cts.		53½ cts.		53¾ cts.	
Lbs.	Amt.	Lbs.	Amt.	Lbs.	Amt.	Lbs.	Amt.
1	$ .00	1	$ .00	1	$ .00	1	$ .00
2	.01	2	.01	2	.01	2	.01
3	.01	3	.01	3	.01	3	.01
4	.02	4	.02	4	.02	4	.02
5	.02	5	.02	5	.02	5	.02
6	.03	6	.03	6	.03	6	.03
7	.03	7	.03	7	.03	7	.03
8	.04	8	.04	8	.04	8	.04
9	.04	9	.04	9	.04	9	.04
10	.05	10	.05	10	.05	10	.05
20	.10	20	.10	20	.10	20	.10
30	.15	30	.15	30	.16	30	.16
40	.21	40	.21	40	.21	40	.21
50	.26	50	.26	50	.26	50	.26
60	.31	60	.31	60	.32	60	.32
70	.37	70	.37	70	.37	70	.37
80	.42	80	.42	80	.42	80	.43
90	.47	90	.47	90	.48	90	.48
100	.53	100	.53	100	.53	100	.53
200	1.06	200	1.06	200	1.07	200	1.07
300	1.59	300	1.59	300	1.60	300	1.61
400	2.12	400	2.13	400	2.14	400	2.15
500	2.65	500	2.66	500	2.67	500	2.68
600	3.18	600	3.19	600	3.21	600	3.22
700	3.71	700	3.72	700	3.74	700	3.76
800	4.24	800	4.26	800	4.28	800	4.30
900	4.77	900	4.79	900	4.81	900	4.83
1000	5.30	1000	5.32	1000	5.35	1000	5.37
1100	5.83	1100	5.85	1100	5.88	1100	5.91
1200	6.35	1200	6.39	1200	6.42	1200	6.45
1300	6.89	1300	6.92	1300	6.95	1300	6.98
1400	7.42	1400	7.45	1400	7.49	1400	7.52
1500	7.95	1500	7.98	1500	8.02	1500	8.06
1600	8.48	1600	8.52	1600	8.56	1600	8.60
1700	9.01	1700	9.05	1700	9.09	1700	9.13
1800	9.54	1800	9.58	1800	9.63	1800	9.67
1900	10.07	1900	10.11	1900	10.16	1900	10.21
2000	10.60	2000	10.65	2000	10.70	2000	10.75
2100	11.13	2100	11.18	2100	11.23	2100	11.28
2200	11.66	2200	11.71	2200	11.77	2200	11.83
2300	12.19	2300	12.24	2300	12.30	2300	12.36
2400	12.72	2400	12.78	2400	12.84	2400	12.90
2500	13.25	2500	13.31	2500	13.37	2500	13.43
2600	13.78	2600	13.84	2600	13.91	2600	13.97
2700	14.31	2700	14.37	2700	14.44	2700	14.51
2800	14.84	2800	14.91	2800	14.98	2800	15.05
2900	15.37	2900	15.44	2900	15.61	2900	15.68
3000	15.90	3000	15.97	3000	16.05	3000	16.12
3100	16.43	3100	16.50	3100	16.58	3100	16.66
3200	16.96	3200	17.04	3200	17.12	3200	17.20
3300	17.49	3300	17.57	3300	17.65	3300	17.73
3400	18.02	3400	18.10	3400	18.19	3400	18.27
3500	18.55	3500	18.63	3500	18.72	3500	18.81
3600	19.08	3600	19.17	3600	19.26	3600	19.35
3700	19.61	3700	19.70	3700	19.79	3700	19.88
3800	20.14	3800	20.23	3800	20.33	3800	20.42
3900	20.67	3900	20.76	3900	20.86	3900	20.96
4000	21.20	4000	21.30	4000	21.40	4000	21.50

54 cts.		54¼ cts.		54½ cts.		54¾ cts.	
Lbs.	Amt.	Lbs.	Amt.	Lbs.	Amt.	Lbs.	Amt.
1	$ .00	1	$ .00	1	$ .00	1	$ .00
2	.01	2	.01	2	.01	2	.01
3	.01	3	.01	3	.01	3	.01
4	.02	4	.02	4	.02	4	.02
5	.02	5	.02	5	.02	5	.02
6	.03	6	.03	6	.03	6	.03
7	.03	7	.03	7	.03	7	.03
8	.04	8	.04	8	.04	8	.04
9	.04	9	.04	9	.04	9	.04
10	.05	10	.05	10	.05	10	.05
20	.10	20	.10	20	.10	20	.10
30	.16	30	.16	30	.16	30	.16
40	.21	40	.21	40	.21	40	.21
50	.27	50	.27	50	.27	50	.27
60	.32	60	.32	60	.32	60	.32
70	.37	70	.37	70	.38	70	.38
80	.43	80	.43	80	.43	80	.43
90	.48	90	.48	90	.49	90	.49
100	.54	100	.54	100	.54	100	.54
200	1.08	200	1.08	200	1.09	200	1.09
300	1.62	300	1.62	300	1.63	300	1.64
400	2.16	400	2.17	400	2.18	400	2.19
500	2.70	500	2.71	500	2.72	500	2.73
600	3.24	600	3.25	600	3.27	600	3.28
700	3.78	700	3.79	700	3.81	700	3.83
800	4.32	800	4.34	800	4.36	800	4.38
900	4.86	900	4.88	900	4.90	900	4.92
1000	5.40	1000	5.42	1000	5.45	1000	5.47
1100	5.94	1100	5.95	1100	5.99	1100	6.02
1200	6.48	1200	6.51	1200	6.54	1200	6.57
1300	7.02	1300	7.05	1300	7.08	1300	7.11
1400	7.56	1400	7.59	1400	7.63	1400	7.66
1500	8.10	1500	8.13	1500	8.17	1500	8.21
1600	8.64	1600	8.68	1600	8.72	1600	8.76
1700	9.18	1700	9.22	1700	9.26	1700	9.30
1800	9.72	1800	9.76	1800	9.81	1800	9.85
1900	10.26	1900	10.30	1900	10.35	1900	10.40
2000	10.80	2000	10.85	2000	10.90	2000	10.95
2100	11.34	2100	11.39	2100	11.44	2100	11.49
2200	11.88	2200	11.93	2200	11.99	2200	12.04
2300	12.42	2300	12.47	2300	12.53	2300	12.59
2400	12.96	2400	13.02	2400	13.08	2400	13.14
2500	13.50	2500	13.56	2500	13.62	2500	13.68
2600	14.04	2600	14.10	2600	14.17	2600	14.23
2700	14.58	2700	14.64	2700	14.71	2700	14.78
2800	15.12	2800	15.19	2800	15.26	2800	15.33
2900	15.66	2900	15.73	2900	15.80	2900	15.87
3000	16.20	3000	16.27	3000	16.35	3000	16.42
3100	16.74	3100	16.81	3100	16.89	3100	16.97
3200	17.28	3200	17.36	3200	17.44	3200	17.52
3300	17.82	3300	17.90	3300	17.98	3300	18.06
3400	18.36	3400	18.44	3400	18.53	3400	18.61
3500	18.90	3500	18.98	3500	19.07	3500	19.16
3600	19.44	3600	19.53	3600	19.62	3600	19.71
3700	19.98	3700	20.07	3700	20.16	3700	20.25
3800	20.52	3800	20.61	3800	20.71	3800	20.80
3900	21.06	3900	21.15	3900	21.25	3900	21.35
4000	21.60	4000	21.70	4000	21.80	4000	21.90

55 cts.		55¼ cts.		55½ cts.		55¾ cts.	
Lbs.	Amt.	Lbs.	Amt.	Lbs.	Amt.	Lbs.	Amt.
1	$ .00	1	$ .00	1	$ .00	1	$ .00
2	.01	2	.01	2	.01	2	.01
3	.01	3	.01	3	.01	3	.01
4	.02	4	.02	4	.02	4	.02
5	.02	5	.02	5	.02	5	.02
6	.03	6	.03	6	.03	6	.03
7	.03	7	.03	7	.03	7	.03
8	.04	8	.04	8	.04	8	.04
9	.04	9	.04	9	.04	9	.04
10	.05	10	.05	10	.05	10	.05
20	.11	20	.11	20	.11	20	.11
30	.16	30	.16	30	.16	30	.16
40	.22	40	.22	40	.22	40	.22
50	.27	50	.27	50	.27	50	.27
60	.33	60	.33	60	.33	60	.33
70	.38	70	.38	70	.38	70	.38
80	.44	80	.44	80	.44	80	.44
90	.49	90	.49	90	.49	90	.50
100	.55	100	.55	100	.55	100	.55
200	1.10	200	1.10	200	1.11	200	1.11
300	1.65	300	1.65	300	1.66	300	1.67
400	2.20	400	2.21	400	2.22	400	2.23
500	2.75	500	2.76	500	2.77	500	2.78
600	3.30	600	3.31	600	3.33	600	3.34
700	3.85	700	3.86	700	3.88	700	3.90
800	4.40	800	4.42	800	4.44	800	4.46
900	4.95	900	4.97	900	4.99	900	5.01
1000	5.50	1000	5.52	1000	5.55	1000	5.57
1100	6.05	1100	6.07	1100	6.10	1100	6.13
1200	6.60	1200	6.63	1200	6.66	1200	6.69
1300	7.15	1300	7.18	1300	7.21	1300	7.24
1400	7.70	1400	7.73	1400	7.77	1400	7.80
1500	8.25	1500	8.28	1500	8.32	1500	8.36
1600	8.80	1600	8.84	1600	8.88	1600	8.92
1700	9.35	1700	9.39	1700	9.43	1700	9.47
1800	9.90	1800	9.94	1800	9.99	1800	10.03
1900	10.45	1900	10.49	1900	10.54	1900	10.59
2000	11.00	2000	11.05	2000	11.10	2000	11.15
2100	11.55	2100	11.60	2100	11.65	2100	11.70
2200	12.10	2200	12.15	2200	12.21	2200	12.26
2300	12.65	2300	12.70	2300	12.76	2300	12.82
2400	13.20	2400	13.26	2400	13.32	2400	13.38
2500	13.75	2500	13.81	2500	13.87	2500	13.93
2600	14.30	2600	14.36	2600	14.43	2600	14.49
2700	14.85	2700	14.91	2700	14.98	2700	15.05
2800	15.40	2800	15.47	2800	15.54	2800	15.61
2900	15.95	2900	16.02	2900	16.09	2900	16.16
3000	16.50	3000	16.57	3000	16.65	3000	16.72
3100	17.05	3100	17.12	3100	17.20	3100	17.28
3200	17.60	3200	17.68	3200	17.76	3200	17.84
3300	18.15	3300	18.23	3300	18.31	3300	18.39
3400	18.70	3400	18.78	3400	18.87	3400	18.95
3500	19.25	3500	19.33	3500	19.42	3500	19.51
3600	19.80	3600	19.89	3600	19.98	3600	20.07
3700	20.35	3700	20.44	3700	20.53	3700	20.62
3800	20.90	3800	20.99	3800	21.09	3800	21.18
3900	21.45	3900	21.54	3900	21.64	3900	21.74
4000	22.00	4000	22.10	4000	22.20	4000	22.30

56 cts.		56¼ cts.		56½ cts.		56¾ cts.	
Lbs.	Amt.	Lbs.	Amt.	Lbs.	Amt.	Lbs.	Amt.
1	$ .00	1	$ .00	1	$ .00	1	$ .00
2	.01	2	.01	2	.01	2	.01
3	.01	3	.01	3	.01	3	.01
4	.02	4	.02	4	.02	4	.02
5	.02	5	.02	5	.02	5	.02
6	.03	6	.03	6	.03	6	.03
7	.03	7	.03	7	.03	7	.03
8	.04	8	.04	8	.04	8	.04
9	.05	9	.05	9	.05	9	.05
10	.05	10	.05	10	.05	10	.05
20	.11	20	.11	20	.11	20	.11
30	.16	30	.16	30	.16	30	.17
40	.22	40	.22	40	.22	40	.22
50	.28	50	.28	50	.28	50	.28
60	.33	60	.33	60	.33	60	.34
70	.39	70	.39	70	.39	70	.39
80	.44	80	.45	80	.45	80	.45
90	.50	90	.50	90	.50	90	.51
100	.56	100	.56	100	.56	100	.56
200	1.12	200	1.12	200	1.13	200	1.13
300	1.68	300	1.68	300	1.69	300	1.70
400	2.24	400	2.25	400	2.26	400	2.27
500	2.80	500	2.81	500	2.82	500	2.83
600	3.36	600	3.37	600	3.39	600	3.40
700	3.92	700	3.93	700	3.95	700	3.97
800	4.48	800	4.50	800	4.52	800	4.54
900	5.04	900	5.06	900	5.08	900	5.10
1000	5.60	1000	5.62	1000	5.65	1000	5.67
1100	6.16	1100	6.18	1100	6.21	1100	6.24
1200	6.72	1200	6.75	1200	6.78	1200	6.81
1300	7.28	1300	7.31	1300	7.34	1300	7.37
1400	7.84	1400	7.87	1400	7.91	1400	7.94
1500	8.40	1500	8.43	1500	8.47	1500	8.51
1600	8.96	1600	9.00	1600	9.04	1600	9.08
1700	9.52	1700	9.56	1700	9.60	1700	9.64
1800	10.08	1800	10.12	1800	10.17	1800	10.21
1900	10.64	1900	10.68	1900	10.73	1900	10.78
2000	11.20	2000	11.25	2000	11.30	2000	11.35
2100	11.76	2100	11.81	2100	11.86	2100	11.91
2200	12.32	2200	12.37	2200	12.43	2200	12.48
2300	12.88	2300	12.93	2300	12.99	2300	13.05
2400	13.44	2400	13.50	2400	13.56	2400	13.62
2500	14.00	2500	14.06	2500	14.12	2500	14.18
2600	14.56	2600	14.62	2600	14.69	2600	14.75
2700	15.12	2700	15.18	2700	15.25	2700	15.32
2800	15.68	2800	15.75	2800	15.82	2800	15.89
2900	16.24	2900	16.31	2900	16.38	2900	16.45
3000	16.80	3000	16.87	3000	16.95	3000	17.02
3100	17.36	3100	17.43	3100	17.51	3100	17.59
3200	17.92	3200	18.00	3200	18.08	3200	18.16
3300	18.48	3300	18.56	3300	18.64	3300	18.72
3400	19.04	3400	19.12	3400	19.21	3400	19.29
3500	19.60	3500	19.68	3500	19.77	3500	19.86
3600	20.16	3600	20.25	3600	20.34	3600	20.43
3700	20.72	3700	20.81	3700	20.90	3700	20.99
3800	21.28	3800	21.37	3800	21.47	3800	21.56
3900	21.84	3900	21.93	3900	22.03	3900	22.13
4000	22.40	4000	22.50	4000	22.60	4000	22.70

57 cts.		57¼ cts.		57½ cts.		57¾ cts.	
Lbs.	Amt.	Lbs.	Amt.	Lbs.	Amt.	Lbs.	Amt.
1	$ .00	1	$ .00	1	$ .00	1	$ .00
2	.01	2	.01	2	.01	2	.01
3	.01	3	.01	3	.01	3	.01
4	.02	4	.02	4	.02	4	.02
5	.02	5	.02	5	.02	5	.02
6	.03	6	.03	6	.03	6	.03
7	.03	7	.04	7	.04	7	.04
8	.04	8	.04	8	.04	8	.04
9	.05	9	.05	9	.05	9	.05
10	.05	10	.05	10	.05	10	.05
20	.11	20	.11	20	.11	20	.11
30	.17	30	.17	30	.17	30	.17
40	.22	40	.22	40	.23	40	.23
50	.28	50	.28	50	.28	50	.28
60	.34	60	.34	60	.34	60	.34
70	.39	70	.40	70	.40	70	.40
80	.45	80	.45	80	.46	80	.46
90	.51	90	.51	90	.51	90	.51
100	.57	100	.57	100	.57	100	.57
200	1.14	200	1.14	200	1.15	200	1.15
300	1.71	300	1.71	300	1.72	300	1.73
400	2.28	400	2.29	400	2.30	400	2.31
500	2.85	500	2.86	500	2.87	500	2.88
600	3.42	600	3.43	600	3.45	600	3.46
700	3.99	700	4.00	700	4.02	700	4.04
800	4.56	800	4.58	800	4.60	800	4.62
900	5.13	900	5.15	900	5.17	900	5.19
1000	5.70	1000	5.72	1000	5.75	1000	5.77
1100	6.27	1100	6.29	1100	6.32	1100	6.35
1200	6.84	1200	6.87	1200	6.90	1200	6.93
1300	7.41	1300	7.44	1300	7.47	1300	7.50
1400	7.98	1400	8.01	1400	8.05	1400	8.08
1500	8.55	1500	8.58	1500	8.62	1500	8.66
1600	9.12	1600	9.16	1600	9.20	1600	9.24
1700	9.69	1700	9.73	1700	9.77	1700	9.81
1800	10.26	1800	10.30	1800	10.35	1800	10.39
1900	10.83	1900	10.87	1900	10.92	1900	10.97
2000	11.40	2000	11.45	2000	11.50	2000	11.55
2100	11.97	2100	12.02	2100	12.07	2100	12.12
2200	12.54	2200	12.59	2200	12.65	2200	12.70
2300	13.11	2300	13.16	2300	13.22	2300	13.28
2400	13.68	2400	13.74	2400	13.80	2400	13.86
2500	14.25	2500	14.31	2500	14.37	2500	14.43
2600	14.82	2600	14.88	2600	14.95	2600	15.01
2700	15.39	2700	15.45	2700	15.52	2700	15.57
2800	15.96	2800	16.03	2800	16.10	2800	16.17
2900	16.53	2900	16.60	2900	16.67	2900	16.74
3000	17.10	3000	17.17	3000	17.25	3000	17.32
3100	17.67	3100	17.74	3100	17.82	3100	17.90
3200	18.24	3200	18.32	3200	18.40	3200	18.48
3300	18.81	3300	18.89	3300	18.97	3300	19.05
3400	19.38	3400	19.46	3400	19.55	3400	19.63
3500	19.95	3500	20.03	3500	20.12	3500	20.21
3600	20.52	3600	20.61	3600	20.70	3600	20.79
3700	21.09	3700	21.18	3700	21.27	3700	21.36
3800	21.66	3800	21.75	3800	21.85	3800	21.94
3900	22.23	3900	22.32	3900	22.42	3900	22.42
4000	22.80	4000	22.90	4000	23.00	4000	23.10

58 cts.		58¼ cts.		58½ cts.		58¾ cts.	
Lbs.	Amt.	Lbs.	Amt.	Lbs.	Amt.	Lbs.	Amt.
1	$ .00	1	$ .00	1	$ .00	1	$ .00
2	.01	2	.01	2	.01	2	.01
3	.01	3	.01	3	.01	3	.01
4	.02	4	.02	4	.02	4	.02
5	.02	5	.02	5	.02	5	.02
6	.03	6	.03	6	.03	6	.03
7	.04	7	.04	7	.04	7	.04
8	.04	8	.04	8	.04	8	.04
9	.05	9	.05	9	.05	9	.05
10	.05	10	.05	10	.05	10	.05
20	.11	20	.11	20	.11	20	.11
30	.17	30	.17	30	.17	30	.17
40	.23	40	.23	40	.23	40	.23
50	.29	50	.29	50	.29	50	.29
60	.34	60	.34	60	.35	60	.35
70	.40	70	.40	70	.40	70	.41
80	.46	80	.46	80	.46	80	.47
90	.52	90	.52	90	.52	90	.52
100	.58	100	.58	100	.58	100	.58
200	1.16	200	1.16	200	1.17	200	1.17
300	1.74	300	1.74	300	1.75	300	1.76
400	2.32	400	2.33	400	2.34	400	2.35
500	2.90	500	2.91	500	2.92	500	2.93
600	3.48	600	3.49	600	3.51	600	3.52
700	4.06	700	4.07	700	4.09	700	4.11
800	4.64	800	4.66	800	4.68	800	4.70
900	5.22	900	5.24	900	5.26	900	5.28
1000	5.80	1000	5.82	1000	5.85	1000	5.87
1100	6.38	1100	6.40	1100	6.43	1100	6.46
1200	6.96	1200	6.99	1200	7.02	1200	7.05
1300	7.54	1300	7.57	1300	7.60	1300	7.63
1400	8.12	1400	8.15	1400	8.19	1400	8.22
1500	8.70	1500	8.73	1500	8.77	1500	8.81
1600	9.28	1600	9.32	1600	9.36	1600	9.40
1700	9.86	1700	9.90	1700	9.94	1700	9.98
1800	10.44	1800	10.48	1800	10.53	1800	10.57
1900	11.02	1900	11.06	1900	11.11	1900	11.16
2000	11.60	2000	11.65	2000	11.70	2000	11.75
2100	12.18	2100	12.23	2100	12.28	2100	12.33
2200	12.76	2200	12.81	2200	12.87	2200	12.92
2300	13.34	2300	13.39	2300	13.45	2300	13.51
2400	13.92	2400	13.98	2400	14.04	2400	14.10
2500	14.50	2500	14.56	2500	14.62	2500	14.68
2600	15.08	2600	15.14	2600	15.21	2600	15.27
2700	15.66	2700	15.72	2700	15.79	2700	15.86
2800	16.24	2800	16.31	2800	16.38	2800	16.45
2900	16.82	2900	16.89	2900	16.96	2900	17.03
3000	17.40	3000	17.47	3000	17.55	3000	17.62
3100	17.98	3100	18.05	3100	18.13	3100	18.21
3200	18.56	3200	18.64	3200	18.72	3200	18.80
3300	19.14	3300	19.22	3300	19.30	3300	19.38
3400	19.72	3400	19.80	3400	19.89	3400	19.97
3500	20.30	3500	20.38	3500	20.47	3500	20.56
3600	20.88	3600	20.97	3600	21.06	3600	21.15
3700	21.46	3700	21.55	3700	21.64	3700	21.73
3800	22.04	3800	22.13	3800	22.23	3800	22.32
3900	22.62	3900	22.71	3900	22.81	3900	22.91
4000	23.20	4000	23.30	4000	23.40	4000	23.50

59 cts.		59¼ cts.		59½ cts.		59¾ cts.	
Lbs.	Amt.	Lbs.	Amt.	Lbs.	Amt.	Lbs.	Amt.
1	$ .00	1	$ .00	1	$ .00	1	$ .00
2	.01	2	.01	2	.01	2	.01
3	.01	3	.01	3	.01	3	.01
4	.02	4	.02	4	.02	4	.02
5	.02	5	.02	5	.02	5	.02
6	.03	6	.03	6	.03	6	.03
7	.04	7	.04	7	.04	7	.04
8	.04	8	.04	8	.04	8	.04
9	.05	9	.05	9	.05	9	.05
10	.05	10	.05	10	.05	10	.05
20	.11	20	.11	20	.11	20	.11
30	.17	30	.17	30	.17	30	.17
40	.23	40	.23	40	.23	40	.23
50	.29	50	.29	50	.29	50	.29
60	.35	60	.35	60	.35	60	.35
70	.41	70	.41	70	.41	70	.41
80	.47	80	.47	80	.47	80	.47
90	.53	90	.53	90	.53	90	.53
100	.59	100	.59	100	.59	100	.59
200	1.18	200	1.18	200	1.19	200	1.19
300	1.77	300	1.77	300	1.78	300	1.79
400	2.36	400	2.37	400	2.38	400	2.39
500	2.95	500	2.96	500	2.97	500	2.98
600	3.54	600	3.55	600	3.57	600	3.58
700	4.13	700	4.14	700	4.16	700	4.18
800	4.72	800	4.74	800	4.76	800	4.78
900	5.31	900	5.33	900	5.35	900	5.37
1000	5.90	1000	5.92	1000	5.95	1000	5.97
1100	6.49	1100	6.51	1100	6.54	1100	6.57
1200	7.08	1200	7.11	1200	7.14	1200	7.17
1300	7.67	1300	7.70	1300	7.73	1300	7.76
1400	8.26	1400	8.29	1400	8.33	1400	8.36
1500	8.85	1500	8.88	1500	8.92	1500	8.96
1600	9.44	1600	9.48	1600	9.52	1600	9.56
1700	10.03	1700	10.07	1700	10.11	1700	10.15
1800	10.62	1800	10.66	1800	10.71	1800	10.75
1900	11.21	1900	11.25	1900	11.30	1900	11.35
2000	11.80	2000	11.85	2000	11.90	2000	11.95
2100	12.39	2100	12.44	2100	12.49	2100	12.54
2200	12.98	2200	13.03	2200	13.09	2200	13.14
2300	13.57	2300	13.62	2300	13.68	2300	13.74
2400	14.16	2400	14.22	2400	14.28	2400	14.34
2500	14.75	2500	14.81	2500	14.87	2500	14.93
2600	15.34	2600	15.40	2600	15.47	2600	15.53
2700	15.93	2700	15.99	2700	16.06	2700	16.13
2800	16.52	2800	16.59	2800	16.66	2800	16.73
2900	17.11	2900	17.18	2900	17.25	2900	17.22
3000	17.70	3000	17.77	3000	17.85	3000	17.92
3100	18.29	3100	18.36	3100	18.44	3100	18.52
3200	18.88	3200	18.96	3200	19.04	3200	19.12
3300	19.47	3300	19.55	3300	19.63	3300	19.71
3400	20.06	3400	20.14	3400	20.23	3400	20.31
3500	20.65	3500	20.73	3500	20.82	3500	20.91
3600	21.24	3600	21.33	3600	21.42	3600	21.51
3700	21.83	3700	21.92	3700	22.01	3700	22.10
3800	22.42	3800	22.51	3800	22.61	3800	22.70
3900	23.01	3900	23.10	3900	23.20	3900	23.30
4000	23.60	4000	23.70	4000	23.80	4000	23.90

60 cts.		60¼ cts.		60½ cts.		60¾ cts.	
Lbs.	Amt.	Lbs.	Amt.	Lbs.	Amt.	Lbs.	Amt.
1	$ .00	1	$ .00	1	$ .00	1	$ .00
2	.01	2	.01	2	.01	2	.01
3	.01	3	.01	3	.01	3	.01
4	.02	4	.02	4	.02	4	.02
5	.03	5	.03	5	.03	5	.03
6	.03	6	.03	6	.03	6	.03
7	.04	7	.04	7	.04	7	.04
8	.04	8	.04	8	.04	8	.04
9	.05	9	.05	9	.05	9	.05
10	.06	10	.06	10	.06	10	.06
20	.12	20	.12	20	.12	20	.12
30	.18	30	.18	30	.18	30	.18
40	.24	40	.24	40	.24	40	.24
50	.30	50	.30	50	.30	50	.30
60	.36	60	.36	60	.36	60	.36
70	.42	70	.42	70	.42	70	.42
80	.48	80	.48	80	.48	80	.48
90	.54	90	.54	90	.54	90	.54
100	.60	100	.60	100	.60	100	.60
200	1.20	200	1.20	200	1.21	200	1.21
300	1.80	300	1.80	300	1.81	300	1.82
400	2.40	400	2.41	400	2.42	400	2.43
500	3.00	500	3.01	500	3.02	500	3.03
600	3.60	600	3.61	600	3.63	600	3.64
700	4.20	700	4.21	700	4.23	700	4.25
800	4.80	800	4.82	800	4.84	800	4.86
900	5.40	900	5.42	900	5.44	900	5.46
1000	6.00	1000	6.02	1000	6.05	1000	6.07
1100	6.60	1100	6.62	1100	6.65	1100	6.68
1200	7.20	1200	7.23	1200	7.26	1200	7.29
1300	7.80	1300	7.83	1300	7.86	1300	7.89
1400	8.40	1400	8.43	1400	8.47	1400	8.50
1500	9.00	1500	9.03	1500	9.07	1500	9.11
1600	9.60	1600	9.64	1600	9.68	1600	9.72
1700	10.20	1700	10.24	1700	10.28	1700	10.32
1800	10.80	1800	10.84	1800	10.89	1800	10.93
1900	11.40	1900	11.44	1900	11.49	1900	11.54
2000	12.00	2000	12.05	2000	12.10	2000	12.15
2100	12.60	2100	12.65	2100	12.70	2100	12.75
2200	13.20	2200	13.25	2200	13.31	2200	13.36
2300	13.80	2300	13.85	2300	13.91	2300	13.97
2400	14.40	2400	14.46	2400	14.52	2400	14.58
2500	15.00	2500	15.06	2500	15.12	2500	15.18
2600	15.60	2600	15.66	2600	15.73	2600	15.79
2700	16.20	2700	16.26	2700	16.33	2700	16.40
2800	16.80	2800	16.87	2800	16.94	2800	17.01
2900	17.40	2900	17.47	2900	17.54	2900	17.61
3000	18.00	3000	18.07	3000	18.15	3000	18.22
3100	18.60	3100	18.67	3100	18.75	3100	18.83
3200	19.20	3200	19.28	3200	19.36	3200	19.44
3300	19.80	3300	19.88	3300	19.96	3300	20.04
3400	20.40	3400	20.48	3400	20.57	3400	20.65
3500	21.00	3500	21.08	3500	21.17	3500	21.26
3600	21.60	3600	21.69	3600	21.78	3600	21.87
3700	22.20	3700	22.29	3700	22.38	3700	22.47
3800	22.80	3800	22.89	3800	22.99	3800	23.08
3900	23.40	3900	23.49	3900	23.59	3900	23.69
4000	24.00	4000	24.10	4000	24.20	4000	24.30

61 cts.		61¼ cts.		61½ cts.		61¾ cts.	
Lbs.	Amt.	Lbs.	Amt.	Lbs.	Amt.	Lbs.	Amt.
1	$ .00	1	$ .00	1	$ .00	1	$ .00
2	.01	2	.01	2	.01	2	.01
3	.01	3	.01	3	.01	3	.01
4	.02	4	.02	4	.02	4	.02
5	.03	5	.03	5	.03	5	.03
6	.03	6	.03	6	.03	6	.03
7	.04	7	.04	7	.04	7	.04
8	.04	8	.04	8	.04	8	.04
9	.05	9	.05	9	.05	9	.05
10	.06	10	.06	10	.06	10	.06
20	.12	20	.12	20	.12	20	.12
30	.18	30	.18	30	.18	30	.18
40	.24	40	.24	40	.24	40	.24
50	.30	50	.30	50	.30	50	.30
60	.36	60	.36	60	.36	60	.37
70	.42	70	.42	70	.43	70	.43
80	.48	80	.49	80	.49	80	.49
90	.54	90	.55	90	.55	90	.55
100	.61	100	.61	100	.61	100	.61
200	1.22	200	1.22	200	1.23	200	1.23
300	1.83	300	1.83	300	1.84	300	1.85
400	2.44	400	2.45	400	2.46	400	2.47
500	3.05	500	3.06	500	3.07	500	3.08
600	3.66	600	3.67	600	3.69	600	3.70
700	4.27	700	4.28	700	4.30	700	4.32
800	4.88	800	4.90	800	4.92	800	4.94
900	5.49	900	5.51	900	5.53	900	5.55
1000	6.10	1000	6.12	1000	6.15	1000	6.17
1100	6.71	1100	6.73	1100	6.76	1100	6.79
1200	7.32	1200	7.35	1200	7.38	1200	7.41
1300	7.93	1300	7.96	1300	7.99	1300	8.02
1400	8.54	1400	8.57	1400	8.61	1400	8.64
1500	9.15	1500	9.18	1500	9.22	1500	9.26
1600	9.76	1600	9.80	1600	9.84	1600	9.88
1700	10.37	1700	10.41	1700	10.45	1700	10.49
1800	10.98	1800	11.02	1800	11.07	1800	11.11
1900	11.59	1900	11.63	1900	11.68	1900	11.73
2000	12.20	2000	12.25	2000	12.30	2000	12.35
2100	12.81	2100	12.86	2100	12.91	2100	12.96
2200	13.42	2200	13.47	2200	13.53	2200	13.58
2300	14.03	2300	14.08	2300	14.14	2300	14.20
2400	14.64	2400	14.70	2400	14.76	2400	14.82
2500	15.25	2500	15.31	2500	15.37	2500	15.43
2600	15.86	2600	15.92	2600	15.99	2600	16.05
2700	16.47	2700	16.53	2700	16.60	2700	16.67
2800	17.08	2800	17.15	2800	17.22	2800	17.29
2900	17.69	2900	17.76	2900	17.83	2900	17.90
3000	18.30	3000	18.37	3000	18.45	3000	18.52
3100	18.91	3100	18.98	3100	19.06	3100	19.14
3200	19.52	3200	19.60	3200	19.68	3200	19.76
3300	20.13	3300	20.21	3300	20.29	3300	20.37
3400	20.74	3400	20.82	3400	20.91	3400	20.99
3500	21.35	3500	21.43	3500	21.52	3500	21.61
3600	21.96	3600	22.05	3600	22.14	3600	22.23
3700	22.57	3700	22.66	3700	22.75	3700	22.84
3800	23.18	3800	23.27	3800	23.37	3800	23.46
3900	23.79	3900	23.88	3900	23.98	3900	24.08
4000	24.40	4000	24.50	4000	24.60	4000	24.70

62 cts.		62¼ cts.		62½ cts.		62¾ cts.	
Lbs.	Amt.	Lbs.	Amt.	Lbs.	Amt.	Lbs.	Amt.
1	$ .00	1	$ .00	1	$ .00	1	$ .00
2	.01	2	.01	2	.01	2	.01
3	.01	3	.01	3	.01	3	.01
4	.02	4	.02	4	.02	4	.02
5	.03	5	.03	5	.03	5	.03
6	.03	6	.03	6	.03	6	.03
7	.04	7	.04	7	.04	7	.04
8	.04	8	.04	8	.05	8	.05
9	.05	9	.05	9	.05	9	.05
10	.06	10	.06	10	.06	10	.06
20	.12	20	.12	20	.12	20	.12
30	.18	30	.18	30	.18	30	.18
40	.24	40	.24	40	.25	40	.25
50	.31	50	.31	50	.31	50	.31
60	.37	60	.37	60	.37	60	.37
70	.43	70	.43	70	.43	70	.43
80	.49	80	.49	80	.50	80	.50
90	.55	90	.56	90	.56	90	.56
100	.62	100	.62	100	.62	100	.62
200	1.24	200	1.24	200	1.25	200	1.25
300	1.86	300	1.86	300	1.87	300	1.88
400	2.48	400	2.49	400	2.50	400	2.51
500	3.10	500	3.11	500	3.12	500	3.13
600	3.72	600	3.73	600	3.75	600	3.76
700	4.34	700	4.35	700	4.37	700	4.39
800	4.96	800	4.98	800	5.00	800	5.02
900	5.58	900	5.60	900	5.62	900	5.64
1000	6.20	1000	6.22	1000	6.25	1000	6.27
1100	6.82	1100	6.84	1100	6.87	1100	6.90
1200	7.44	1200	7.47	1200	7.50	1200	7.53
1300	8.06	1300	8.09	1300	8.12	1300	8.15
1400	8.68	1400	8.71	1400	8.75	1400	8.78
1500	9.30	1500	9.33	1500	9.37	1500	9.41
1600	9.92	1600	9.96	1600	10.00	1600	10.04
1700	10.54	1700	10.58	1700	10.62	1700	10.66
1800	11.16	1800	11.20	1800	11.25	1800	11.29
1900	11.78	1900	11.82	1900	11.87	1900	11.92
2000	12.40	2000	12.45	2000	12.50	2000	12.55
2100	13.02	2100	13.07	2100	13.12	2100	13.17
2200	13.64	2200	13.69	2200	13.75	2200	13.80
2300	14.26	2300	14.31	2300	14.37	2300	14.43
2400	14.88	2400	14.94	2400	15.00	2400	15.06
2500	15.50	2500	15.56	2500	15.62	2500	15.68
2600	16.12	2600	16.18	2600	16.25	2600	16.31
2700	16.74	2700	16.80	2700	16.87	2700	16.94
2800	17.36	2800	17.43	2800	17.50	2800	17.57
2900	17.98	2900	18.05	2900	18.12	2900	18.19
3000	18.60	3000	18.67	3000	18.75	3000	18.82
3100	19.22	3100	19.29	3100	19.37	3100	19.45
3200	19.84	3200	19.92	3200	20.00	3200	20.08
3300	20.46	3300	20.54	3300	20.62	3300	20.70
3400	21.08	3400	21.16	3400	21.25	3400	21.33
3500	21.70	3500	21.78	3500	21.87	3500	21.96
3600	22.32	3600	22.41	3600	22.50	3600	22.59
3700	22.94	3700	23.03	3700	23.12	3700	23.21
3800	23.56	3800	23.65	3800	23.75	3800	23.84
3900	24.18	3900	24.27	3900	24.37	3900	24.47
4000	24.80	4000	24.90	4000	25.00	4000	25.10

63 cts.		63¼ cts.		63½ cts.		63¾ cts.	
Lbs.	Amt.	Lbs.	Amt.	Lbs.	Amt.	Lbs.	Amt.
1	$ .00	1	$ .00	1	$ .00	1	$ .00
2	.01	2	.01	2	.01	2	.01
3	.01	3	.01	3	.01	3	.01
4	.02	4	.02	4	.02	4	.02
5	.03	5	.03	5	.03	5	.03
6	.03	6	.03	6	.03	6	.03
7	.04	7	.04	7	.04	7	.04
8	.05	8	.05	8	.05	8	.05
9	.05	9	.05	9	.05	9	.05
10	.06	10	.06	10	.06	10	.06
20	.12	20	.12	20	.12	20	.12
30	.18	30	.18	30	.19	30	.19
40	.25	40	.25	40	.25	40	.25
50	.31	50	.31	50	.31	50	.31
60	.37	60	.37	60	.38	60	.38
70	.44	70	.44	70	.44	70	.44
80	.50	80	.50	80	.50	80	.51
90	.56	90	.56	90	.57	90	.57
100	.63	100	.63	100	.63	100	.63
200	1.26	200	1.26	200	1.27	200	1.27
300	1.89	300	1.89	300	1.90	300	1.91
400	2.52	400	2.53	400	2.54	400	2.55
500	3.15	500	3.16	500	3.17	500	3.18
600	3.78	600	3.79	600	3.81	600	3.82
700	4.41	700	4.42	700	4.44	700	4.46
800	5.04	800	5.06	800	5.08	800	5.10
900	5.67	900	5.69	900	5.71	900	5.73
1000	6.30	1000	6.32	1000	6.35	1000	6.37
1100	6.93	1100	6.95	1100	6.98	1100	7.01
1200	7.56	1200	7.59	1200	7.62	1200	7.65
1300	8.19	1300	8.22	1300	8.25	1300	8.28
1400	8.82	1400	8.85	1400	8.89	1400	8.92
1500	9.45	1500	9.48	1500	9.52	1500	9.56
1600	10.08	1600	10.12	1600	10.16	1600	10.20
1700	10.71	1700	10.75	1700	10.79	1700	10.83
1800	11.34	1800	11.38	1800	11.43	1800	11.47
1900	11.97	1900	12.01	1900	12.06	1900	12.11
2000	12.60	2000	12.65	2000	12.70	2000	12.75
2100	13.23	2100	13.28	2100	13.33	2100	13.38
2200	13.86	2200	13.91	2200	13.97	2200	14.02
2300	14.49	2300	14.54	2300	14.60	2300	14.66
2400	15.12	2400	15.18	2400	15.24	2400	15.30
2500	15.75	2500	15.81	2500	15.87	2500	15.93
2600	16.38	2600	16.44	2600	16.51	2600	16.57
2700	17.01	2700	17.07	2700	17.14	2700	17.21
2800	17.64	2800	17.71	2800	17.78	2800	17.85
2900	18.27	2900	18.34	2900	18.41	2900	18.48
3000	18.90	3000	18.97	3000	19.05	3000	19.12
3100	19.53	3100	19.60	3100	19.68	3100	19.76
3200	20.16	3200	20.24	3200	20.32	3200	20.40
3300	20.79	3300	20.87	3300	20.95	3300	21.03
3400	21.42	3400	21.50	3400	21.59	3400	21.67
3500	22.05	3500	22.13	3500	22.22	3500	22.31
3600	22.68	3600	22.77	3600	22.86	3600	22.95
3700	23.31	3700	23.40	3700	23.49	3700	23.58
3800	23.94	3800	24.03	3800	24.13	3800	24.22
3900	24.57	3900	24.66	3900	24.76	3900	24.86
4000	25.20	4000	25.30	4000	25.40	4000	25.50

64 cts.		64¼ cts.		64½ cts.		64¾ cts.	
Lbs.	Amt.	Lbs.	Amt.	Lbs.	Amt.	Lbs.	Amt.
1	$ .00	1	$ .00	1	$ .00	1	$ .00
2	.01	2	.01	2	.01	2	.01
3	.01	3	.01	3	.01	3	.01
4	.02	4	.02	4	.02	4	.02
5	.03	5	.03	5	.03	5	.03
6	.03	6	.03	6	.03	6	.03
7	.04	7	.04	7	.04	7	.04
8	.05	8	.05	8	.05	8	.05
9	.05	9	.05	9	.05	9	.05
10	.06	10	.06	10	.06	10	.06
20	.12	20	.12	20	.12	20	.12
30	.19	30	.19	30	.19	30	.19
40	.25	40	.25	40	.25	40	.25
50	.32	50	.32	50	.32	50	.32
60	.38	60	.38	60	.38	60	.38
70	.44	70	.44	70	.45	70	.45
80	.51	80	.51	80	.51	80	.51
90	.57	90	.57	90	.58	90	.58
100	.64	100	.64	100	.64	100	.64
200	1.28	200	1.28	200	1.29	200	1.29
300	1.92	300	1.92	300	1.93	300	1.94
400	2.56	400	2.57	400	2.58	400	2.59
500	3.20	500	3.21	500	3.22	500	3.23
600	3.84	600	3.85	600	3.87	600	3.88
700	4.48	700	4.49	700	4.51	700	4.53
800	5.12	800	5.14	800	5.16	800	5.18
900	5.76	900	5.78	900	5.80	900	5.82
1000	6.40	1000	6.42	1000	6.45	1000	6.47
1100	7.04	1100	7.06	1100	7.09	1100	7.12
1200	7.68	1200	7.71	1200	7.74	1200	7.77
1300	8.32	1300	8.35	1300	8.38	1300	8.41
1400	8.96	1400	8.99	1400	9.03	1400	9.06
1500	9.60	1500	9.63	1500	9.67	1500	9.71
1600	10.24	1600	10.28	1600	10.32	1600	10.36
1700	10.88	1700	10.92	1700	10.96	1700	11.00
1800	11.52	1800	11.56	1800	11.61	1800	11.65
1900	12.16	1900	12.20	1900	12.25	1900	12.30
2000	12.80	2000	12.85	2000	12.90	2000	12.95
2100	13.44	2100	13.49	2100	13.54	2100	13.59
2200	14.08	2200	14.13	2200	14.19	2200	14.24
2300	14.72	2300	14.77	2300	14.83	2300	14.89
2400	15.36	2400	15.42	2400	15.48	2400	15.54
2500	16.00	2500	16.06	2500	16.12	2500	16.18
2600	16.64	2600	16.70	2600	16.77	2600	16.83
2700	17.28	2700	17.34	2700	17.41	2700	17.48
2800	17.92	2800	17.99	2800	18.06	2800	18.13
2900	18.56	2900	18.63	2900	18.70	2900	18.77
3000	19.20	3000	19.27	3000	19.35	3000	19.42
3100	19.84	3100	19.91	3100	19.98	3100	20.06
3200	20.48	3200	20.56	3200	20.64	3200	20.72
3300	21.12	3300	21.20	3300	21.28	3300	21.36
3400	21.76	3400	21.84	3400	21.93	3400	22.01
3500	22.40	3500	22.48	3500	22.57	3500	22.66
3600	23.04	3600	23.13	3600	23.22	3600	23.31
3700	23.68	3700	23.77	3700	23.86	3700	23.95
3800	24.32	3800	24.41	3800	24.51	3800	24.60
3900	24.96	3900	25.05	3900	25.15	3900	25.25
4000	25.60	4000	25.70	4000	25.80	4000	25.90

65 cts.		65¼ cts.		65½ cts.		65¾ cts.	
Lbs.	Amt.	Lbs.	Amt.	Lbs.	Amt.	Lbs.	Amt.
1	$ .00	1	$ .00	1	$ .00	1	$ .00
2	.01	2	.01	2	.01	2	.01
3	.01	3	.01	3	.01	3	.01
4	.02	4	.02	4	.02	4	.02
5	.03	5	.03	5	.03	5	.03
6	.03	6	.03	6	.03	6	.03
7	.04	7	.04	7	.04	7	.04
8	.05	8	.05	8	.05	8	.05
9	.05	9	.05	9	.05	9	.05
10	.06	10	.06	10	.06	10	.06
20	.13	20	.13	20	.13	20	.13
30	.19	30	.19	30	.19	30	.19
40	.26	40	.26	40	.26	40	.26
50	.32	50	.32	50	.32	50	.32
60	.39	60	.39	60	.39	60	.39
70	.45	70	.45	70	.45	70	.46
80	.52	80	.52	80	.52	80	.52
90	.58	90	.58	90	.58	90	.59
100	.65	100	.65	100	.65	100	.65
200	1.30	200	1.30	200	1.31	200	1.31
300	1.95	300	1.95	300	1.96	300	1.97
400	2.60	400	2.61	400	2.62	400	2.63
500	3.25	500	3.26	500	3.27	500	3.28
600	3.90	600	3.91	600	3.93	600	3.94
700	4.55	700	4.56	700	4.58	700	4.60
800	5.20	800	5.22	800	5.24	800	5.26
900	5.85	900	5.87	900	5.89	900	5.91
1000	6.50	1000	6.52	1000	6.55	1000	6.57
1100	7.15	1100	7.17	1100	7.20	1100	7.23
1200	7.80	1200	7.83	1200	7.86	1200	7.89
1300	8·45	1300	8.48	1300	8.51	1300	8.54
1400	9.10	1400	9.13	1400	9.17	1400	9.20
1500	9.75	1500	9.78	1500	9.82	1500	9.86
1600	10.40	1600	10.44	1600	10.48	1600	10.52
1700	11.05	1700	11.09	1700	11.13	1700	11.17
1800	11.70	1800	11.74	1800	11.79	1800	11.83
1900	12.35	1900	12.39	1900	12.44	1900	12.49
2000	13.00	2000	13.05	2000	13.10	2000	13.15
2100	13.65	2100	13.70	2100	13.75	2100	13.80
2200	14.30	2200	14.35	2200	14.41	2200	14.46
2300	14.95	2300	15.00	2300	15.06	2300	15.12
2400	15.60	2400	15.66	2400	15.72	2400	15.78
2500	16.25	2500	16.31	2500	16.37	2500	16.43
2600	16.90	2600	16.96	2600	17.03	2600	17.09
2700	17.55	2700	17.61	2700	17.68	2700	17.75
2800	18.20	2800	18.27	2800	18.34	2800	18.41
2900	18.85	2900	18.92	2900	18.99	2900	19.06
3000	19.50	3000	19.57	3000	19.65	3000	19.72
3100	20.15	3100	20.22	3100	20.30	3100	20.38
3200	20.80	3200	20.88	3200	20.96	3200	21.04
3300	21.45	3300	21.53	3300	21.61	3300	21.69
3400	22.10	3400	22.18	3400	22.27	3400	22.35
3500	22.75	3500	22.83	3500	22.92	3500	23.01
3600	23.40	3600	23.49	3600	23.58	3600	23.67
3700	24.05	3700	24.14	3700	24.23	3700	24.32
3800	24.70	3800	24.79	3800	24.89	3800	24.98
3900	25.35	3900	25.44	3900	25.54	3900	25.64
4000	26.00	4000	26.10	4000	26.20	4000	26.30

66 cts.		66¼ cts.		66½ cts.		66¾ cts.	
Lbs.	Amt.	Lbs.	Amt.	Lbs.	Amt.	Lbs.	Amt.
1	$ .00	1	$ .00	1	$ .00	1	$ .00
2	.01	2	.01	2	.01	2	.01
3	.01	3	.01	3	.01	3	.01
4	.02	4	.02	4	.02	4	.02
5	.03	5	.03	5	.03	5	.03
6	.03	6	.03	6	.03	6	.03
7	.04	7	.04	7	.04	7	.04
8	.05	8	.05	8	.05	8	.05
9	.05	9	.05	9	.05	9	.05
10	.06	10	.06	10	.06	10	.06
20	.13	20	.13	20	.13	20	.13
30	.19	30	.19	30	.19	30	.20
40	.26	40	.26	40	.26	40	.26
50	.33	50	.33	50	.33	50	.33
60	.39	60	.39	60	.39	60	.40
70	.46	70	.46	70	.46	70	.46
80	.52	80	.53	80	.53	80	.53
90	.59	90	.59	90	.59	90	.60
100	.66	100	.66	100	.66	100	.66
200	1.32	200	1.32	200	1.33	200	1.33
300	1.98	300	1.98	300	1.99	300	2.00
400	2.64	400	2.65	400	2.66	400	2.67
500	3.30	500	3.31	500	3.32	500	3.33
600	3.96	600	3.97	600	3.99	600	4.00
700	4.62	700	4.63	700	4.65	700	4.67
800	5.28	800	5.30	800	5.32	800	5.34
900	5.94	900	5.96	900	5.98	900	6.00
1000	6.60	1000	6.62	1000	6.65	1000	6.67
1100	7.26	1100	7.28	1100	7.31	1100	7.34
1200	7.92	1200	7.95	1200	7.98	1200	8.01
1300	8.58	1300	8.61	1300	8.64	1300	8.67
1400	9.24	1400	9.27	1400	9.31	1400	9.34
1500	9.90	1500	9.93	1500	9.97	1500	10.01
1600	10.56	1600	10.60	1600	10.64	1600	10.68
1700	11.22	1700	11.26	1700	11.30	1700	11.34
1800	11.88	1800	11.92	1800	11.97	1800	12.01
1900	12.54	1900	12.58	1900	12.63	1900	12.68
2000	13.20	2000	13.25	2000	13.30	2000	13.35
2100	13.86	2100	13.91	2100	13.96	2100	14.01
2200	14.52	2200	14.57	2200	14.63	2200	14.68
2300	15.18	2300	15.23	2300	15.29	2300	15.35
2400	15.84	2400	15.90	2400	15.96	2400	16.02
2500	16.50	2500	16.56	2500	16.62	2500	16.68
2600	17.16	2600	17.22	2600	17.29	2600	17.35
2700	17.82	2700	17.88	2700	17.95	2700	18.02
2800	18.48	2800	18.55	2800	18.62	2800	18.69
2900	19.14	2900	19.21	2900	19.28	2900	19.35
3000	19.80	3000	19.87	3000	19.95	3000	20.02
3100	20.46	3100	20.53	3100	20.61	3100	20.69
3200	21.12	3200	21.20	3200	21.28	3200	21.36
3300	21.78	3300	21.86	3300	21.94	3300	22.02
3400	22.44	3400	22.52	3400	22.61	3400	22.69
3500	23.10	3500	23.18	3500	23.27	3500	23.36
3600	23.76	3600	23.85	3600	23.94	3600	24.03
3700	24.42	3700	24.51	3700	24.60	3700	24.69
3800	25.08	3800	25.17	3800	25.27	3800	25.36
3900	25.74	3900	25.83	3900	25.93	3900	26.03
4000	26.40	4000	26.50	4000	26.60	4000	26.70

67 cts.		67¼ cts.		67½ cts.		67¾ cts.	
Lbs.	Amt.	Lbs.	Amt.	Lbs.	Amt.	Lbs.	Amt.
1	$ .00	1	$ .00	1	$ .00	1	$ .00
2	.01	2	.01	2	.01	2	.01
3	.02	3	.02	3	.02	3	.02
4	.02	4	.02	4	.02	4	.02
5	.03	5	.03	5	.03	5	.03
6	.04	6	.04	6	.04	6	.04
7	.04	7	.04	7	.04	7	.04
8	.05	8	.05	8	.05	8	.05
9	.06	9	.06	9	.06	9	.06
10	.06	10	.06	10	.06	10	.06
20	.13	20	.13	20	.13	20	.13
30	.20	30	.20	30	.20	30	.20
40	.26	40	.26	40	.27	40	.27
50	.33	50	.33	50	.33	50	.33
60	.40	60	.40	60	.40	60	.40
70	.46	70	.47	70	.47	70	.47
80	.53	80	.53	80	.54	80	.54
90	.60	90	.60	90	.60	90	.60
100	.67	100	.67	100	.67	100	.67
200	1.34	200	1.34	200	1.35	200	1.35
300	2.01	300	2.01	300	2.02	300	2.03
400	2.68	400	2.69	400	2.70	400	2.71
500	3.35	500	3.36	500	3.37	500	3.38
600	4.02	600	4.03	600	4.05	600	4.06
700	4.69	700	4.70	700	4.72	700	4.74
800	5.36	800	5.38	800	5.40	800	5.42
900	6.03	900	6.05	900	6.07	900	6.09
1000	6.70	1000	6.72	1000	6.75	1000	6.77
1100	7.37	1100	7.39	1100	7.42	1100	7.45
1200	8.04	1200	8.07	1200	8.10	1200	8.13
1300	8.71	1300	8.74	1300	8.77	1300	8.80
1400	9.38	1400	9.41	1400	9.45	1400	9.48
1500	10.05	1500	10.08	1500	10.12	1500	10.16
1600	10.72	1600	10.76	1600	10.80	1600	10.84
1700	11.39	1700	11.43	1700	11.47	1700	11.51
1800	12.06	1800	12.10	1800	12.15	1800	12.19
1900	12.73	1900	12.77	1900	12.82	1900	12.87
2000	13.40	2000	13.45	2000	13.50	2000	13.55
2100	14.07	2100	14.12	2100	14.17	2100	14.22
2200	14.74	2200	14.79	2200	14.85	2200	14.90
2300	15.41	2300	15.46	2300	15.52	2300	15.58
2400	16.08	2400	16.14	2400	16.20	2400	16.26
2500	16.75	2500	16.81	2500	16.87	2500	16.93
2600	17.42	2600	17.48	2600	17.55	2600	17.61
2700	18.09	2700	18.15	2700	18.22	2700	18.29
2800	18.76	2800	18.83	2800	18.90	2800	18.97
2900	19.43	2900	19.50	2900	19.57	2900	19.64
3000	20.10	3000	20.17	3000	20.25	3000	20.32
3100	20.77	3100	20.84	3100	20.92	3100	21.00
3200	21.44	3200	21.52	3200	21.60	3200	21.68
3300	22.11	3300	22.19	3300	22.27	3300	22.35
3400	22.78	3400	22.86	3400	22.95	3400	23.03
3500	23.45	3500	23.53	3500	23.62	3500	23.71
3600	24.12	3600	24.21	3600	24.30	3600	24.39
3700	24.79	3700	24.88	3700	24.97	3700	25.06
3800	25.46	3800	25.55	3800	25.65	3800	25.74
3900	26.13	3900	26.22	3900	26.32	3900	26.42
4000	26.80	4000	26.90	4000	27.00	4000	27.10

68 cts.		68¼ cts.		68½ cts.		68¾ cts.	
Lbs.	Amt.	Lbs.	Amt.	Lbs.	Amt.	Lbs.	Amt.
1	$ .00	1	$ .00	1	$ .00	1	$ .00
2	.01	2	.01	2	.01	2	.01
3	.02	3	.02	3	.02	3	.02
4	.02	4	.02	4	.02	4	.02
5	.03	5	.03	5	.03	5	.03
6	.04	6	.04	6	.04	6	.04
7	.04	7	.04	7	.04	7	.04
8	.05	8	.05	8	.05	8	.05
9	.06	9	.06	9	.06	9	.06
10	.06	10	.06	10	.06	10	.06
20	.13	20	.13	20	.13	20	.13
30	.20	30	.20	30	.20	30	.20
40	.27	40	.27	40	.27	40	.27
50	.34	50	.34	50	.34	50	.34
60	.40	60	.40	60	.41	60	.41
70	.47	70	.47	70	.47	70	.48
80	.54	80	.54	80	.54	80	.55
90	.61	90	.61	90	.61	90	.61
100	.68	100	.68	100	.68	100	.68
200	1.36	200	1.36	200	1.37	200	1.37
300	2.04	300	2.04	300	2.05	300	2.06
400	2.72	400	2.73	400	2.74	400	2.75
500	3.40	500	3.41	500	3.42	500	3.43
600	4.08	600	4.09	600	4.11	600	4.12
700	4.76	700	4.77	700	4.79	700	4.81
800	5.44	800	5.46	800	5.48	800	5.50
900	6.12	900	6.14	900	6.16	900	6.18
1000	6.80	1000	6.82	1000	6.85	1000	6.87
1100	7.48	1100	7.50	1100	7.53	1100	7.56
1200	8.16	1200	8.19	1200	8.22	1200	8.25
1300	8.84	1300	8.87	1300	8.90	1300	8.93
1400	9.52	1400	9.55	1400	9.59	1400	9.62
1500	10.20	1500	10.23	1500	10.27	1500	10.31
1600	10.88	1600	10.92	1600	10.96	1600	11.00
1700	11.56	1700	11.60	1700	11.64	1700	11.68
1800	12.24	1800	12.28	1800	12.33	1800	12.37
1900	12.92	1900	12.96	1900	13.01	1900	13.06
2000	13.60	2000	13.65	2000	13.70	2000	13.75
2100	14.28	2100	14.33	2100	14.38	2100	14.43
2200	14.96	2200	15.01	2200	15.07	2200	15.12
2300	15.64	2300	15.69	2300	15.75	2300	15.81
2400	16.32	2400	16.38	2400	16.44	2400	16.50
2500	17.00	2500	17.06	2500	17.12	2500	17.18
2600	17.68	2600	17.74	2600	17.81	2600	17.87
2700	18.36	2700	18.42	2700	18.49	2700	18.56
2800	19.04	2800	19.11	2800	19.18	2800	19.25
2900	19.72	2900	19.79	2900	19.86	2900	19.93
3000	20.40	3000	20.47	3000	20.55	3000	20.62
3100	21.08	3100	21.15	3100	21.23	3100	21.31
3200	21.76	3200	21.84	3200	21.92	3200	22.00
3300	22.44	3300	22.52	3300	22.60	3300	22.68
3400	23.12	3400	23.20	3400	23.29	3400	23.37
3500	23.80	3500	23.88	3500	23.97	3500	24.06
3600	24.48	3600	24.57	3600	24.66	3600	24.75
3700	25.16	3700	25.25	3700	25.34	3700	25.43
3800	25.84	3800	25.93	3800	26.03	3800	26.12
3900	26.52	3900	26.61	3900	26.71	3900	26.81
4000	27.20	4000	27.30	4000	27.40	4000	27.50

69 cts.		69¼ cts.		69½ cts.		69¾ cts.	
Lbs.	Amt.	Lbs.	Amt.	Lbs.	Amt.	Lbs.	Amt.
1	$ .00	1	$ .00	1	$ .00	1	$ .00
2	.01	2	.01	2	.01	2	.01
3	.02	3	.02	3	.02	3	.02
4	.02	4	.02	4	.02	4	.02
5	.03	5	.03	5	.03	5	.03
6	.04	6	.04	6	.04	6	.04
7	.04	7	.04	7	.04	7	.04
8	.05	8	.05	8	.05	8	.05
9	.06	9	.06	9	.06	9	.06
10	.06	10	.06	10	.06	10	.06
20	.13	20	.13	20	.13	20	.13
30	.20	30	.20	30	.20	30	.20
40	.27	40	.27	40	.27	40	.27
50	.34	50	.34	50	.34	50	.34
60	.41	60	.41	60	.41	60	.41
70	.48	70	.48	70	.48	70	.48
80	.55	80	.55	80	.55	80	.55
90	.62	90	.62	90	.62	90	.62
100	.69	100	.69	100	.69	100	.69
200	1.38	200	1.38	200	1.39	200	1.39
300	2.07	300	2.07	300	2.08	300	2.09
400	2.76	400	2.77	400	2.78	400	2.79
500	3.45	500	3.46	500	3.47	500	3.48
600	4.14	600	4.15	600	4.17	600	4.18
700	4.83	700	4.84	700	4.86	700	4.88
800	5.52	800	5.54	800	5.56	800	5.58
900	6.21	900	6.23	900	6.25	900	6.27
1000	6.90	1000	6.92	1000	6.95	1000	6.97
1100	7.59	1100	7.61	1100	7.64	1100	7.67
1200	8.28	1200	8.31	1200	8.34	1200	8.37
1300	8.97	1300	9.00	1300	9.03	1300	9.06
1400	9.66	1400	9.69	1400	9.73	1400	9.76
1500	10.35	1500	10.38	1500	10.42	1500	10.46
1600	11.04	1600	11.08	1600	11.12	1600	11.16
1700	11.73	1700	11.77	1700	11.81	1700	11.85
1800	12.42	1800	12.46	1800	12.51	1800	12.55
1900	13.11	1900	13.15	1900	13.20	1900	13.25
2000	13.80	2000	13.85	2000	13.90	2000	13.95
2100	14.49	2100	14.54	2100	14.59	2100	14.64
2200	15.18	2200	15.23	2200	15.29	2200	15.34
2300	15.87	2300	15.92	2300	15.98	2300	16.04
2400	16.56	2400	16.62	2400	16.68	2400	16.74
2500	17.25	2500	17.31	2500	17.37	2500	17.43
2600	17.94	2600	18.00	2600	18.07	2600	18.13
2700	18.63	2700	18.69	2700	18.76	2700	18.83
2800	19.32	2800	19.39	2800	19.46	2800	19.53
2900	20.01	2900	20.08	2900	20.15	2900	20.22
3000	20.70	3000	20.77	3000	20.85	3000	20.92
3100	21.39	3100	21.46	3100	21.54	3100	21.62
3200	22.08	3200	22.16	3200	22.24	3200	22.32
3300	22.77	3300	22.85	3300	22.93	3300	23.01
3400	23.46	3400	23.54	3400	23.63	3400	23.71
3500	24.15	3500	24.23	3500	24.32	3500	24.41
3600	24.84	3600	24.93	3600	25.02	3600	25.11
3700	25.53	3700	25.62	3700	25.71	3700	25.80
3800	26.22	3800	26.31	3800	26.41	3800	26.50
3900	26.91	3900	27.00	3900	27.10	3900	27.20
4000	27.60	4000	27.70	4000	27.80	4000	27.90

70 cts.		70¼ cts.		70½ cts.		70¾ cts.	
Lbs.	Amt.	Lbs.	Amt.	Lbs.	Amt.	Lbs.	Amt.
1	$ .00	1	$ .00	1	$ .00	1	$ .00
2	.01	2	.01	2	.01	2	.01
3	.02	3	.02	3	.02	3	.02
4	.02	4	.02	4	.02	4	.02
5	.03	5	.03	5	.03	5	.03
6	.04	6	.04	6	.04	6	.04
7	.04	7	.04	7	.04	7	.04
8	.05	8	.05	8	.05	8	.05
9	.06	9	.06	9	.06	9	.06
10	.07	10	.07	10	.07	10	.07
20	.14	20	.14	20	.14	20	.14
30	.21	30	.21	30	.21	30	.21
40	.28	40	.28	40	.28	40	.28
50	.35	50	.35	50	.35	50	.35
60	.42	60	.42	60	.42	60	.42
70	.49	70	.49	70	.49	70	.49
80	.56	80	.56	80	.56	80	.56
90	.63	90	.63	90	.63	90	.63
100	.70	100	.70	100	.70	100	.70
200	1.40	200	1.40	200	1.41	200	1.41
300	2.10	300	2.10	300	2.11	300	2.12
400	2.80	400	2.81	400	2.82	400	2.83
500	3.50	500	3.51	500	3.52	500	3.53
600	4.20	600	4.21	600	4.23	600	4.24
700	4.90	700	4.91	700	4.93	700	4.95
800	5.60	800	5.62	800	5.64	800	5.66
900	6.30	900	6.32	900	6.34	900	6.36
1000	7.00	1000	7.02	1000	7.05	1000	7.07
1100	7.70	1100	7.72	1100	7.75	1100	7.78
1200	8.40	1200	8.43	1200	8.46	1200	8.49
1300	9.10	1300	9.13	1300	9.16	1300	9.19
1400	9.80	1400	9.83	1400	9.87	1400	9.90
1500	10.50	1500	10.53	1500	10.57	1500	10.61
1600	11.20	1600	11.24	1600	11.28	1600	11.32
1700	11.90	1700	11.94	1700	11.98	1700	12.02
1800	12.60	1800	12.64	1800	12.69	1800	12.73
1900	13.30	1900	13.34	1900	13.39	1900	13.44
2000	14.00	2000	14.05	2000	14.10	2000	14.15
2100	14.70	2100	14.75	2100	14.80	2100	14.85
2200	15.40	2200	15.45	2200	15.51	2200	15.56
2300	16.10	2300	16.15	2300	16.21	2300	16.27
2400	16.80	2400	16.86	2400	16.92	2400	16.98
2500	17.50	2500	17.56	2500	17.62	2500	17.68
2600	18.20	2600	18.26	2600	18.33	2600	18.39
2700	18.90	2700	18.96	2700	19.03	2700	19.10
2800	19.60	2800	19.67	2800	19.74	2800	19.81
2900	20.30	2900	20.37	2900	20.44	2900	20.51
3000	21.00	3000	21.07	3000	21.15	3000	21.22
3100	21.70	3100	21.77	3100	21.85	3100	21.93
3200	22.40	3200	22.48	3200	22.56	3200	22.64
3300	23.10	3300	23.18	3300	23.26	3300	23.34
3400	23.80	3400	23.88	3400	23.97	3400	24.05
3500	24.50	3500	24.58	3500	24.67	3500	24.76
3600	25.20	3600	25.29	3600	25.38	3600	25.47
3700	25.90	3700	25.99	3700	26.08	3700	26.17
3800	26.60	3800	26.69	3800	26.79	3800	26.88
3900	27.30	3900	27.39	3900	27.49	3900	27.59
4000	28.00	4000	28.10	4000	28.20	4000	28.30

71 cts.		71¼ cts.		71½ cts.		71¾ cts.	
Lbs.	Amt.	Lbs.	Amt.	Lbs.	Amt.	Lbs.	Amt.
1	$ .00	1	$ .00	1	$ .00	1	$ .00
2	.01	2	.01	2	.01	2	.01
3	.02	3	.02	3	.02	3	.02
4	.02	4	.02	4	.02	4	.02
5	.03	5	.03	5	.03	5	.03
6	.04	6	.04	6	.04	6	.04
7	.04	7	.04	7	.05	7	.05
8	.05	8	.05	8	.05	8	.05
9	.06	9	.06	9	.06	9	.06
10	.07	10	.07	10	.07	10	.07
20	.14	20	.14	20	.14	20	.14
30	.21	30	.21	30	.21	30	.21
40	.28	40	.28	40	.28	40	.28
50	.35	50	.35	50	.35	50	.35
60	.42	60	.42	60	.42	60	.43
70	.49	70	.49	70	.50	70	.50
80	.56	80	.56	80	.57	80	.57
90	.63	90	.64	90	.64	90	.64
100	.71	100	.71	100	.71	100	.71
200	1.42	200	1.42	200	1.43	200	1.43
300	2.13	300	2.13	300	2.14	300	2.15
400	2.84	400	2.85	400	2.86	400	2.87
500	3.55	500	3.56	500	3.57	500	3.58
600	4.26	600	4.27	600	4.29	600	4.30
700	4.97	700	4.98	700	5.00	700	5.02
800	5.68	800	5.70	800	5.72	800	5.74
900	6.39	900	6.41	900	6.43	900	6.45
1000	7.10	1000	7.12	1000	7.15	1000	7.17
1100	7.81	1100	7.83	1100	7.86	1100	7.89
1200	8.52	1200	8.55	1200	8.58	1200	8.61
1300	9.23	1300	9.26	1300	9.29	1300	9.32
1400	9.94	1400	9.97	1400	10.01	1400	10.04
1500	10.65	1500	10.68	1500	10.72	1500	10.76
1600	11.36	1600	11.40	1600	11.44	1600	11.48
1700	12.07	1700	12.11	1700	12.15	1700	12.19
1800	12.78	1800	12.82	1800	12.87	1800	12.91
1900	13.49	1900	13.53	1900	13.58	1900	13.63
2000	14.20	2000	14.25	2000	14.30	2000	14.35
2100	14.91	2100	14.96	2100	15.01	2100	15.06
2200	15.62	2200	15.67	2200	15.73	2200	15.78
2300	16.33	2300	16.38	2300	16.44	2300	16.50
2400	17.04	2400	17.10	2400	17.16	2400	17.22
2500	17.75	2500	17.81	2500	17.87	2500	17.93
2600	18.46	2600	18.52	2600	18.59	2600	18.65
2700	19.17	2700	19.23	2700	19.30	2700	19.37
2800	19.88	2800	19.95	2800	20.02	2800	20.09
2900	20.59	2900	20.66	2900	20.73	2900	20.80
3000	21.30	3000	21.37	3000	21.45	3000	21.52
3100	22.01	3100	22.08	3100	22.16	3100	22.24
3200	22.72	3200	22.80	3200	22.88	3200	22.96
3300	23.43	3300	23.51	3300	23.59	3300	23.67
3400	24.14	3400	24.22	3400	24.31	3400	24.39
3500	24.85	3500	24.93	3500	25.02	3500	25.11
3600	25.56	3600	25.65	3600	25.74	3600	25.83
3700	26.27	3700	26.36	3700	26.45	3700	26.54
3800	26.98	3800	27.07	3800	27.17	3800	27.26
3900	27.69	3900	27.78	3900	27.88	3900	27.98
4000	28.40	4000	28.50	4000	28.60	4000	28.70

72 cts.		72¼ cts.		72½ cts.		72¾ cts.	
Lbs.	Amt.	Lbs.	Amt.	Lbs.	Amt.	Lbs.	Amt.
1	$ .00	1	$ .00	1	$ .00	1	$ .00
2	.01	2	.01	2	.01	2	.01
3	.02	3	.02	3	.02	3	.02
4	.02	4	.02	4	.02	4	.02
5	.03	5	.03	5	.03	5	.03
6	.04	6	.04	6	.04	6	.04
7	.05	7	.05	7	.05	7	.05
8	.05	8	.05	8	.05	8	.05
9	.06	9	.06	9	.06	9	.06
10	.07	10	.07	10	.07	10	.07
20	.14	20	.14	20	.14	20	.14
30	.21	30	.21	30	.21	30	.21
40	.28	40	.28	40	.29	40	.29
50	.36	50	.36	50	.36	50	.36
60	.43	60	.43	60	.43	60	.43
70	.50	70	.50	70	.50	70	.50
80	.57	80	.57	80	.58	80	.58
90	.64	90	.64	90	.65	90	.65
100	.72	100	.72	100	.72	100	.72
200	1.44	200	1.44	200	1.45	200	1.45
300	2.16	300	2.16	300	2.17	300	2.18
400	2.88	400	2.89	400	2.90	400	2.91
500	3.60	500	3.61	500	3.62	500	3.63
600	4.32	600	4.33	600	4.35	600	4.36
700	5.04	700	5.05	700	5.07	700	5.09
800	5.76	800	5.78	800	5.80	800	5.82
900	6.48	900	6.50	900	6.52	900	6.54
1000	7.20	1000	7.22	1000	7.25	1000	7.27
1100	7.92	1100	7.94	1100	7.97	1100	8.00
1200	8.64	1200	8.67	1200	8.70	1200	8.73
1300	9.36	1300	9.39	1300	9.42	1300	9.45
1400	10.08	1400	10.11	1400	10.15	1400	10.18
1500	10.80	1500	10.83	1500	10.87	1500	10.91
1600	11.52	1600	11.56	1600	11.60	1600	11.64
1700	12.24	1700	12.28	1700	12.32	1700	12.36
1800	12.96	1800	13.00	1800	13.05	1800	13.09
1900	13.68	1900	13.72	1900	13.77	1900	13.82
2000	14.40	2000	14.45	2000	14.50	2000	14.55
2100	15.12	2100	15.17	2100	15.22	2100	15.27
2200	15.84	2200	15.89	2200	15.95	2200	16.00
2300	16.56	2300	16.61	2300	16.67	2300	16.73
2400	17.28	2400	17.34	2400	17.40	2400	17.46
2500	18.00	2500	18.06	2500	18.12	2500	18.18
2600	18.72	2600	18.78	2600	18.85	2600	18.91
2700	19.44	2700	19.50	2700	19.57	2700	19.64
2800	20.16	2800	20.23	2800	20.30	2800	20.37
2900	20.88	2900	20.95	2900	21.02	2900	21.09
3000	21.60	3000	21.67	3000	21.75	3000	21.82
3100	22.32	3100	22.39	3100	22.37	3100	22.45
3200	23.04	3200	23.12	3200	23.20	3200	23.25
3300	23.76	3300	23.84	3300	23.92	3300	24.00
3400	24.48	3400	24.56	3400	24.65	3400	24.73
3500	25.20	3500	25.29	3500	25.37	3500	25.46
3600	25.92	3600	26.01	3600	26.10	3600	26.19
3700	26.64	3700	26.73	3700	26.82	3700	26.91
3800	27.36	3800	27.45	3800	27.55	3800	27.64
3900	28.08	3900	28.17	3900	28.27	3900	28.37
4000	28.80	4000	28.90	4000	29.00	4000	29.10

73 cts.		73¼ cts.		73½ cts.		73¾ cts.	
Lbs.	Amt.	Lbs.	Amt.	Lbs.	Amt.	Lbs.	Amt.
1	$ .00	1	$ .00	1	$ .00	1	$ .00
2	.01	2	.01	2	.01	2	.01
3	.02	3	.02	3	.02	3	.02
4	.02	4	.02	4	.02	4	.02
5	.03	5	.03	5	.03	5	.03
6	.04	6	.04	6	.04	6	.04
7	.05	7	.05	7	.05	7	.05
8	.05	8	.05	8	.05	8	.05
9	.06	9	.06	9	.06	9	.06
10	.07	10	.07	10	.07	10	.07
20	.14	20	.14	20	.14	20	.14
30	.21	30	.21	30	.22	30	.22
40	.29	40	.29	40	.29	40	.29
50	.36	50	.36	50	.36	50	.36
60	.43	60	.43	60	.44	60	.44
70	.51	70	.51	70	.51	70	.51
80	.58	80	.58	80	.58	80	.59
90	.65	90	.65	90	.66	90	.66
100	.73	100	.73	100	.73	100	.73
200	1.46	200	1.46	200	1.47	200	1.47
300	2.19	300	2.19	300	2.20	300	2.21
400	2.92	400	2.93	400	2.94	400	2.95
500	3.65	500	3.66	500	3.67	500	3.68
600	4.38	600	4.39	600	4.41	600	4.42
700	5.11	700	5.12	700	5.14	700	5.16
800	5.84	800	5.86	800	5.88	800	5.90
900	6.57	900	6.59	900	6.61	900	6.63
1000	7.30	1000	7.32	1000	7.35	1000	7.37
1100	8.03	1100	8.05	1100	8.08	1100	8.11
1200	8.76	1200	8.79	1200	8.82	1200	8.85
1300	9.49	1300	9.52	1300	9.55	1300	9.58
1400	10.22	1400	10.25	1400	10.29	1400	10.32
1500	10.95	1500	10.98	1500	11.02	1500	11.06
1600	11.68	1600	11.72	1600	11.76	1600	11.80
1700	12.41	1700	12.45	1700	12.49	1700	12.53
1800	13.14	1800	13.18	1800	13.23	1800	13.27
1900	13.87	1900	13.91	1900	13.96	1900	14.01
2000	14.60	2000	14.65	2000	14.70	2000	14.75
2100	15.33	2100	15.38	2100	15.43	2100	15.48
2200	16.06	2200	16.11	2200	16.17	2200	16.22
2300	16.79	2300	16.84	2300	16.90	2300	16.96
2400	17.52	2400	17.58	2400	17.64	2400	17.70
2500	18.25	2500	18.31	2500	18.37	2500	18.43
2600	18.98	2600	19.04	2600	19.11	2600	19.17
2700	19.71	2700	19.77	2700	19.84	2700	19.91
2800	20.44	2800	20.51	2800	20.58	2800	20.65
2900	21.17	2900	21.24	2900	21.31	2900	21.38
3000	21.90	3000	21.97	3000	22.05	3000	22.12
3100	22.63	3100	22.70	3100	21.78	3100	22.86
3200	23.36	3200	23.44	3200	23.52	3200	23.60
3300	24.09	3300	24.17	3300	24.25	3300	24.33
3400	24.82	3400	24.90	3400	24.99	3400	25.07
3500	25.55	3500	25.63	3500	25.72	3500	25.81
3600	26.28	3600	26.37	3600	26.46	3600	26.55
3700	27.01	3700	27.10	3700	27.19	3700	27.28
3800	27.74	3800	27.83	3800	27.93	3800	28.02
3900	28.47	3900	28.56	3900	28.65	3900	28.76
4000	29.20	4000	29.30	4000	29.40	4000	29.50

74 cts.		74¼ cts.		74½ cts.		74¾ cts.	
Lbs.	Amt.	Lbs.	Amt.	Lbs.	Amt.	Lbs.	Amt.
1	$ .00	1	$ .00	1	$ .00	1	$ .00
2	.01	2	.01	2	.01	2	.01
3	.02	3	.02	3	.02	3	.02
4	.02	4	.02	4	.02	4	.02
5	.03	5	.03	5	.03	5	.03
6	.04	6	.04	6	.04	6	.04
7	.05	7	.05	7	.05	7	.05
8	.05	8	.05	8	.05	8	.05
9	.06	9	.06	9	.06	9	.06
10	.07	10	.07	10	.07	10	.07
20	.14	20	.14	20	.14	20	.14
30	.22	30	.22	30	.22	30	.22
40	.29	40	.29	40	.29	40	.29
50	.37	50	.37	50	.37	50	.37
60	.44	60	.44	60	.44	60	.44
70	.51	70	.51	70	.52	70	.52
80	.59	80	.59	80	.59	80	.59
90	.66	90	.66	90	.67	90	.67
100	.74	100	.74	100	.74	100	.74
200	1.48	200	1.48	200	1.49	200	1.49
300	2.22	300	2.22	300	2.23	300	2.24
400	2.96	400	2.97	400	2.98	400	2.99
500	3.70	500	3.71	500	3.72	500	3.73
600	4.44	600	4.45	600	4.47	600	4.48
700	5.18	700	5.19	700	5.21	700	5.23
800	5.92	800	5.94	800	5.96	800	5.98
900	6.66	900	6.68	900	6.70	900	6.72
1000	7.40	1000	7.42	1000	7.45	1000	7.47
1100	8.14	1100	8.16	1100	8.19	1100	8.22
1200	8.88	1200	8.91	1200	8.94	1200	8.97
1300	9.62	1300	9.65	1300	9.68	1300	9.71
1400	10.36	1400	10.39	1400	10.43	1400	10.46
1500	11.10	1500	11.13	1500	11.17	1500	11.21
1600	11.84	1600	11.88	1600	11.92	1600	11.96
1700	12.58	1700	12.62	1700	12.66	1700	12.70
1800	13.32	1800	13.36	1800	13.41	1800	13.45
1900	14.06	1900	14.10	1900	14.15	1900	14.20
2000	14.80	2000	14.85	2000	14.90	2000	14.95
2100	15.54	2100	15.59	2100	15.64	2100	15.69
2200	16.28	2200	16.33	2200	16.39	2200	16.44
2300	17.02	2300	17.07	2300	17.13	2300	17.19
2400	17.76	2400	17.82	2400	17.88	2400	17.94
2500	18.50	2500	18.56	2500	18.62	2500	18.68
2600	19.24	2600	19.30	2600	19.37	2600	19.43
2700	19.98	2700	20.04	2700	20.11	2700	20.18
2800	20.72	2800	20.79	2800	20.86	2800	20.93
2900	21.46	2900	21.53	2900	21.60	2900	21.67
3000	22.20	3000	22.27	3000	22.35	3000	22.42
3100	22.94	3100	23.01	3100	23.09	3100	23.17
3200	23.68	3200	23.76	3200	23.84	3200	23.92
3300	24.42	3300	24.50	3300	24.58	3300	24.66
3400	25.16	3400	25.24	3400	25.33	3400	25.41
3500	25.90	3500	25.98	3500	26.07	3500	26.16
3600	26.64	3600	26.73	3600	26.82	3600	26.91
3700	27.38	3700	27.47	3700	27.56	3700	27.65
3800	28.12	3800	28.21	3800	28.31	3800	28.40
3900	28.86	3900	28.95	3900	29.05	3900	29.15
4000	29.60	4000	29.70	4000	29.80	4000	29.90

75 cts.		75¼ cts.		75½ cts.		75¾ cts.	
Lbs.	Amt.	Lbs.	Amt.	Lbs.	Amt.	Lbs.	Amt.
1	$ .00	1	$ .00	1	$ .00	1	$ .00
2	.01	2	.01	2	.01	2	.01
3	.02	3	.02	3	.02	3	.02
4	.03	4	.03	4	.03	4	.03
5	.03	5	.03	5	.03	5	.03
6	.04	6	.04	6	.04	6	.04
7	.05	7	.05	7	.05	7	.05
8	.06	8	.06	8	.06	8	.06
9	.06	9	.06	9	.06	9	.06
10	.07	10	.07	10	.07	10	.07
20	.15	20	.15	20	.15	20	.15
30	.22	30	.22	30	.22	30	.22
40	.30	40	.30	40	.30	40	.30
50	.37	50	.37	50	.37	50	.37
60	.45	60	.45	60	.45	60	.45
70	.52	70	.52	70	.52	70	.53
80	.60	80	.60	80	.60	80	.60
90	.67	90	.67	90	.67	90	.68
100	.75	100	.75	100	.75	100	.75
200	1.50	200	1.50	200	1.51	200	1.51
300	2.25	300	2.25	300	2.26	300	2.27
400	3.00	400	3.01	400	3.02	400	3.03
500	3.75	500	3.76	500	3.77	500	3.78
600	4.50	600	4.51	600	4.53	600	4.54
700	5.25	700	5.26	700	5.28	700	5.30
800	6.00	800	6.02	800	6.04	800	6.06
900	6.75	900	6.77	900	6.79	900	6.81
1000	7.50	1000	7.52	1000	7.55	1000	7.57
1100	8.25	1100	8.27	1100	8.30	1100	8.33
1200	9.00	1200	9.03	1200	9.06	1200	9.09
1300	9.75	1300	9.78	1300	9.81	1300	9.84
1400	10.50	1400	10.53	1400	10.57	1400	10.60
1500	11.25	1500	11.28	1500	11.32	1500	11.36
1600	12.00	1600	12.04	1600	12.08	1600	12.12
1700	12.75	1700	12.79	1700	12.83	1700	12.87
1800	13.50	1800	13.54	1800	13.59	1800	13.63
1900	14.25	1900	14.29	1900	14.34	1900	14.39
2000	15.00	2000	15.05	2000	15.10	2000	15.15
2100	15.75	2100	15.80	2100	15.85	2100	15.90
2200	16.50	2200	16.55	2200	16.61	2200	16.66
2300	17.25	2300	17.30	2300	17.36	2300	17.42
2400	18.00	2400	18.06	2400	18.12	2400	18.18
2500	18.75	2500	18.81	2500	18.87	2500	18.93
2600	19.50	2600	19.56	2600	19.63	2600	19.69
2700	20.25	2700	20.31	2700	20.38	2700	20.45
2800	21.00	2800	21.07	2800	21.14	2800	21.21
2900	21.75	2900	21.82	2900	21.89	2900	21.96
3000	22.50	3000	22.57	3000	22.65	3000	22.72
3100	23.25	3100	23.32	3100	23.40	3100	23.48
3200	24.00	3200	24.08	3200	24.16	3200	24.24
3300	24.75	3300	24.83	3300	24.91	3300	24.99
3400	25.50	3400	25.58	3400	25.67	3400	25.75
3500	26.25	3500	26.33	3500	26.42	3500	26.51
3600	27.00	3600	27.09	3600	27.18	3600	27.27
3700	27.75	3700	27.84	3700	27.93	3700	28.02
3800	28.50	3800	28.59	3800	28.69	3800	28.78
3900	29.25	3900	29.34	3900	29.44	3900	29.54
4000	30.00	4000	30.10	4000	30.20	4000	30.30

76 cts.		76¼ cts.		76½ cts.		76¾ cts.	
Lbs.	Amt.	Lbs.	Amt.	Lbs.	Amt.	Lbs.	Amt.
1	$ .00	1	$ .00	1	$ .00	1	$ .00
2	.01	2	.01	2	.01	2	.01
3	.02	3	.02	3	.02	3	.02
4	.03	4	.03	4	.03	4	.03
5	.03	5	.03	5	.03	5	.03
6	.04	6	.04	6	.04	6	.04
7	.05	7	.05	7	.05	7	.05
8	.06	8	.06	8	.06	8	.06
9	.06	9	.06	9	.06	9	.06
10	.07	10	.07	10	.07	10	.07
20	.15	20	.15	20	.15	20	.15
30	.22	30	.22	30	.22	30	.23
40	.30	40	.30	40	.30	40	.30
50	.38	50	.38	50	.38	50	.38
60	.45	60	.45	60	.45	60	.46
70	.53	70	.53	70	.53	70	.53
80	.60	80	.61	80	.61	80	.61
90	.68	90	.68	90	.68	90	.69
100	.76	100	.76	100	.76	100	.76
200	1.52	200	1.52	200	1.53	200	1.53
300	2.28	300	2.28	300	2.29	300	2.30
400	3.04	400	3.05	400	3.06	400	3.07
500	3.80	500	3.81	500	3.82	500	3.83
600	4.56	600	4.57	600	4.59	600	4.60
700	5.32	700	5.33	700	5.35	700	5.37
800	6.08	800	6.10	800	6.12	800	6.14
900	6.84	900	6.86	900	6.88	900	6.90
1000	7.60	1000	7.62	1000	7.65	1000	7.67
1100	8.36	1100	8.38	1100	8.41	1100	8.44
1200	9.12	1200	9.15	1200	9.18	1200	9.21
1300	9.88	1300	9.91	1300	9.94	1300	9.97
1400	10.64	1400	10.67	1400	10.71	1400	10.74
1500	11.40	1500	11.43	1500	11.47	1500	11.51
1600	12.16	1600	12.20	1600	12.24	1600	12.28
1700	12.92	1700	12.96	1700	13.00	1700	13.04
1800	13.68	1800	13.72	1800	13.77	1800	13.81
1900	14.44	1900	14.48	1900	14.53	1900	14.58
2000	15.20	2000	15.25	2000	15.30	2000	15.35
2100	15.96	2100	16.01	2100	16.06	2100	16.11
2200	16.72	2200	16.77	2200	16.83	2200	16.88
2300	17.48	2300	17.53	2300	17.59	2300	17.65
2400	18.24	2400	18.30	2400	18.36	2400	18.42
2500	19.00	2500	19.06	2500	19.12	2500	19.18
2600	19.76	2600	19.82	2600	19.89	2600	19.95
2700	20.52	2700	20.58	2700	20.65	2700	20.72
2800	21.28	2800	21.35	2800	21.42	2800	21.49
2900	22.04	2900	22.11	2900	22.18	2900	22.25
3000	22.80	3000	22.87	3000	22.95	3000	23.02
3100	23.56	3100	23.63	3100	23.71	3100	23.79
3200	24.32	3200	24.40	3200	24.48	3200	24.56
3300	25.08	3300	25.16	3300	25.24	3300	25.32
3400	25.84	3400	25.92	3400	26.01	3400	26.09
3500	26.60	3500	26.68	3500	26.77	3500	26.86
3600	27.36	3600	27.45	3600	27.54	3600	27.63
3700	28.12	3700	28.21	3700	28.30	3700	28.39
3800	28.88	3800	28.97	3800	29.07	3800	29.16
3900	29.64	3900	29.73	3900	29.83	3900	29.93
4000	30.40	4000	30.50	4000	30.60	4000	30.70

77 cts.		77¼ cts.		77½ cts.		77¾ cts.	
Lbs.	Amt.	Lbs.	Amt.	Lbs.	Amt.	Lbs.	Amt.
1	$ .00	1	$ .00	1	$ .00	1	$ .00
2	.01	2	.01	2	.01	2	.01
3	.02	3	.02	3	.02	3	.02
4	.03	4	.03	4	.03	4	.03
5	.03	5	.03	5	.03	5	.03
6	.04	6	.04	6	.04	6	.04
7	.05	7	.05	7	.05	7	.05
8	.06	8	.06	8	.06	8	.06
9	.06	9	.06	9	.06	9	.06
10	.07	10	.07	10	.07	10	.07
20	.15	20	.15	20	.15	20	.15
30	.23	30	.23	30	.23	30	.23
40	.30	40	.30	40	.31	40	.31
50	.38	50	.38	50	.38	50	.38
60	.46	60	.46	60	.46	60	.46
70	.53	70	.54	70	.54	70	.54
80	.61	80	.61	80	.62	80	.62
90	.69	90	.69	90	.69	90	.69
100	.77	100	.77	100	.77	100	.77
200	1.54	200	1.54	200	1.55	200	1.55
300	2.31	300	2.31	300	2.32	300	2.33
400	3.08	400	3.09	400	3.10	400	3.11
500	3.85	500	3.86	500	3.87	500	3.88
600	4.62	600	4.63	600	4.65	600	4.66
700	5.39	700	5.40	700	5.42	700	5.44
800	6.16	800	6.18	800	6.20	800	6.22
900	6.93	900	6.95	900	6.97	900	6.99
1000	7.70	1000	7.72	1000	7.75	1000	7.77
1100	8.47	1100	8.49	1100	8.52	1100	8.55
1200	9.24	1200	9.27	1200	9.30	1200	9.33
1300	10.01	1300	10.04	1300	10.07	1300	10.10
1400	10.78	1400	10.81	1400	10.85	1400	10.88
1500	11.55	1500	11.58	1500	11.62	1500	11.66
1600	12.32	1600	12.36	1600	12.40	1600	12.44
1700	13.09	1700	13.13	1700	13.17	1700	13.21
1800	13.86	1800	13.90	1800	13.95	1800	13.99
1900	14.63	1900	14.67	1900	14.72	1900	14.77
2000	15.40	2000	15.45	2000	15.50	2000	15.55
2100	16.17	2100	16.22	2100	16.27	2100	16.32
2200	16.94	2200	16.99	2200	17.05	2200	17.10
2300	17.71	2300	17.76	2300	17.82	2300	17.88
2400	18.48	2400	18.54	2400	18.60	2400	18.66
2500	19.25	2500	19.31	2500	19.37	2500	19.43
2600	20.02	2600	20.08	2600	20.15	2600	20.21
2700	20.79	2700	20.85	2700	20.92	2700	20.99
2800	21.56	2800	21.63	2800	21.70	2800	21.77
2900	22.33	2900	22.40	2900	22.47	2900	22.54
3000	23.10	3000	23.17	3000	23.25	3000	23.32
3100	23.87	3100	23.94	3100	24.02	3100	24.10
3200	24.64	3200	24.72	3200	24.80	3200	24.88
3300	25.11	3300	25.19	3300	25.27	3300	25.35
3400	26.18	3400	26.26	3400	26.35	3400	26.43
3500	26.95	3500	27.03	3500	27.12	3500	27.21
3600	27.72	3600	27.81	3600	27.90	3600	27.99
3700	28.49	3700	28.58	3700	28.67	3700	28.76
3800	29.26	3800	29.35	3800	29.45	3800	29.54
3900	30.03	3900	30.12	3900	30.22	3900	30.32
4000	30.80	4000	30.90	4000	31.00	4000	31.10

78 cts.		78¼ cts.		78½ cts.		78¾ cts.	
Lbs.	Amt.	Lbs.	Amt.	Lbs.	Amt.	Lbs.	Amt.
1	$ .00	1	$ .00	1	$ .00	1	$ .00
2	.01	2	.01	2	.01	2	.01
3	.02	3	.02	3	.02	3	.02
4	.03	4	.03	4	.03	4	.03
5	.03	5	.03	5	.03	5	.03
6	.04	6	.04	6	.04	6	.04
7	.05	7	.05	7	.05	7	.05
8	.06	8	.06	8	.06	8	.06
9	.07	9	.07	9	.07	9	.07
10	.07	10	.07	10	.07	10	.07
20	.15	20	.15	20	.15	20	.15
30	.23	30	.23	30	.23	30	.23
40	.31	40	.31	40	.31	40	.31
50	.39	50	.39	50	.39	50	.39
60	.46	60	.46	60	.47	60	.47
70	.54	70	.54	70	.54	70	.55
80	.62	80	.62	80	.62	80	.63
90	.70	90	.70	90	.70	90	.70
100	.78	100	.78	100	.78	100	.78
200	1.56	200	1.56	200	1.57	200	1.57
300	2.34	300	2.34	300	2.35	300	2.36
400	3.12	400	3.13	400	3.14	400	3.15
500	3.90	500	3.91	500	3.92	500	3.93
600	4.68	600	4.69	600	4.71	600	4.72
700	5.46	700	5.47	700	5.49	700	5.51
800	6.24	800	6.26	800	6.28	800	6.30
900	7.02	900	7.04	900	7.06	900	7.08
1000	7.80	1000	7.82	1000	7.85	1000	7.87
1100	8.58	1100	8.60	1100	8.63	1100	8.66
1200	9.36	1200	9.39	1200	9.42	1200	9.45
1300	10.14	1300	10.17	1300	10.20	1300	10.23
1400	10.92	1400	10.95	1400	10.99	1400	11.02
1500	11.70	1500	11.73	1500	11.77	1500	11.81
1600	12.48	1600	12.52	1600	12.56	1600	12.60
1700	13.26	1700	13.30	1700	13.34	1700	13.38
1800	14.04	1800	14.08	1800	14.13	1800	14.17
1900	14.82	1900	14.86	1900	14.91	1900	14.96
2000	15.60	2000	15.65	2000	15.70	2000	15.75
2100	16.38	2100	16.43	2100	16.48	2100	16.53
2200	17.16	2200	17.21	2200	17.27	2200	17.32
2300	17.94	2300	17.99	2300	18.05	2300	18.11
2400	18.72	2400	18.78	2400	18.84	2400	18.90
2500	19.50	2500	19.56	2500	19.62	2500	19.68
2600	20.28	2600	20.34	2600	20.41	2600	20.47
2700	21.06	2700	21.12	2700	21.19	2700	21.26
2800	21.84	2800	21.91	2800	21.98	2800	22.05
2900	22.62	2900	22.69	2900	22.76	2900	22.83
3000	23.40	3000	23.47	3000	23.55	3000	23.62
3100	24.18	3100	24.25	3100	24.33	3100	24.41
3200	24.96	3200	25.04	3200	25.12	3200	25.20
3300	25.74	3300	25.82	3300	25.90	3300	25.98
3400	26.52	3400	26.60	3400	26.69	3400	26.77
3500	27.30	3500	27.38	3500	27.47	3500	27.56
3600	28.08	3600	28.17	3600	28.26	3600	28.35
3700	28.86	3700	28.95	3700	29.04	3700	29.13
3800	29.64	3800	29.73	3800	29.83	3800	29.92
3900	30.42	3900	30.51	3900	30.61	3900	30.71
4000	31.20	4000	31.30	4000	31.40	4000	31.50

79 cts.		79¼ cts.		79½ cts.		79¾ cts.	
Lbs.	Amt.	Lbs.	Amt.	Lbs.	Amt.	Lbs.	Amt.
1	$ .00	1	$ .00	1	$ .00	1	$ .00
2	.01	2	.01	2	.01	2	.01
3	.02	3	.02	3	.02	3	.02
4	.03	4	.03	4	.03	4	.03
5	.03	5	.03	5	.03	5	.03
6	.04	6	.04	6	.04	6	.04
7	.05	7	.05	7	.05	7	.05
8	.06	8	.06	8	.06	8	.06
9	.07	9	.07	9	.07	9	.07
10	.07	10	.07	10	.07	10	.07
20	.15	20	.15	20	.15	20	.15
30	.23	30	.23	30	.23	30	.23
40	.31	40	.31	40	.31	40	.31
50	.39	50	.39	50	.39	50	.39
60	.47	60	.47	60	.47	60	.47
70	.55	70	.55	70	.55	70	.55
80	.63	80	.63	80	.63	80	.63
90	.71	90	.71	90	.71	90	.71
100	.79	100	.79	100	.79	100	.79
200	1.58	200	1.58	200	1.59	200	1.59
300	2.37	300	2.37	300	2.38	300	2.39
400	3.16	400	3.17	400	3.18	400	3.19
500	3.95	500	3.96	500	3.97	500	3.98
600	4.74	600	4.75	600	4.77	600	4.78
700	5.53	700	5.54	700	5.56	700	5.58
800	6.32	800	6.34	800	6.36	800	6.38
900	7.11	900	7.13	900	7.15	900	7.17
1000	7.90	1000	7.92	1000	7.95	1000	7.97
1100	8.69	1100	8.71	1100	8.74	1100	8.77
1200	9.48	1200	9.51	1200	9.54	1200	9.57
1300	10.27	1300	10.30	1300	10.33	1300	10.36
1400	11.06	1400	11.09	1400	11.13	1400	11.16
1500	11.85	1500	11.88	1500	11.92	1500	11.96
1600	12.64	1600	12.68	1600	12.72	1600	12.76
1700	13.43	1700	13.47	1700	13.51	1700	13.55
1800	14.22	1800	14.26	1800	14.31	1800	14.35
1900	15.01	1900	15.05	1900	15.10	1900	15.15
2000	15.80	2000	15.85	2000	15.90	2000	15.95
2100	16.59	2100	16.64	2100	16.69	2100	16.74
2200	17.38	2200	17.43	2200	17.49	2200	17.54
2300	18.17	2300	18.22	2300	18.28	2300	18.34
2400	18.96	2400	19.02	2400	19.08	2400	19.14
2500	19.75	2500	19.81	2500	19.87	2500	19.93
2600	20.54	2600	20.60	2600	20.67	2600	20.73
2700	21.33	2700	21.39	2700	21.46	2700	21.53
2800	22.12	2800	22.19	2800	22.26	2800	22.33
2900	22.91	2900	22.98	2900	23.05	2900	23.12
3000	23.70	3000	23.77	3000	23.85	3000	23.92
3100	24.49	3100	24.56	3100	24.64	3100	24.72
3200	25.28	3200	25.36	3200	25.44	3200	25.52
3300	26.07	3300	26.15	3300	26.23	3300	26.31
3400	26.86	3400	26.94	3400	27.03	3400	27.11
3500	27.65	3500	27.73	3500	27.82	3500	27.91
3600	28.44	3600	28.53	3600	28.62	3600	28.71
3700	29.23	3700	29.32	3700	29.41	3700	29.50
3800	30.02	3800	30.11	3800	30.21	3800	30.30
3900	30.81	3900	30.90	3900	31.00	3900	31.10
4000	31.60	4000	31.70	4000	31.80	4000	31.90

80 cts.		80¼ cts.		80½ cts.		80¾ cts.	
Lbs.	Amt.	Lbs.	Amt.	Lbs.	Amt.	Lbs.	Amt.
1	$ .00	1	$ .00	1	$ .00	1	$ .00
2	.01	2	.01	2	.01	2	.01
3	.02	3	.02	3	.02	3	.02
4	.03	4	.03	4	.03	4	.03
5	.04	5	.04	5	.04	5	.04
6	.04	6	.04	6	.04	6	.04
7	.05	7	.05	7	.05	7	.05
8	.06	8	.06	8	.06	8	.06
9	.07	9	.07	9	.07	9	.07
10	.08	10	.08	10	.08	10	.08
20	.16	20	.16	20	.16	20	.16
30	.24	30	.24	30	.24	30	.24
40	.32	40	.32	40	.32	40	.32
50	.40	50	.40	50	.40	50	.40
60	.48	60	.48	60	.48	60	.48
70	.56	70	.56	70	.56	70	.56
80	.64	80	.64	80	.64	80	.64
90	.72	90	.72	90	.72	90	.72
100	.80	100	.80	100	.80	100	.80
200	1.60	200	1.60	200	1.61	200	1.61
300	2.40	300	2.40	300	2.41	300	2.42
400	3.20	400	3.21	400	3.22	400	3.23
500	4.00	500	4.01	500	4.02	500	4.03
600	4.80	600	4.81	600	4.83	600	4.84
700	5.60	700	5.61	700	5.63	700	5.65
800	6.40	800	6.42	800	6.44	800	6.46
900	7.20	900	7.22	900	7.24	900	7.26
1000	8.00	1000	8.02	1000	8.05	1000	8.07
1100	8.80	1100	8.82	1100	8.85	1100	8.88
1200	9.60	1200	9.63	1200	9.66	1200	9.69
1300	10.40	1300	10.43	1300	10.46	1300	10.49
1400	11.20	1400	11.23	1400	11.27	1400	11.30
1500	12.00	1500	12.03	1500	12.07	1500	12.11
1600	12.80	1600	12.84	1600	12.88	1600	12.92
1700	13.60	1700	13.64	1700	13.68	1700	13.72
1800	14.40	1800	14.44	1800	14.49	1800	14.53
1900	15.20	1900	15.24	1900	15.29	1900	15.34
2000	16.00	2000	16.05	2000	16.10	2000	16.15
2100	16.80	2100	16.85	2100	16.90	2100	16.95
2200	17.60	2200	17.65	2200	17.71	2200	17.76
2300	18.40	2300	18.45	2300	18.51	2300	18.57
2400	19.20	2400	19.26	2400	19.32	2400	19.38
2500	20.00	2500	20.06	2500	20.12	2500	20.18
2600	20.80	2600	20.86	2600	20.93	2600	20.99
2700	21.60	2700	21.66	2700	21.73	2700	21.80
2800	22.40	2800	22.47	2800	22.54	2800	22.61
2900	23.20	2900	23.27	2900	23.34	2900	23.41
3000	24.00	3000	24.07	3000	24.15	3000	24.22
3100	24.80	3100	24.87	3100	24.95	3100	25.03
3200	25.60	3200	25.68	3200	25.76	3200	25.84
3300	26.40	3300	26.48	3300	26.56	3300	26.63
3400	27.20	3400	27.28	3400	27.37	3400	27.45
3500	28.00	3500	28.08	3500	28.17	3500	28.26
3600	28.80	3600	28.89	3600	28.98	3600	29.07
3700	29.60	3700	29.69	3700	29.78	3700	29.87
3800	30.40	3800	30.49	3800	30.59	3800	30.68
3900	31.20	3900	31.29	3900	31.39	3900	31.49
4000	32.00	4000	32.10	4000	32.20	4000	32.30

81 cts.		81¼ cts.		81½ cts.		81¾ cts.	
Lbs.	Amt.	Lbs.	Amt.	Lbs.	Amt.	Lbs.	Amt.
1	$ .00	1	$ .00	1	$ .00	1	$ .00
2	.01	2	.01	2	.01	2	.01
3	.02	3	.02	3	.02	3	.02
4	.03	4	.03	4	.03	4	.03
5	.04	5	.04	5	.04	5	.04
6	.04	6	.04	6	.04	6	.04
7	.05	7	.05	7	.05	7	.05
8	.06	8	.06	8	.06	8	.06
9	.07	9	.07	9	.07	9	.07
10	.08	10	.08	10	.08	10	.08
20	.16	20	.16	20	.16	20	.16
30	.24	30	.24	30	.24	30	.24
40	.32	40	.32	40	.32	40	.32
50	.40	50	.40	50	.40	50	.40
60	.48	60	.48	60	.48	60	.49
70	.56	70	.56	70	.57	70	.57
80	.64	80	.65	80	.65	80	.65
90	.72	90	.73	90	.73	90	.73
100	.81	100	.81	100	.81	100	.81
200	1.62	200	1.62	200	1.63	200	1.63
300	2.43	300	2.43	300	2.44	300	2.45
400	3.24	400	3.25	400	3.26	400	3.27
500	4.05	500	4.06	500	4.07	500	4.08
600	4.86	600	4.87	600	4.89	600	4.90
700	5.67	700	5.68	700	5.70	700	5.72
800	6.48	800	6.50	800	6.52	800	6.54
900	7.29	900	7.31	900	7.33	900	7.35
1000	8.10	1000	8.12	1000	8.15	1000	8.17
1100	8.91	1100	8.93	1100	8.96	1100	8.99
1200	9.72	1200	9.75	1200	9.78	1200	9.81
1300	10.53	1300	10.56	1300	10.59	1300	10.62
1400	11.34	1400	11.37	1400	11.41	1400	11.44
1500	12.15	1500	12.18	1500	12.22	1500	12.26
1600	12.96	1600	13.00	1600	13.04	1600	13.08
1700	13.77	1700	13.81	1700	13.85	1700	13.89
1800	14.58	1800	14.62	1800	14.67	1800	14.71
1900	15.39	1900	15.43	1900	15.48	1900	15.53
2000	16.20	2000	16.25	2000	16.30	2000	16.35
2100	17.01	2100	17.06	2100	17.11	2100	17.16
2200	17.82	2200	17.87	2200	17.93	2200	17.98
2300	18.63	2300	18.68	2300	18.74	2300	18.86
2400	19.44	2400	19.50	2400	19.56	2400	19.62
2500	20.25	2500	20.31	2500	20.37	2500	20.43
2600	21.06	2600	21.12	2600	21.19	2600	21.25
2700	22.87	2700	21.93	2700	22.00	2700	22.07
2800	22.68	2800	22.75	2800	22.82	2800	22.89
2900	23.49	2900	23.56	2900	23.63	2900	23.70
3000	24.30	3000	24.37	3000	24.45	3000	24.52
3100	25.11	3100	25.18	3100	25.26	3100	25.34
3200	25.92	3200	26.00	3200	26.08	3200	26.16
3300	26.73	3300	26.81	3300	26.89	3300	26.97
3400	27.54	3400	27.62	3400	27.71	3400	27.79
3500	28.35	3500	28.43	3500	28.52	3500	28.61
3600	29.16	3600	29.25	3600	29.34	3600	29.43
3700	29.97	3700	30.06	3700	30.15	3700	30.24
3800	30.78	3800	30.87	3800	30.97	3800	31.06
3900	31.59	3900	31.68	3900	31.78	3900	31.88
4000	32.40	4000	32.50	4000	32.60	4000	32.70

82 cts.		82¼ cts.		82½ cts.		82¾ cts.	
Lbs.	Amt.	Lbs.	Amt.	Lbs.	Amt.	Lbs.	Amt.
1	$ .00	1	$ .00	1	$ .00	1	$ .00
2	.01	2	.01	2	.01	2	.01
3	.02	3	.02	3	.02	3	.02
4	.03	4	.03	4	.03	4	.03
5	.04	5	.04	5	.04	5	.04
6	.04	6	.04	6	.04	6	.04
7	.05	7	.05	7	.05	7	.05
8	.06	8	.06	8	.06	8	.06
9	.07	9	.07	9	.07	9	.07
10	.08	10	.08	10	.08	10	.08
20	.16	20	.16	20	.16	20	.16
30	.24	30	.24	30	.24	30	.24
40	.32	40	.32	40	.33	40	.33
50	.41	50	.41	50	.41	50	.41
60	.49	60	.49	60	.49	60	.49
70	.57	70	.57	70	.57	70	.57
80	.65	80	.65	80	.66	80	.66
90	.73	90	.74	90	.74	90	.74
100	.82	100	.82	100	.82	100	.82
200	1.64	200	1.64	200	1.65	200	1.65
300	2.46	300	2.46	300	2.47	300	2.48
400	3.28	400	3.29	400	3.30	400	3.31
500	4.10	500	4.11	500	4.12	500	4.13
600	4.92	600	4.93	600	4.95	600	4.96
700	5.74	700	5.75	700	5.77	700	5.79
800	6.56	800	6.58	800	6.60	800	6.62
900	7.38	900	7.40	900	7.42	900	7.44
1000	8.20	1000	8.22	1000	8.25	1000	8.27
1100	9.02	1100	9.04	1100	9.07	1100	9.10
1200	9.84	1200	9.87	1200	9.90	1200	9.93
1300	10.66	1300	10.69	1300	10.72	1300	10.75
1400	11.48	1400	11.51	1400	11.55	1400	11.58
1500	12.30	1500	12.33	1500	12.37	1500	12.41
1600	13.12	1600	13.16	1600	13.20	1600	13.24
1700	13.94	1700	13.98	1700	14.02	1700	14.06
1800	14.76	1800	14.80	1800	14.85	1800	14.89
1900	15.58	1900	15.62	1900	15.67	1900	15.72
2000	16.40	2000	16.45	2000	16.50	2000	16.55
2100	17.22	2100	17.27	2100	17.32	2100	17.37
2200	18.04	2200	18.09	2200	18.15	2200	18.20
2300	18.86	2300	18.91	2300	18.97	2300	19.03
2400	19.68	2400	19.74	2400	19.80	2400	19.86
2500	20.50	2500	20.56	2500	20.62	2500	20.68
2600	21.32	2600	21.38	2600	21.45	2600	21.51
2700	22.14	2700	22.20	2700	22.27	2700	22.34
2800	22.96	2800	23.03	2800	23.10	2800	23.17
2900	23.78	2900	23.85	2900	23.92	2900	23.99
3000	24.60	3000	24.67	3000	24.75	3000	24.82
3100	25.42	3100	25.49	3100	25.57	3100	25.65
3200	26.24	3200	26.32	3200	26.40	3200	26.48
3300	27.06	3300	27.14	3300	27.22	3300	27.30
3400	27.88	3400	27.96	3400	28.05	3400	28.13
3500	28.70	3500	28.78	3500	28.87	3500	28.96
3600	29.52	3600	29.61	3600	29.70	3600	29.79
3700	30.34	3700	30.43	3700	30.52	3700	30.61
3800	31.16	3800	31.25	3800	31.35	3800	31.44
3900	31.98	3900	32.07	3900	32.17	3900	32.27
4000	32.80	4000	32.90	4000	33.00	4000	33.10

83 cts.		83¼ cts.		83½ cts.		83¾ cts.	
Lbs.	Amt.	Lbs.	Amt.	Lbs.	Amt.	Lbs.	Amt.
1	$ .00	1	$ .00	1	$ .00	1	$ .00
2	.01	2	.01	2	.01	2	.01
3	.02	3	.02	3	.02	3	.02
4	.03	4	.03	4	.03	4	.03
5	.04	5	.04	5	.04	5	.04
6	.04	6	.04	6	.04	6	.04
7	.05	7	.05	7	.05	7	.05
8	.06	8	.06	8	.06	8	.06
9	.07	9	.07	9	.07	9	.07
10	.08	10	.08	10	.08	10	.08
20	.16	20	.16	20	.16	20	.16
30	.24	30	.24	30	.25	30	.25
40	.33	40	.33	40	.33	40	.33
50	.41	50	.41	50	.41	50	.41
60	.49	60	.49	60	.50	60	.50
70	.58	70	.58	70	.58	70	.58
80	.66	80	.66	80	.66	80	.67
90	.74	90	.74	90	.75	90	.75
100	.83	100	.83	100	.83	100	.83
200	1.66	200	1.66	200	1.67	200	1.67
300	2.49	300	2.49	300	2.50	300	2.51
400	3.32	400	3.33	400	3.34	400	3.35
500	4.15	500	4.16	500	4.17	500	4.18
600	4.98	600	4.99	600	5.01	600	5.02
700	5.81	700	5.82	700	5.84	700	5.86
800	6.64	800	6.66	800	6.68	800	6.70
900	7.47	900	7.49	900	7.51	900	7.53
1000	8.30	1000	8.32	1000	8.35	1000	8.37
1100	9.13	1100	9.15	1100	9.18	1100	9.21
1200	9.96	1200	9.99	1200	10.02	1200	10.05
1300	10.79	1300	10.82	1300	10.85	1300	10.88
1400	11.62	1400	11.65	1400	11.69	1400	11.72
1500	12.45	1500	12.48	1500	12.52	1500	12.56
1600	13.28	1600	13.32	1600	13.36	1600	13.40
1700	14.11	1700	14.15	1700	14.19	1700	14.23
1800	14.94	1800	14.98	1800	15.03	1800	15.07
1900	15.77	1900	15.81	1900	15.86	1900	15.91
2000	16.60	2000	16.65	2000	16.70	2000	16.75
2100	17.43	2100	17.48	2100	17.53	2100	17.58
2200	18.26	2200	18.31	2200	18.37	2200	18.42
2300	19.09	2300	19.14	2300	19.20	2300	19.26
2400	19.92	2400	19.98	2400	20.04	2400	20.10
2500	20.75	2500	20.81	2500	20.87	2500	20.93
2600	21.58	2600	21.64	2600	21.71	2600	21.77
2700	22.41	2700	22.47	2700	22.54	2700	22.61
2800	23.24	2800	23.31	2800	23.38	2800	23.45
2900	24.07	2900	24.14	2900	24.21	2900	24.28
3000	24.90	3000	24.97	3000	25.05	3000	25.12
3100	25.73	3100	25.80	3100	25.88	3100	25.96
3200	26.56	3200	26.64	3200	26.72	3200	26.80
3300	27.39	3300	27.47	3300	27.55	3300	27.63
3400	28.22	3400	28.30	3400	28.39	3400	28.47
3500	29.05	3500	29.13	3500	29.22	3500	29.31
3600	29.88	3600	29.97	3600	30.06	3600	30.15
3700	30.71	3700	30.80	3700	30.89	3700	30.98
3800	31.54	3800	31.63	3800	31.73	3800	31.82
3900	32.37	3900	32.46	3900	32.56	3900	32.66
4000	33.20	4000	33.30	4000	33.40	4000	33.50

84 cts.		84¼ cts.		84½ cts.		84¾ cts.	
Lbs.	Amt.	Lbs.	Amt.	Lbs.	Amt.	Lbs.	Amt.
1	$ .00	1	$ .00	1	$ .00	1	$ .00
2	.01	2	.01	2	.01	2	.01
3	.02	3	.02	3	.02	3	.02
4	.03	4	.03	4	.03	4	.03
5	.04	5	.04	5	.04	5	.04
6	.05	6	.05	6	.05	6	.05
7	.05	7	.05	7	.05	7	.05
8	.06	8	.06	8	.06	8	.06
9	.07	9	.07	9	.07	9	.07
10	.08	10	.08	10	.08	10	.08
20	.16	20	.16	20	.16	20	.16
30	.25	30	.25	30	.25	30	.25
40	.33	40	.33	40	.33	40	.33
50	.42	50	.42	50	.42	50	.42
60	.50	60	.50	60	.50	60	.50
70	.58	70	.58	70	.59	70	.59
80	.67	80	.67	80	.67	80	.67
90	.75	90	.75	90	.76	90	.76
100	.84	100	.84	100	.84	100	.84
200	1.68	200	1.68	200	1.69	200	1.69
300	2.52	300	2.52	300	2.53	300	2.54
400	3.36	400	3.37	400	3.38	400	3.39
500	4.20	500	4.21	500	4.22	500	4.23
600	5.04	600	5.05	600	5.07	600	5.08
700	5.88	700	5.89	700	5.91	700	5.93
800	6.72	800	6.74	800	6.76	800	6.78
900	7.56	900	7.58	900	7.60	900	7.62
1000	8.40	1000	8.42	1000	8.45	1000	8.47
1100	9.24	1100	9.26	1100	9.29	1100	9.32
1200	10.08	1200	10.11	1200	10.14	1200	10.17
1300	10.92	1300	10.95	1300	10.98	1300	11.01
1400	11.76	1400	11.79	1400	11.83	1400	11.86
1500	12.60	1500	12.63	1500	12.67	1500	12.71
1600	13.44	1600	13.48	1600	13.52	1600	13.56
1700	14.28	1700	14.32	1700	14.36	1700	14.40
1800	15.12	1800	15.16	1800	15.21	1800	15.25
1900	15.96	1900	16.00	1900	16.05	1900	16.10
2000	16.80	2000	16.85	2000	16.90	2000	16.95
2100	17.64	2100	17.69	2100	17.74	2100	17.79
2200	18.48	2200	18.53	2200	18.59	2200	18.64
2300	19.32	2300	19.37	2300	19.43	2300	19.49
2400	20.16	2400	20.22	2400	20.28	2400	20.34
2500	21.00	2500	21.06	2500	21.12	2500	21.18
2600	21.84	2600	21.90	2600	21.97	2600	22.03
2700	22.68	2700	22.74	2700	22.81	2700	22.88
2800	23.52	2800	23.59	2800	23.66	2800	23.73
2900	24.36	2900	24.43	2900	24.50	2900	24.57
3000	25.20	3000	25.27	3000	25.35	3000	25.42
3100	26.04	3100	26.11	3100	26.19	3100	26.27
3200	26.88	3200	26.96	3200	27.04	3200	27.12
3300	27.72	3300	27.80	3300	27.88	3300	27.96
3400	28.56	3400	28.64	3400	28.73	3400	28.81
3500	29.40	3500	29.48	3500	29.57	3500	29.66
3600	30.24	3600	30.33	3600	30.42	3600	30.51
3700	31.08	3700	31.17	3700	31.26	3700	31.35
3800	31.92	3800	32.01	3800	32.11	3800	32.20
3900	32.76	3900	32.85	3900	32.95	3900	33.05
4000	33.60	4000	33.70	4000	33.80	4000	33.90

85 cts.		85¼ cts.		85½ cts.		85¾ cts.	
Lbs.	Amt.	Lbs.	Amt.	Lbs.	Amt.	Lbs.	Amt.
1	$ .00	1	$ .00	1	$ .00	1	$ .00
2	.01	2	.01	2	.01	2	.01
3	.02	3	.02	3	.02	3	.02
4	.03	4	.03	4	.03	4	.03
5	.04	5	.04	5	.04	5	.04
6	.05	6	.05	6	.05	6	.05
7	.05	7	.05	7	.05	7	.05
8	.06	8	.06	8	.06	8	.06
9	.07	9	.07	9	.07	9	.07
10	.08	10	.08	10	.08	10	.08
20	.17	20	.17	20	.17	20	.17
30	.25	30	.25	30	.25	30	.25
40	.34	40	.34	40	.34	40	.34
50	.42	50	.42	50	.42	50	.42
60	.51	60	.51	60	.51	60	.51
70	.59	70	.59	70	.59	70	.60
80	.68	80	.68	80	.68	80	.68
90	.76	90	.76	90	.76	90	.77
100	.85	100	.85	100	.85	100	.85
200	1.70	200	1.70	200	1.71	200	1.71
300	2.55	300	2.55	300	2.56	300	2.57
400	3.40	400	3.41	400	3.42	400	3.43
500	4.25	500	4.26	500	4.27	500	4.28
600	5.10	600	5.11	600	5.13	600	5.14
700	5.95	700	5.96	700	5.98	700	6.00
800	6.80	800	6.82	800	6.84	800	6.86
900	7.65	900	7.67	900	7.69	900	7.71
1000	8.50	1000	8.52	1000	8.55	1000	8.57
1100	9.35	1100	9.37	1100	9.40	1100	9.43
1200	10.20	1200	10.23	1200	10.26	1200	10.29
1300	11.05	1300	11.08	1300	11.11	1300	11.14
1400	11.90	1400	11.93	1400	11.97	1400	12.00
1500	12.75	1500	12.78	1500	12.82	1500	12.86
1600	13.60	1600	13.64	1600	13.68	1600	13.72
1700	14.45	1700	14.49	1700	14.53	1700	14.57
1800	15.30	1800	15.34	1800	15.39	1800	15.43
1900	16.15	1900	16.19	1900	16.24	1900	16.29
2000	17.00	2000	17.05	2000	17.10	2000	17.15
2100	17.85	2100	17.90	2100	17.95	2100	18.00
2200	18.70	2200	18.75	2200	18.81	2200	18.86
2300	19.55	2300	19.60	2300	19.66	2300	19.72
2400	20.40	2400	20.46	2400	20.52	2400	20.58
2500	21.25	2500	21.31	2500	21.37	2500	21.43
2600	22.10	2600	22.16	2600	22.23	2600	22.29
2700	22.95	2700	23.01	2700	23.08	2700	23.15
2800	23.80	2800	23.87	2800	23.94	2800	24.01
2900	24.65	2900	24.72	2900	24.79	2900	24.86
3000	25.50	3000	25.57	3000	25.65	3000	25.72
3100	26.35	3100	26.42	3100	26.50	3100	26.58
3200	27.20	3200	27.28	3200	27.36	3200	27.44
3300	28.05	3300	28.13	3300	28.21	3300	28.29
3400	28.90	3400	28.98	3400	29.07	3400	29.15
3500	29.75	3500	29.83	3500	29.92	3500	30.01
3600	30.60	3600	30.69	3600	30.78	3600	30.87
3700	31.45	3700	31.54	3700	31.63	3700	31.72
3800	32.30	3800	32.39	3800	32.49	3800	32.58
3900	33.15	3900	33.24	3900	33.34	3900	33.44
4000	34.00	4000	34.10	4000	34.20	4000	34.30

86 cts.		86¼ cts.		86½ cts.		86¾ cts.	
Lbs.	Amt.	Lbs.	Amt.	Lbs.	Amt.	Lbs.	Amt.
1	$ .00	1	$ .00	1	$ .00	1	$ .00
2	.01	2	.01	2	.01	2	.01
3	.02	3	.02	3	.02	3	.02
4	.03	4	.03	4	.03	4	.03
5	.04	5	.04	5	.04	5	.04
6	.05	6	.05	6	.05	6	.05
7	.06	7	.06	7	.06	7	.06
8	.06	8	.06	8	.06	8	.06
9	.07	9	.07	9	.07	9	.07
10	.08	10	.08	10	.08	10	.08
20	.17	20	.17	20	.17	20	.17
30	.25	30	.25	30	.25	30	.26
40	.34	40	.34	40	.34	40	.34
50	.43	50	.43	50	.43	50	.43
60	.51	60	.51	60	.51	60	.52
70	.60	70	.60	70	.60	70	.60
80	.68	80	.69	80	.69	80	.69
90	.77	90	.77	90	.77	90	.78
100	.86	100	.86	100	.86	100	.86
200	1.72	200	1.72	200	1.73	200	1.73
300	2.58	300	2.58	300	2.59	300	2.60
400	3.44	400	3.45	400	3.46	400	3.47
500	4.30	500	4.31	500	4.32	500	4.33
600	5.16	600	5.17	600	5.19	600	5.20
700	6.02	700	6.03	700	6.05	700	6.07
800	6.88	800	6.90	800	6.92	800	6.94
900	7.74	900	7.76	900	7.78	900	7.80
1000	8.60	1000	8.62	1000	8.65	1000	8.67
1100	9.46	1100	9.48	1100	9.51	1100	9.54
1200	10.32	1200	10.35	1200	10.38	1200	10.41
1300	11.18	1300	11.21	1300	11.24	1300	11.27
*1400	12.04	1400	12.07	1400	12.11	1400	12.14
1500	12.90	1500	12.93	1500	12.97	1500	13.01
1600	13.76	1600	13.80	1600	13.84	1600	13.88
1700	14.62	1700	14.66	1700	14.70	1700	14.74
1800	15.48	1800	15.52	1800	15.57	1800	15.61
1900	16.34	1900	16.38	1900	16.43	1900	16.48
2000	17.20	2000	17.25	2000	17.30	2000	17.35
2100	18.06	2100	18.11	2100	18.16	2100	18.21
2200	18.92	2200	18.97	2200	19.03	2200	19.08
2300	19.78	2300	19.83	2300	19.89	2300	19.95
2400	20.64	2400	20.70	2400	20.76	2400	20.82
2500	21.50	2500	21.56	2500	21.62	2500	21.68
2600	22.36	2600	22.42	2600	22.49	2600	22.55
2700	23.22	2700	23.28	2700	23.35	2700	23.42
2800	24.08	2800	24.15	2800	24.22	2800	24.29
2900	24.94	2900	25.01	2900	25.08	2900	25.15
3000	25.80	3000	25.87	3000	25.95	3000	26.02
3100	26.66	3100	26.73	3100	26.81	3100	26.89
3200	27.52	3200	27.60	3200	27.68	3200	27.76
3300	28.38	3300	28.46	3300	28.54	3300	28.62
3400	29.24	3400	29.32	3400	29.41	3400	29.49
3500	30.10	3500	30.18	3500	30.27	3500	30.36
3600	30.96	3600	31.05	3600	31.14	3600	31.23
3700	31.82	3700	31.91	3700	32.00	3700	32.09
3800	32.68	3800	32.77	3800	32.88	3800	32.97
3900	33.54	3900	33.63	3900	33.73	3900	33.83
4000	34.40	4000	34.50	4000	34.60	4000	34.70

87 cts.		87¼ cts.		87½ cts.		87¾ cts.	
Lbs.	Amt.	Lbs.	Amt.	Lbs.	Amt.	Lbs.	Amt.
1	$ .00	1	$ .00	1	$ .00	1	$ .00
2	.01	2	.01	2	.01	2	.01
3	.02	3	.02	3	.02	3	.02
4	.03	4	.03	4	.03	4	.03
5	.04	5	.04	5	.04	5	.04
6	.05	6	.05	6	.05	6	.05
7	.06	7	.06	7	.06	7	.06
8	.06	8	.06	8	.07	8	.07
9	.07	9	.07	9	.07	9	.07
10	.08	10	.08	10	.08	10	.08
20	.17	20	.17	20	.17	20	.17
30	.26	30	.26	30	.26	30	.26
40	.34	40	.34	40	.35	40	.35
50	.43	50	.43	50	.43	50	.43
60	.52	60	.52	60	.52	60	.52
70	.60	70	.60	70	.61	70	.61
80	.69	80	.69	80	.70	80	.70
90	.78	90	.78	90	.78	90	.78
100	.87	100	.87	100	.87	100	.87
200	1.74	200	1.74	200	1.75	200	1.75
300	2.61	300	2.61	300	2.62	300	2.63
400	3.48	400	3.49	400	3.50	400	3.51
500	4.35	500	4.36	500	4.37	500	4.38
600	5.22	600	5.23	600	5.25	600	5.26
700	6.09	700	6.10	700	6.12	700	6.14
800	6.96	800	6.98	800	7.00	800	7.02
900	7.83	900	7.85	900	7.87	900	7.89
1000	8.70	1000	8.72	1000	8.75	1000	8.77
1100	9.57	1100	9.59	1100	9.62	1100	9.65
1200	10.44	1200	10.47	1200	10.50	1200	10.53
1300	11.31	1300	11.34	1300	11.37	1300	11.40
1400	12.18	1400	12.21	1400	12.25	1400	12.28
1500	13.05	1500	13.08	1500	13.12	1500	13.16
1600	13.92	1600	13.96	1600	14.00	1600	14.04
1700	14.79	1700	14.83	1700	14.87	1700	14.91
1800	15.66	1800	15.70	1800	15.75	1800	15.79
1900	16.53	1900	16.57	1900	16.62	1900	16.67
2000	17.40	2000	17.45	2000	17.50	2000	17.55
2100	18.27	2100	18.32	2100	18.37	2100	18.42
2200	19.14	2200	19.19	2200	19.25	2200	19.30
2300	20.01	2300	20.06	2300	20.12	2300	20.18
2400	20.88	2400	20.94	2400	21.00	2400	21.06
2500	21.75	2500	21.81	2500	21.87	2500	21.93
2600	22.62	2600	22.68	2600	22.75	2600	22.81
2700	23.49	2700	23.55	2700	23.62	2700	23.69
2800	24.36	2800	24.43	2800	24.50	2800	24.57
2900	25.23	2900	25.30	2900	25.37	2900	25.44
3000	26.10	3000	26.17	3000	26.25	3000	26.32
3100	26.97	3100	27.04	3100	27.12	3100	27.20
3200	27.84	3200	27.92	3200	28.00	3200	28.08
3300	28.71	3300	28.79	3300	28.87	3300	28.95
3400	29.58	3400	29.66	3400	29.75	3400	29.83
3500	30.45	3500	30.53	3500	30.62	3500	30.71
3600	31.32	3600	31.41	3600	31.50	3600	31.59
3700	32.19	3700	32.28	3700	32.37	3700	32.46
3800	33.06	3800	33.15	3800	33.25	3800	33.34
3900	33.93	3900	34.02	3900	34.12	3900	34.22
4000	34.80	4000	34.90	4000	35.00	4000	35.10

88 cts.		88¼ cts.		88½ cts.		88¾ cts.	
Lbs.	Amt.	Lbs.	Amt.	Lbs.	Amt.	Lbs.	Amt.
1	$ .00	1	$ .00	1	$ .00	1	$ .00
2	.01	2	.01	2	.01	2	.01
3	.02	3	.02	3	.02	3	.02
4	.03	4	.03	4	.03	4	.03
5	.04	5	.04	5	.04	5	.04
6	.05	6	.05	6	.05	6	.05
7	.06	7	.06	7	.06	7	.06
8	.07	8	.07	8	.07	8	.07
9	.07	9	.07	9	.07	9	.07
10	.08	10	.08	10	.08	10	.08
20	.17	20	.17	20	.17	20	.17
30	.26	30	.26	30	.26	30	.26
40	.35	40	.35	40	.35	40	.35
50	.44	50	.44	50	.44	50	.44
60	.52	60	.52	60	.53	60	.53
70	.61	70	.61	70	.61	70	.62
80	.70	80	.70	80	.70	80	.71
90	.79	90	.79	90	.79	90	.79
100	.88	100	.88	100	.88	100	.88
200	1.76	200	1.76	200	1.77	200	1.77
300	2.64	300	2.64	300	2.65	300	2.66
400	3.52	400	3.53	400	3.54	400	3.55
500	4.40	500	4.41	500	4.42	500	4.43
600	5.28	600	5.29	600	5.31	600	5.32
700	6.16	700	6.17	700	6.19	700	6.21
800	7.04	800	7.06	800	7.08	800	7.10
900	7.92	900	7.94	900	7.96	900	7.98
1000	8.80	1000	8.82	1000	8.85	1000	8.87
1100	9.68	1100	9.70	1100	9.73	1100	9.76
1200	10.56	1200	10.59	1200	10.62	1200	10.65
1300	11.44	1300	11.47	1300	11.50	1300	11.53
1400	12.32	1400	12.35	1400	12.39	1400	12.42
1500	13.20	1500	13.23	1500	13.27	1500	13.31
1600	14.08	1600	14.12	1600	14.16	1600	14.20
1700	14.96	1700	15.00	1700	15.04	1700	15.08
1800	15.84	1800	15.88	1800	15.93	1800	15.97
1900	16.72	1900	16.76	1900	16.81	1900	16.86
2000	17.60	2000	17.65	2000	17.70	2000	17.75
2100	18.48	2100	18.53	2100	18.58	2100	18.63
2200	19.36	2200	19.41	2200	19.47	2200	19.52
2300	20.24	2300	20.29	2300	20.35	2300	20.41
2400	21.12	2400	21.18	2400	21.24	2400	21.30
2500	22.00	2500	22.06	2500	22.12	2500	22.18
2600	22.88	2600	22.94	2600	23.01	2600	23.07
2700	23.76	2700	23.82	2700	23.89	2700	23.96
2800	24.64	2800	24.71	2800	24.78	2800	24.85
2900	25.52	2900	25.59	2900	25.66	2900	25.73
3000	26.40	3000	26.47	3000	26.55	3000	26.62
3100	27.28	3100	27.35	3100	27.43	3100	27.51
3200	28.16	3200	28.24	3200	28.32	3200	28.40
3300	29.04	3300	29.12	3300	29.20	3300	29.28
3400	29.92	3400	30.00	3400	30.09	3400	30.17
3500	30.80	3500	30.88	3500	30.97	3500	31.06
3600	31.68	3600	31.77	3600	31.86	3600	31.95
3700	32.56	3700	32.65	3700	32.74	3700	32.83
3800	33.44	3800	33.53	3800	33.63	3800	33.72
3900	34.32	3900	34.41	3900	34.51	3900	34.61
4000	35.20	4000	35.30	4000	35.40	4000	35.50

89 cts.		89¼ cts.		89½ cts.		89¾ cts.	
bs.	Amt.	Lbs.	Amt.	Lbs.	Amt.	Lbs.	Amt.
1	$ .00	1	$ .00	1	$ .00	1	$ .00
2	.01	2	.01	2	.01	2	.01
3	.02	3	.02	3	.02	3	.02
4	.03	4	.03	4	.03	4	.03
5	.04	5	.04	5	.04	5	.04
6	.05	6	.05	6	.05	6	.05
7	.06	7	.06	7	.06	7	.06
8	.07	8	.07	8	.07	8	.07
9	.08	9	.08	9	.08	9	.08
10	.08	10	.08	10	.08	10	.08
20	.17	20	.17	20	.17	20	.17
30	.26	30	.26	30	.26	30	.26
40	.35	40	.35	40	.35	40	.35
50	.44	50	.44	50	.44	50	.44
60	.53	60	.53	60	.53	60	.53
70	.62	70	.62	70	.62	70	.62
80	.71	80	.71	80	.71	80	.71
90	.80	90	.80	90	.80	90	.80
100	.89	100	.89	100	.89	100	.89
200	1.78	200	1.78	200	1.79	200	1.79
300	2.67	300	2.67	300	2.68	300	2.69
400	3.56	400	3.57	400	3.58	400	3.59
500	4.45	500	4.46	500	4.47	500	4.48
600	5.34	600	5.35	600	5.37	600	5.38
700	6.23	700	6.24	700	6.26	700	6.28
800	7.12	800	7.14	800	7.16	800	7.18
900	8.01	900	8.03	900	8.05	900	8.07
000	8.90	1000	8.92	1000	8.95	1000	8.97
100	9.79	1100	9.81	1100	9.84	1100	9.87
200	10.68	1200	10.71	1200	10.74	1200	10.77
300	11.57	1300	11.60	1300	11.63	1300	11.66
400	12.46	1400	12.49	1400	12.53	1400	12.56
500	13.35	1500	13.38	1500	13.42	1500	13.46
600	14.24	1600	14.28	1600	14.32	1600	14.36
700	15.13	1700	15.17	1700	15.21	1700	15.25
800	16.02	1800	16.06	1800	16.11	1800	16.15
900	16.91	1900	16.95	1900	17.00	1900	17.05
000	17.80	2000	17.85	2000	17.90	2000	17.95
100	18.69	2100	18.74	2100	18.79	2100	18.84
200	19.58	2200	19.63	2200	19.69	2200	19.74
300	20.47	2300	20.52	2300	20.58	2300	20.64
400	21.36	2400	21.42	2400	21.48	2400	21.54
500	22.25	2500	22.31	2500	22.37	2500	22.43
600	23.14	2600	23.20	2600	23.27	2600	23.33
700	24.03	2700	24.09	2700	24.16	2700	24.23
800	24.92	2800	24.99	2800	25.06	2800	25.13
900	25.81	2900	25.88	2900	25.95	2900	26.02
000	26.70	3000	26.77	3000	26.85	3000	26.92
100	27.59	3100	27.66	3100	27.74	3100	27.82
200	28.48	3200	28.56	3200	28.64	3200	28.72
300	29.37	3300	29.45	3300	29.53	3300	29.61
400	30.26	3400	30.34	3400	30.43	3400	30.51
500	31.15	3500	31.23	3500	31.32	3500	31.41
600	32.04	3600	32.13	3600	32.22	3600	32.31
700	32.93	3700	33.02	3700	33.11	3700	33.20
800	33.82	3800	33.91	3800	34.01	3800	34.10
900	34.71	3900	34.80	3900	34.90	3900	35.00
000	35.60	4000	35.70	4000	35.80	4000	35.90

90 cts.		90¼ cts.		90½ cts.		90¾ cts.	
Lbs.	Amt.	Lbs.	Amt.	Lbs.	Amt.	Lbs.	Amt.
1	$ .00	1	$ .00	1	$ .00	1	$ .00
2	.01	2	.01	2	.01	2	.01
3	.02	3	.02	3	.02	3	.02
4	.03	4	.03	4	.03	4	.03
5	.04	5	.04	5	.04	5	.04
6	.05	6	.05	6	.05	6	.05
7	.06	7	.06	7	.06	7	.06
8	.07	8	.07	8	.07	8	.07
9	.08	9	.08	9	.08	9	.08
10	.09	10	.09	10	.09	10	.09
20	.18	20	.18	20	.18	20	.18
30	.27	30	.27	30	.27	30	.27
40	.36	40	.36	40	.36	40	.36
50	.45	50	.45	50	.45	50	.45
60	.54	60	.54	60	.54	60	.54
70	.63	70	.63	70	.63	70	.63
80	.72	80	.72	80	.72	80	.72
90	.81	90	.81	90	.81	90	.81
100	.90	100	.90	100	.90	100	.90
200	1.80	200	1.80	200	1.81	200	1.81
300	2.70	300	2.70	300	2.71	300	2.72
400	3.60	400	3.61	400	3.62	400	3.63
500	4.50	500	4.51	500	4.52	500	4.53
600	5.40	600	5.41	600	5.43	600	5.44
700	6.30	700	6.31	700	6.33	700	6.35
800	7.20	800	7.22	800	7.24	800	7.26
900	8.10	900	8.12	900	8.14	900	8.16
1000	9.00	1000	9.02	1000	9.05	1000	9.07
1100	9.90	1100	9.92	1100	9.95	1100	9.98
1200	10.80	1200	10.83	1200	10.86	1200	10.89
1300	11.70	1300	11.73	1300	11.76	1300	11.79
1400	12.60	1400	12.63	1400	12.67	1400	12.70
1500	13.50	1500	13.53	1500	13.57	1500	13.61
1600	14.40	1600	14.44	1600	14.48	1600	14.52
1700	15.30	1700	15.34	1700	15.38	1700	15.42
1800	16.20	1800	16.24	1800	16.29	1800	16.33
1900	17.10	1900	17.14	1900	17.19	1900	17.24
2000	18.00	2000	18.05	2000	18.10	2000	18.15
2100	18.90	2100	18.95	2100	19.00	2100	19.05
2200	19.80	2200	19.85	2200	19.91	2200	19.96
2300	20.70	2300	20.75	2300	20.81	2300	20.87
2400	21.60	2400	21.66	2400	21.72	2400	21.78
2500	22.50	2500	22.56	2500	22.62	2500	22.68
2600	23.40	2600	23.46	2600	23.53	2600	23.59
2700	24.30	2700	24.36	2700	24.43	2700	24.50
2800	25.20	2800	25.27	2800	25.34	2800	25.41
2900	26.10	2900	26.17	2900	26.24	2900	26.31
3000	27.00	3000	27.07	3000	27.15	3000	27.22
3100	27.90	3100	27.97	3100	28.05	3100	28.13
3200	28.80	3200	28.88	3200	28.96	3200	29.04
3300	29.70	3300	29.78	3300	29.86	3300	29.94
3400	30.60	3400	30.68	3400	30.77	3400	30.85
3500	31.50	3500	31.58	3500	31.67	3500	31.76
3600	32.40	3600	32.49	3600	32.58	3600	32.67
3700	33.30	3700	33.39	3700	33.48	3700	33.57
3800	34.20	3800	34.29	3800	34.39	3800	34.48
3900	35.10	3900	35.19	3900	35.29	3900	35.39
4000	36.00	4000	36.10	4000	36.20	4000	36.30

91 cts.		91¼ cts.		91½ cts.		91¾ cts.	
Lbs.	Amt.	Lbs.	Amt.	Lbs.	Amt.	Lbs.	Amt.
1	$ .00	1	$ .00	1	$ .00	1	$ .00
2	.01	2	.01	2	.01	2	.01
3	.02	3	.02	3	.02	3	.02
4	.03	4	.03	4	.03	4	.03
5	.04	5	.04	5	.04	5	.04
6	.05	6	.05	6	.05	6	.05
7	.06	7	.06	7	.06	7	.06
8	.07	8	.07	8	.07	8	.07
9	.08	9	.08	9	.08	9	.08
10	.09	10	.09	10	.09	10	.09
20	.18	20	.18	20	.18	20	.18
30	.27	30	.27	30	.27	30	.27
40	.36	40	.36	40	.36	40	.36
50	.45	50	.45	50	.45	50	.45
60	.54	60	.54	60	.54	60	.55
70	.63	70	.63	70	.64	70	.64
80	.72	80	.73	80	.73	80	.73
90	.81	90	.82	90	.82	90	.82
100	.91	100	.91	100	.91	100	.91
200	1.82	200	1.82	200	1.83	200	1.83
300	2.73	300	2.73	300	2.74	300	2.75
400	3.64	400	3.65	400	3.66	400	3.67
500	4.55	500	4.56	500	4.57	500	4.58
600	5.46	600	5.47	600	5.49	600	5.50
700	6.37	700	6.38	700	6.40	700	6.42
800	7.28	800	7.30	800	7.32	800	7.34
900	8.19	900	8.21	900	8.23	900	8.25
1000	9.10	1000	9.12	1000	9.15	1000	9.17
1100	10.01	1100	10.03	1100	10.06	1100	10.09
1200	10.92	1200	10.95	1200	10.98	1200	11.01
1300	11.83	1300	11.86	1300	11.89	1300	11.92
1400	12.74	1400	12.77	1400	12.81	1400	12.84
1500	13.65	1500	13.68	1500	13.72	1500	13.76
1600	14.56	1600	14.60	1600	14.64	1600	14.68
1700	15.47	1700	15.51	1700	15.55	1700	15.59
1800	16.38	1800	16.42	1800	16.47	1800	16.51
1900	17.29	1900	17.33	1900	17.38	1900	17.43
2000	18.20	2000	18.25	2000	18.30	2000	18.35
2100	19.11	2100	19.16	2100	19.21	2100	19.26
2200	20.02	2200	20.07	2200	20.13	2200	20.18
2300	20.93	2300	20.98	2300	21.04	2300	21.10
2400	21.84	2400	21.90	2400	21.96	2400	22.02
2500	22.75	2500	22.81	2500	22.87	2500	22.93
2600	23.66	2600	23.72	2600	23.79	2600	23.85
2700	24.57	2700	24.63	2700	24.70	2700	24.77
2800	25.48	2800	25.55	2800	25.62	2800	25.69
2900	26.39	2900	26.46	2900	26.53	2900	26.60
3000	27.30	3000	27.37	3000	27.45	3000	27.52
3100	28.21	3100	28.28	3100	28.36	3100	28.44
3200	29.12	3200	29.20	3200	29.28	3200	29.36
3300	30.03	3300	30.11	3300	30.19	3300	30.27
3400	30.94	3400	31.02	3400	31.11	3400	31.19
3500	31.85	3500	31.93	3500	32.02	3500	32.11
3600	32.76	3600	32.85	3600	32.94	3600	33.03
3700	33.67	3700	33.76	3700	33.85	3700	33.94
3800	34.58	3800	34.67	3800	34.77	3800	34.86
3900	35.49	3900	35.58	3900	35.68	3900	35.78
4000	36.40	4000	36.50	4000	36.60	4000	36.70

92 cts.		92¼ cts.		92½ cts.		92¾ cts.	
Lbs.	Amt.	Lbs.	Amt.	Lbs.	Amt.	Lbs.	Amt.
1	$ .00	1	$ .00	1	$ .00	1	$ .00
2	.01	2	.01	2	.01	2	.01
3	.02	3	.02	3	.02	3	.02
4	.03	4	.03	4	.03	4	.03
5	.04	5	.04	5	.04	5	.04
6	.05	6	.05	6	.05	6	.05
7	.06	7	.06	7	.06	7	.06
8	.07	8	.07	8	.07	8	.07
9	.08	9	.08	9	.08	9	.08
10	.09	10	.09	10	.09	10	.09
20	.18	20	.18	20	.18	20	.18
30	.27	30	.27	30	.27	30	.27
40	.36	40	.36	40	.37	40	.37
50	.46	50	.46	50	.46	50	.46
60	.55	60	.55	60	.55	60	.55
70	.64	70	.64	70	.64	70	.65
80	.73	80	.73	80	.74	80	.74
90	.82	90	.83	90	.83	90	.83
100	.92	100	.92	100	.92	100	.92
200	1.84	200	1.84	200	1.85	200	1.85
300	2.76	300	2.76	300	2.77	300	2.78
400	3.68	400	3.69	400	3.70	400	3.71
500	4.60	500	4.61	500	4.62	500	4.63
600	5.52	600	5.53	600	5.55	600	5.56
700	6.44	700	6.45	700	6.47	700	6.49
800	7.36	800	7.38	800	7.40	800	7.42
900	8.28	900	8.30	900	8.32	900	8.34
1000	9.20	1000	9.22	1000	9.25	1000	9.27
1100	10.12	1100	10.14	1100	10.17	1100	10.20
1200	11.04	1200	11.07	1200	11.10	1200	11.13
1300	11.96	1300	11.99	1300	12.02	1300	12.05
1400	12.88	1400	12.91	1400	12.95	1400	12.98
1500	13.80	1500	13.83	1500	13.87	1500	13.91
1600	14.72	1600	14.76	1600	14.80	1600	14.84
1700	15.64	1700	15.68	1700	15.72	1700	15.76
1800	16.56	1800	16.60	1800	16.65	1800	16.69
1900	17.48	1900	17.52	1900	17.57	1900	17.62
2000	18.40	2000	18.45	2000	18.50	2000	18.55
2100	19.32	2100	19.37	2100	19.42	2100	19.47
2200	20.24	2200	20.29	2200	20.35	2200	20.40
2300	21.16	2300	21.21	2300	21.27	2300	21.33
2400	22.08	2400	22.14	2400	22.20	2400	22.26
2500	23.00	2500	23.06	2500	23.12	2500	23.18
2600	23.92	2600	23.98	2600	24.05	2600	24.11
2700	24.84	2700	24.90	2700	24.97	2700	25.04
2800	25.76	2800	25.83	2800	25.90	2800	25.97
2900	26.68	2900	26.75	2900	26.82	2900	26.89
3000	27.60	3000	27.67	3000	27.75	3000	27.82
3100	28.52	3100	28.59	3100	28.67	3100	28.75
3200	29.44	3200	29.52	3200	29.60	3200	29.68
3300	30.36	3300	30.44	3300	30.52	3300	30.60
3400	31.28	3400	31.36	3400	31.45	3400	31.53
3500	32.20	3500	32.28	3500	32.37	3500	32.46
3600	33.12	3600	33.21	3600	33.30	3600	33.39
3700	34.04	3700	34.13	3700	34.22	3700	34.31
3800	34.96	3800	35.05	3800	35.15	3800	35.24
3900	35.88	3900	35.97	3900	36.07	3900	36.17
4000	36.80	4000	36.90	4000	37.00	4000	37.10

93 cts.		93¼ cts.		93½ cts.		93¾ cts.	
Lbs.	Amt.	Lbs.	Amt.	Lbs.	Amt.	Lbs.	Amt.
1	$ .00	1	$ .00	1	$ .00	1	$ .00
2	.01	2	.01	2	.01	2	.01
3	.02	3	.02	3	.02	3	.02
4	.03	4	.03	4	.03	4	.03
5	.04	5	.04	5	.04	5	.04
6	.05	6	.05	6	.05	6	.05
7	.06	7	.06	7	.06	7	.06
8	.07	8	.07	8	.07	8	.07
9	.08	9	.08	9	.08	9	.08
10	.09	10	.09	10	.09	10	.09
20	.18	20	.18	20	.18	20	.18
30	.27	30	.27	30	.28	30	.28
40	.37	40	.37	40	.37	40	.37
50	.46	50	.46	50	.46	50	.46
60	.55	60	.55	60	.56	60	.56
70	.65	70	.65	70	.65	70	.65
80	.74	80	.74	80	.74	80	.75
90	.83	90	.83	90	.84	90	.84
100	.93	100	.93	100	.93	100	.93
200	1.86	200	1.86	200	1.87	200	1.87
300	2.79	300	2.79	300	2.80	300	2.81
400	3.72	400	3.73	400	3.74	400	3.75
500	4.65	500	4.66	500	4.67	500	4.68
600	5.58	600	5.59	600	5.61	600	5.62
700	6.51	700	6.52	700	6.51	700	6.56
800	7.44	800	7.46	800	7.48	800	7.50
900	8.37	900	8.39	900	8.41	900	8.43
1000	9.30	1000	9.32	1000	9.35	1000	9.37
1100	10.23	1100	10.25	1100	10.28	1100	10.31
1200	11.16	1200	11.19	1200	11.22	1200	11.25
1300	12.09	1300	12.12	1300	12.15	1300	12.18
1400	13.02	1400	13.05	1400	13.09	1400	13.12
1500	13.95	1500	13.98	1500	14.02	1500	14.06
1600	14.88	1600	14.92	1600	14.96	1600	15.00
1700	15.81	1700	15.85	1700	15.89	1700	15.93
1800	16.74	1800	16.78	1800	16.83	1800	16.87
1900	17.67	1900	17.71	1900	17.76	1900	17.81
2000	18.60	2000	18.65	2000	18.70	2000	18.75
2100	19.53	2100	19.58	2100	19.63	2100	19.68
2200	20.46	2200	20.51	2200	20.57	2200	20.62
2300	21.39	2300	21.44	2300	21.50	2300	21.56
2400	22.32	2400	22.38	2400	22.44	2400	22.50
2500	23.25	2500	23.31	2500	23.37	2500	23.43
2600	24.18	2600	24.24	2600	24.31	2600	24.37
2700	25.11	2700	25.17	2700	25.24	2700	25.31
2800	26.04	2800	26.11	2800	26.18	2800	26.25
2900	26.97	2900	27.04	2900	27.11	2900	27.18
3000	27.90	3000	27.97	3000	28.05	3000	28.12
3100	28.83	3100	28.90	3100	28.98	3100	29.06
3200	29.76	3200	29.84	3200	29.92	3200	30.00
3300	30.69	3300	30.77	3300	30.85	3300	30.93
3400	31.62	3400	31.70	3400	31.79	3400	31.87
3500	32.55	3500	32.63	3500	32.72	3500	32.81
3600	33.48	3600	33.57	3600	33.66	3600	33.75
3700	34.41	3700	34.50	3700	34.59	3700	34.68
3800	35.34	3800	35.43	3800	35.53	3800	35.62
3900	36.27	3900	36.36	3900	36.46	3900	36.56
4000	37.20	4000	37.30	4000	37.40	4000	37.50

94 cts.		94¼ cts.		94½ cts.		94¾ cts.	
Lbs.	Amt.	Lbs.	Amt.	Lbs.	Amt.	Lbs.	Amt.
1	$ .00	1	$ .00	1	$ .00	1	$ .00
2	.01	2	.01	2	.01	2	.01
3	.02	3	.02	3	.02	3	.02
4	.03	4	.03	4	.03	4	.03
5	.04	5	.04	5	.04	5	.04
6	.05	6	.05	6	.05	6	.05
7	.06	7	.06	7	.06	7	.06
8	.07	8	.07	8	.07	8	.07
9	.08	9	.08	9	.08	9	.08
10	.09	10	.09	10	.09	10	.09
20	.18	20	.18	20	.18	20	.18
30	.28	30	.28	30	.28	30	.28
40	.37	40	.37	40	.37	40	.37
50	.47	50	.47	50	.47	50	.47
60	.56	60	.56	60	.56	60	.56
70	.65	70	.65	70	.66	70	.66
80	.75	80	.75	80	.75	80	.75
90	.84	90	.84	90	.85	90	.85
100	.94	100	.94	100	.94	100	.94
200	1.88	200	1.88	200	1.89	200	1.89
300	2.82	300	2.82	300	2.83	300	2.84
400	3.76	400	3.77	400	3.78	400	3.79
500	4.70	500	4.71	500	4.72	500	4.73
600	5.64	600	5.65	600	5.67	600	5.68
700	6.58	700	6.59	700	6.61	700	6.63
800	7.52	800	7.54	800	7.56	800	7.58
900	8.46	900	8.48	900	8.50	900	8.52
1000	9.40	1000	9.42	1000	9.45	1000	9.47
1100	10.34	1100	10.36	1100	10.39	1100	10.42
1200	11.28	1200	11.31	1200	11.34	1200	11.37
1300	12.22	1300	12.25	1300	12.28	1300	12.31
1400	13.16	1400	13.19	1400	13.23	1400	13.26
1500	14.10	1500	14.13	1500	14.17	1500	14.21
1600	15.04	1600	15.08	1600	15.12	1600	15.16
1700	15.98	1700	16.02	1700	16.06	1700	16.10
1800	16.92	1800	16.96	1800	17.01	1800	17.05
1900	17.86	1900	17.90	1900	17.95	1900	18.00
2000	18.80	2000	18.85	2000	18.90	2000	18.95
2100	19.74	2100	19.79	2100	19.84	2100	19.89
2200	20.68	2200	20.73	2200	20.79	2200	20.84
2300	21.62	2300	21.67	2300	21.73	2300	21.79
2400	22.56	2400	22.62	2400	22.68	2400	22.74
2500	23.50	2500	23.56	2500	23.62	2500	23.68
2600	24.44	2600	24.50	2600	24.57	2600	24.63
2700	25.38	2700	25.44	2700	25.51	2700	25.58
2800	26.32	2800	26.39	2800	26.46	2800	26.53
2900	27.26	2900	27.33	2900	27.40	2900	27.47
3000	28.20	3000	28.27	3000	28.35	3000	28.42
3100	29.14	3100	29.21	3100	29.29	3100	29.37
3200	30.08	3200	30.16	3200	30.24	3200	30.32
3300	31.02	3300	31.10	3300	31.18	3300	31.26
3400	31.96	3400	32.04	3400	32.13	3400	32.21
3500	32.90	3500	32.98	3500	33.07	3500	33.16
3600	33.84	3600	33.93	3600	34.02	3600	34.11
3700	34.78	3700	34.87	3700	34.96	3700	35.05
3800	35.72	3800	35.81	3800	35.91	3800	36.00
3900	36.66	3900	36.75	3900	36.85	3900	36.95
4000	37.60	4000	37.70	4000	37.80	4000	37.90

95 cts.		95¼ cts.		95½ cts.		95¾ cts.	
Lbs.	Amt.	Lbs.	Amt.	Lbs.	Amt.	Lbs.	Amt.
1	$ .00	1	$ .00	1	$ .00	1	$ .00
2	.01	2	.01	2	.01	2	.01
3	.02	3	.02	3	.02	3	.02
4	.03	4	.03	4	.03	4	.03
5	.04	5	.04	5	.04	5	.04
6	.05	6	.05	6	.05	6	.05
7	.06	7	.06	7	.06	7	.06
8	.07	8	.07	8	.07	8	.07
9	.08	9	.08	9	.08	9	.08
10	.09	10	.09	10	.09	10	.09
20	.19	20	.19	20	.19	20	.19
30	.28	30	.28	30	.28	30	.28
40	.38	40	.38	40	.38	40	.38
50	.47	50	.47	50	.47	50	.47
60	.57	60	.57	60	.57	60	.57
70	.66	70	.66	70	.66	70	.67
80	.76	80	.76	80	.76	80	.76
90	.85	90	.85	90	.85	90	.86
100	.95	100	.95	100	.95	100	.95
200	1.90	200	1.90	200	1.91	200	1.91
300	2.85	300	2.85	300	2.86	300	2.87
400	3.80	400	3.81	400	3.82	400	3.83
500	4.75	500	4.76	500	4.77	500	4.78
600	5.70	600	5.71	600	5.73	600	5.74
700	6.65	700	6.66	700	6.68	700	6.70
800	7.60	800	7.62	800	7.64	800	7.66
900	8.55	900	8.57	900	8.59	900	8.61
1000	9.50	1000	9.52	1000	9.55	1000	9.57
1100	10.45	1100	10.47	1100	10.50	1100	10.53
1200	11.40	1200	11.43	1200	11.46	1200	11.49
1300	12.35	1300	12.38	1300	12.41	1300	12.44
1400	13.30	1400	13.33	1400	13.37	1400	13.40
1500	14.25	1500	14.28	1500	14.32	1500	14.36
1600	15.20	1600	15.24	1600	15.28	1600	15.32
1700	16.15	1700	16.19	1700	16.23	1700	16.27
1800	17.10	1800	17.14	1800	17.19	1800	17.23
1900	18.05	1900	18.09	1900	18.14	1900	18.19
2000	19.00	2000	19.05	2000	19.10	2000	19.15
2100	19.95	2100	20.00	2100	20.05	2100	20.10
2200	20.90	2200	20.95	2200	21.01	2200	21.06
2300	21.85	2300	21.90	2300	21.96	2300	22.02
2400	22.80	2400	22.86	2400	22.92	2400	22.98
2500	23.75	2500	23.81	2500	23.87	2500	23.93
2600	24.70	2600	24.76	2600	24.83	2600	24.89
2700	25.65	2700	25.71	2700	25.78	2700	25.85
2800	26.60	2800	26.67	2800	26.74	2800	26.81
2900	27.55	2900	27.62	2900	27.69	2900	27.76
3000	28.50	3000	28.57	3000	28.65	3000	28.72
3100	29.45	3100	29.52	3100	29.60	3100	29.68
3200	30.40	3200	30.48	3200	30.56	3200	30.64
3300	31.35	3300	31.43	3300	31.51	3300	31.59
3400	32.30	3400	32.38	3400	32.47	3400	32.55
3500	33.25	3500	33.33	3500	33.42	3500	33.51
3600	34.20	3600	34.29	3600	34.38	3600	34.47
3700	35.15	3700	35.24	3700	35.33	3700	35.42
3800	36.10	3800	36.19	3800	36.29	3800	36.38
3900	37.05	3900	37.14	3900	37.24	3900	37.34
4000	38.00	4000	38.10	4000	38.20	4000	38.30

96 cts.		96¼ cts.		96½ cts.		96¾ cts.	
Lbs.	Amt.	Lbs.	Amt.	Lbs.	Amt.	Lbs.	Amt.
1	$ .00	1	$ .00	1	$ .00	1	$ .00
2	.01		.01	2	.01	2	.01
3	.02	3	.02	3	.02	3	.02
4	.03	4	.03	4	.03	4	.03
5	.04	5	.04	5	.04	5	.04
6	.05	6	.05	6	.05	6	.05
7	.06	7	.06	7	.06	7	.06
8	.07	8	.07	8	.07	8	.07
9	.08	9	.08	9	.08	9	.08
10	.09	10	.09	10	.09	10	.09
20	.19	20	.19	20	.19	20	.19
30	.28	30	.28	30	.28	30	.29
40	.38	40	.38	40	.38	40	.38
50	.48	50	.48	50	.48	50	.48
60	.57	60	.57	60	.57	60	.58
70	.67	70	.67	70	.67	70	.67
80	.76	80	.77	80	.77	80	.77
90	.86	90	.86	90	.86	90	.87
100	.96	100	.96	100	.96	100	.96
200	1.92	200	1.92	200	1.93	200	1.93
300	2.88	300	2.88	300	2.89	300	2.90
400	3.84	400	3.85	400	3.86	400	3.87
500	4.80	500	4.81	500	4.82	500	4.83
600	5.76	600	5.77	600	5.79	600	5.80
700	6.72	700	6.73	700	6.75	700	6.77
800	7.68	800	7.70	800	7.72	800	7.74
900	8.64	900	8.66	900	8.68	900	8.70
1000	9.60	1000	9.62	1000	9.65	1000	9.67
1100	10.56	1100	10.58	1100	10.61	1100	10.64
1200	11.52	1200	11.55	1200	11.58	1200	11.61
1300	12.48	1300	12.51	1300	12.54	1300	12.57
1400	13.44	1400	13.47	1400	13.51	1400	13.54
1500	14.40	1500	14.43	1500	14.47	1500	14.51
1600	15.36	1600	15.40	1600	15.44	1600	15.48
1700	16.32	1700	16.36	1700	16.40	1700	16.44
1800	17.28	1800	17.32	1800	17.37	1800	17.41
1900	18.24	1900	18.28	1900	18.33	1900	18.38
2000	19.20	2000	19.25	2000	19.30	2000	19.35
2100	20.16	2100	20.21	2100	20.26	2100	20.31
2200	21.12	2200	21.17	2200	21.23	2200	21.28
2300	22.08	2300	22.13	2300	22.19	2300	22.25
2400	23.04	2400	23.10	2400	23.16	2400	23.22
2500	24.00	2500	24.06	2500	24.12	2500	24.18
2600	24.96	2600	25.02	2600	25.09	2600	25.15
2700	25.92	2700	25.98	2700	26.05	2700	26.12
2800	26.88	2800	26.95	2800	27.02	2800	27.09
2900	27.84	2900	27.91	2900	27.98	2900	28.05
3000	28.80	3000	28.87	3000	28.95	3000	29.02
3100	29.76	3100	29.83	3100	29.91	3100	29.99
3200	30.72	3200	30.80	3200	30.88	3200	30.96
3300	31.68	3300	31.76	3300	31.84	3300	31.92
3400	32.64	3400	32.72	3400	32.81	3400	32.89
3500	33.60	3500	33.68	3500	33.77	3500	33.86
3600	34.56	3600	34.65	3600	34.74	3600	34.83
3700	35.52	3700	35.61	3700	35.70	3700	35.79
3800	36.48	3800	36.57	3800	36.67	3800	36.76
3900	37.44	3900	37.53	3900	37.63	3900	37.73
4000	38.40	4000	38.50	4000	38.60	4000	38.70

97 cts.		97¼ cts.		97½ cts.		97¾ cts.	
Lbs.	Amt.	Lbs.	Amt.	Lbs.	Amt.	Lbs.	Amt.
1	$ .00	1	$ .00	1	$ .00	1	$ .00
2	.01	2	.01	2	.01	2	.01
3	.02	3	.02	3	.02	3	.02
4	.03	4	.03	4	.03	4	.03
5	.04	5	.04	5	.04	5	.04
6	.05	6	.05	6	.05	6	.05
7	.06	7	.06	7	.06	7	.06
8	.07	8	.07	8	.07	8	.07
9	.08	9	.08	9	.08	9	.08
10	.09	10	.09	10	.09	10	.09
20	.19	20	.19	20	.19	20	.19
30	.29	30	.29	30	.29	30	.29
40	.38	40	.38	40	.39	40	.39
50	.48	50	.48	50	.48	50	.48
60	.58	60	.58	60	.58	60	.58
70	.67	70	.68	70	.68	70	.68
80	.77	80	.77	80	.78	80	.78
90	.87	90	.87	90	.87	90	.87
100	.97	100	.97	100	.97	100	.97
200	1.94	200	1.94	200	1.95	200	1.95
300	2.91	300	2.91	300	2.92	300	2.93
400	3.88	400	3.89	400	3.90	400	3.91
500	4.85	500	4.86	500	4.87	500	4.88
600	5.82	600	5.83	600	5.85	600	5.86
700	6.79	700	6.80	700	6.82	700	6.84
800	7.76	800	7.78	800	7.80	800	7.82
900	8.73	900	8.75	900	8.77	900	8.79
1000	9.70	1000	9.72	1000	9.75	1000	9.77
1100	10.67	1100	10.69	1100	10.72	1100	10.75
1200	11.64	1200	11.67	1200	11.70	1200	11.73
1300	12.61	1300	12.64	1300	12.67	1300	12.70
1400	13.58	1400	13.61	1400	13.65	1400	13.68
1500	14.55	1500	14.58	1500	14.62	1500	14.66
1600	15.52	1600	15.56	1600	15.60	1600	15.64
1700	16.49	1700	16.53	1700	16.57	1700	16.61
1800	17.46	1800	17.50	1800	17.55	1800	17.59
1900	18.43	1900	18.47	1900	18.52	1900	18.57
2000	19.40	2000	19.45	2000	19.50	2000	19.55
2100	20.37	2100	20.42	2100	20.47	2100	20.52
2200	21.34	2200	21.39	2200	21.45	2200	21.50
2300	22.31	2300	22.36	2300	22.42	2300	22.48
2400	23.28	2400	23.34	2400	23.40	2400	23.46
2500	24.25	2500	24.31	2500	24.37	2500	24.43
2600	25.22	2600	25.28	2600	25.35	2600	25.41
2700	26.19	2700	26.25	2700	26.32	2700	26.39
2800	27.16	2800	27.23	2800	27.30	2800	27.37
2900	28.13	2900	28.20	2900	28.27	2900	28.34
3000	29.10	3000	29.17	3000	29.25	3000	29.32
3100	30.07	3100	30.14	3100	30.22	3100	30.30
3200	31.04	3200	31.12	3200	31.20	3200	31.28
3300	32.01	3300	32.09	3300	32.17	3300	32.25
3400	32.98	3400	33.06	3400	33.15	3400	33.23
3500	33.95	3500	34.03	3500	34.12	3500	34.21
3600	34.92	3600	35.01	3600	35.10	3600	35.19
3700	35.89	3700	35.98	3700	36.07	3700	36.16
3800	36.86	3800	36.95	3800	37.05	3800	37.14
3900	37.83	3900	37.92	3900	38.02	3900	38.12
4000	38.80	4000	38.90	4000	39.00	4000	39.10

98 cts.		98¼ cts.		98½ cts.		98¾ cts.	
Lbs.	Amt.	Lbs.	Amt.	Lbs.	Amt.	Lbs.	Amt.
1	$ .00	1	$ .00	1	$ .00	1	$ .00
2	.01	2	.01	2	.01	2	.01
3	.02	3	.02	3	.02	3	.02
4	.03	4	.03	4	.03	4	.03
5	.04	5	.04	5	.04	5	.04
6	.05	6	.05	6	.05	6	.05
7	.06	7	.06	7	.06	7	.06
8	.07	8	.07	8	.07	8	.07
9	.08	9	.08	9	.08	9	.08
10	.09	10	.09	10	.09	10	.09
20	.19	20	.19	20	.19	20	.19
30	.29	30	.29	30	.29	30	.29
40	.39	40	.39	40	.39	40	.39
50	.49	50	.49	50	.49	50	.49
60	.58	60	.58	60	.59	60	.59
70	.68	70	.68	70	.68	70	.69
80	.78	80	.78	80	.78	80	.79
90	.88	90	.88	90	.88	90	.88
100	.98	100	.98	100	.98	100	.98
200	1.96	200	1.96	200	1.97	200	1.97
300	2.94	300	2.94	300	2.95	300	2.96
400	3.92	400	3.93	400	3.94	400	3.95
500	4.90	500	4.91	500	4.92	500	4.93
600	5.88	600	5.89	600	5.91	600	5.92
700	6.86	700	6.87	700	6.89	700	6.91
800	7.84	800	7.86	800	7.88	800	7.90
900	8.82	900	8.84	900	8.86	900	8.88
1000	9.80	1000	9.82	1000	9.85	1000	9.87
1100	10.78	1100	10.80	1100	10.83	1100	10.86
1200	11.76	1200	11.79	1200	11.82	1200	11.85
1300	12.74	1300	12.77	1300	12.80	1300	12.83
1400	13.72	1400	13.75	1400	13.79	1400	13.82
1500	14.70	1500	14.73	1500	14.77	1500	14.81
1600	15.68	1600	15.72	1600	15.76	1600	15.80
1700	16.66	1700	16.70	1700	16.74	1700	16.78
1800	17.64	1800	17.68	1800	17.73	1800	17.77
1900	18.62	1900	18.66	1900	18.71	1900	18.76
2000	19.60	2000	19.65	2000	19.70	2000	19.75
2100	20.58	2100	20.63	2100	20.68	2100	20.73
2200	21.56	2200	21.61	2200	21.67	2200	21.72
2300	22.54	2300	22.59	2300	22.65	2300	22.71
2400	23.52	2400	23.58	2400	23.64	2400	23.70
2500	24.50	2500	24.56	2500	24.62	2500	24.68
2600	25.48	2600	25.54	2600	25.61	2600	25.67
2700	26.46	2700	26.52	2700	26.59	2700	26.66
2800	27.44	2800	27.51	2800	27.58	2800	27.65
2900	28.42	2900	28.49	2900	28.56	2900	28.63
3000	29.40	3000	29.47	3000	29.55	3000	29.62
3100	30.38	3100	30.45	3100	30.53	3100	30.61
3200	31.36	3200	31.44	3200	31.52	3200	31.60
3300	32.34	3300	32.42	3300	32.50	3300	32.58
3400	33.32	3400	33.40	3400	33.49	3400	33.57
3500	34.30	3500	34.38	3500	34.47	3500	34.56
3600	35.28	3600	35.37	3600	35.46	3600	35.55
3700	36.26	3700	36.35	3700	36.44	3700	36.53
3800	37.24	3800	37.33	3800	37.43	3800	37.52
3900	38.22	3900	38.31	3900	38.41	3900	38.51
4000	39.20	4000	39.30	4000	39.40	4000	39.50

99 cts.		99¼ cts.		99½ cts.		99¾ cts.	
Lbs.	Amt.	Lbs.	Amt.	Lbs.	Amt.	Lbs.	Amt.
1	$ .00	1	$ .00	1	$ .00	1	$ .00
2	.01	2	.01	2	.01	2	.01
3	.02	3	.02	3	.02	3	.02
4	.03	4	.03	4	.03	4	.03
5	.04	5	.04	5	.04	5	.04
6	.05	6	.05	6	.05	6	.05
7	.06	7	.06	7	.06	7	.06
8	.07	8	.07	8	.07	8	.07
9	.08	9	.08	9	.08	9	.08
10	.09	10	.09	10	.09	10	.09
20	.19	20	.19	20	.19	20	.19
30	.29	30	.29	30	.29	30	.29
40	.39	40	.39	40	.39	40	.39
50	.49	50	.49	50	.49	50	.49
60	.59	60	.59	60	.59	60	.59
70	.69	70	.69	70	.69	70	.69
80	.79	80	.79	80	.79	80	.79
90	.89	90	.89	90	.89	90	.89
100	.99	100	.99	100	.99	100	.99
200	1.98	200	1.98	200	1.99	200	1.99
300	2.97	300	2.97	300	2.98	300	2.99
400	3.96	400	3.97	400	3.98	400	3.99
500	4.95	500	4.96	500	4.97	500	4.98
600	5.94	600	5.95	600	5.97	600	5.98
700	6.93	700	6.94	700	6.96	700	6.98
800	7.92	800	7.94	800	7.96	800	7.98
900	8.91	900	8.93	900	8.95	900	8.97
1000	9.90	1000	9.92	1000	9.95	1000	9.97
1100	10.89	1100	10.91	1100	10.94	1100	10.97
1200	11.88	1200	11.91	1200	11.94	1200	11.97
1300	12.87	1300	12.90	1300	12.93	1300	12.96
1400	13.86	1400	13.89	1400	13.93	1400	13.96
1500	14.85	1500	14.88	1500	14.92	1500	14.96
1600	15.84	1600	15.88	1600	15.92	1600	15.96
1700	16.83	1700	16.87	1700	16.91	1700	16.95
1800	17.82	1800	17.86	1800	17.91	1800	17.95
1900	18.81	1900	18.85	1900	18.90	1900	18.95
2000	19.80	2000	19.85	2000	19.90	2000	19.95
2100	20.79	2100	20.84	2100	20.89	2100	20.94
2200	21.78	2200	21.83	2200	21.89	2200	21.94
2300	22.77	2300	22.82	2300	22.88	2300	22.94
2400	23.76	2400	23.82	2400	23.88	2400	23.94
2500	24.75	2500	24.81	2500	24.87	2500	24.93
2600	25.74	2600	25.80	2600	25.87	2600	25.93
2700	26.73	2700	26.79	2700	26.86	2700	26.93
2800	27.72	2800	27.79	2800	27.86	2800	27.93
2900	28.71	2900	28.78	2900	28.85	2900	28.92
3000	29.70	3000	29.77	3000	29.85	3000	29.92
3100	30.69	3100	30.76	3100	30.84	3100	30.92
3200	31.68	3200	31.76	3200	31.84	3200	31.92
3300	32.67	3300	32.75	3300	32.83	3300	32.91
3400	33.66	3400	33.74	3400	33.83	3400	33.91
3500	34.65	3500	34.73	3500	34.82	3500	34.91
3600	35.64	3600	35.73	3600	35.82	3600	35.91
3700	36.63	3700	36.72	3700	36.81	3700	36.90
3800	37.62	3800	37.71	3800	37.81	3800	37.90
3900	38.61	3900	38.70	3900	38.80	3900	38.90
4000	39.60	4000	39.70	4000	39.80	4000	39.90

\$1.00		\$1.00¼		\$1.00½		\$1.00¾	
Lbs.	Amt.	Lbs.	Amt.	Lbs.	Amt.	Lbs.	Amt.
1	\$ .01	1	\$ .01	1	\$ .01	1	\$ .01
2	.02	2	.02	2	.02	2	.02
3	.03	3	.03	3	.03	3	.03
4	.04	4	.04	4	.04	4	.04
5	.05	5	.05	5	.05	5	.05
6	.06	6	.06	6	.06	6	.06
7	.07	7	.07	7	.07	7	.07
8	.08	8	.08	8	.08	8	.08
9	.09	9	.09	9	.09	9	.09
10	.10	10	.10	10	.10	10	.10
20	.20	20	.20	20	.20	20	.20
30	.30	30	.30	30	.30	30	.30
40	.40	40	.40	40	.40	40	.40
50	.50	50	.50	50	.50	50	.50
60	.60	60	.60	60	.60	60	.60
70	.70	70	.70	70	.70	70	.70
80	.80	80	.80	80	.80	80	.80
90	.90	90	.90	90	.90	90	.90
100	1.00	100	1.00	100	1.00	100	1.00
200	2.00	200	2.00	200	2.01	200	2.01
300	3.00	300	3.00	300	3.01	300	3.02
400	4.00	400	4.01	400	4.02	400	4.03
500	5.00	500	5.01	500	5.02	500	5.03
600	6.00	600	6.01	600	6.03	600	6.04
700	7.00	700	7.01	700	7.03	700	7.05
800	8.00	800	8.02	800	8.04	800	8.06
900	9.00	900	9.02	900	9.04	900	9.06
1000	10.00	1000	10.02	1000	10.05	1000	10.07
1100	11.00	1100	11.02	1100	11.05	1100	11.08
1200	12.00	1200	12.03	1200	12.05	1200	12.09
1300	13.00	1300	13.03	1300	13.06	1300	13.09
1400	14.00	1400	14.03	1400	14.07	1400	14.10
1500	15.00	1500	15.03	1500	15.07	1500	15.11
1600	16.00	1600	16.04	1600	16.08	1600	16.12
1700	17.00	1700	17.04	1700	17.08	1700	17.12
1800	18.00	1800	18.04	1800	18.09	1800	18.13
1900	19.00	1900	19.04	1900	19.09	1900	19.14
2000	20.00	2000	20.05	2000	20.10	2000	20.15
2100	21.00	2100	21.05	2100	21.10	2100	21.15
2200	22.00	2200	22.05	2200	22.11	2200	22.16
2300	23.00	2300	23.05	2300	23.11	2300	23.17
2400	24.00	2400	24.06	2400	24.12	2400	24.18
2500	25.00	2500	25.06	2500	25.12	2500	25.18
2600	26.00	2600	26.06	2600	26.13	2600	26.19
2700	27.00	2700	27.06	2700	27.13	2700	27.20
2800	28.00	2800	28.07	2800	28.14	2800	28.21
2900	29.00	2900	29.07	2900	29.14	2900	29.21
3000	30.00	3000	30.07	3000	30.15	3000	30.22
3100	31.00	3100	31.07	3100	31.15	3100	31.23
3200	32.00	3200	32.08	3200	32.16	3200	32.24
3300	33.00	3300	33.08	3300	33.16	3300	33.24
3400	34.00	3400	34.08	3400	34.17	3400	34.25
3500	35.00	3500	35.08	3500	35.17	3500	35.26
3600	36.00	3600	36.09	3600	36.18	3600	36.27
3700	37.00	3700	37.09	3700	37.18	3700	37.27
3800	38.00	3800	38.09	3800	38.19	3800	38.28
3900	39.00	3900	39.09	3900	39.19	3900	39.29
4000	40.00	4000	40.10	4000	40.20	4000	40.30

$1.01		$1.01¼		$1.01½		$1.01¾	
Lbs.	Amt.	Lbs.	Amt.	Lbs.	Amt.	Lbs.	Amt.
1	$ .01	1	$ .01	1	$ .01	1	$ .01
2	.02	2	.02	2	.02	2	.02
3	.03	3	.03	3	.03	3	.03
4	.04	4	.04	4	.04	4	.04
5	.05	5	.05	5	.05	5	.05
6	.06	6	.06	6	.06	6	.06
7	.07	7	.07	7	.07	7	.07
8	.08	8	.08	8	.08	8	.08
9	.09	9	.09	9	.09	9	.09
10	.10	10	.10	10	.10	10	.10
20	.20	20	.20	20	.20	20	.20
30	.30	30	.30	30	.30	30	.30
40	.40	40	.40	40	.40	40	.40
50	.50	50	.50	50	.50	50	.50
60	.60	60	.60	60	.60	60	.61
70	.70	70	.70	70	.71	70	.71
80	.80	80	.81	80	.81	80	.81
90	.90	90	.91	90	.91	90	.91
100	1.01	100	1.01	100	1.01	100	1.01
200	2.02	200	2.02	200	2.03	200	2.03
300	3.03	300	3.03	300	3.04	300	3.05
400	4.04	400	4.05	400	4.06	400	4.07
500	5.05	500	5.06	500	5.07	500	5.08
600	6.06	600	6.07	600	6.09	600	6.10
700	7.07	700	7.08	700	7.10	700	7.12
800	8.08	800	8.10	800	8.12	800	8.14
900	9.09	900	9.11	900	9.13	900	9.15
1000	10.10	1000	10.12	1000	10.15	1000	10.17
1100	11.11	1100	11.13	1100	11.16	1100	11.19
1200	12.12	1200	12.15	1200	12.18	1200	12.21
1300	13.13	1300	13.16	1300	13.19	1300	13.22
1400	14.14	1400	14.17	1400	14.21	1400	14.24
1500	15.15	1500	15.18	1500	15.22	1500	15.26
1600	16.16	1600	16.20	1600	16.24	1600	16.28
1700	17.17	1700	17.21	1700	17.25	1700	17.29
1800	18.18	1800	18.22	1800	18.27	1800	18.31
1900	19.19	1900	19.23	1900	19.28	1900	19.33
2000	20.20	2000	20.25	2000	20.30	2000	20.35
2100	21.21	2100	21.26	2100	21.31	2100	21.36
2200	22.22	2200	22.27	2200	22.33	2200	22.38
2300	23.23	2300	23.28	2300	23.34	2300	23.40
2400	24.24	2400	24.30	2400	24.36	2400	24.42
2500	25.25	2500	25.31	2500	25.37	2500	25.43
2600	26.26	2600	26.32	2600	26.39	2600	26.45
2700	27.27	2700	27.33	2700	27.40	2700	27.47
2800	28.28	2800	28.35	2800	28.42	2800	28.49
2900	29.29	2900	29.36	2900	29.43	2900	29.50
3000	30.30	3000	30.37	3000	30.45	3000	30.52
3100	31.31	3100	31.38	3100	31.46	3100	31.54
3200	32.32	3200	32.40	3200	32.48	3200	32.56
3300	33.33	3300	33.41	3300	33.49	3300	33.57
3400	34.34	3400	34.42	3400	34.51	3400	34.59
3500	35.35	3500	35.43	3500	35.52	3500	35.61
3600	36.36	3600	36.45	3600	36.54	3600	36.63
3700	37.37	3700	37.46	3700	37.55	3700	37.64
3800	38.38	3800	38.47	3800	38.57	3800	38.66
3900	39.39	3900	39.48	3900	39.58	3900	39.68
4000	40.40	4000	40.50	4000	40.60	4000	40.70

\$1.02		\$1.02¼		\$1.02½		\$1.02¾	
Lbs.	Amt.	Lbs.	Amt.	Lbs.	Amt.	Lbs.	Amt.
1	\$ .01	1	\$ .01	1	\$ .01	1	\$ .01
2	.02	2	.02	2	.02	2	.02
3	.03	3	.03	3	.03	3	.03
4	.04	4	.04	4	.04	4	.04
5	.05	5	.05	5	.05	5	.05
6	.06	6	.06	6	.06	6	.06
7	.07	7	.07	7	.07	7	.07
8	.08	8	.08	8	.08	8	.08
9	.09	9	.09	9	.09	9	.09
10	.10	10	.10	10	.10	10	.10
20	.20	20	.20	20	.20	20	.20
30	.30	30	.30	30	.30	30	.30
40	.40	40	.40	40	.41	40	.41
50	.51	50	.51	50	.51	50	.51
60	.61	60	.61	60	.61	60	.61
70	.71	70	.71	70	.71	70	.71
80	.81	80	.81	80	.82	80	.82
90	.91	90	.92	90	.92	90	.92
100	1.02	100	1.02	100	1.02	100	1.02
200	2.04	200	2.04	200	2.05	200	2.05
300	3.06	300	3.06	300	3.07	300	3.08
400	4.08	400	4.09	400	4.10	400	4.11
500	5.10	500	5.11	500	5.12	500	5.13
600	6.12	600	6.13	600	6.15	600	6.16
700	7.14	700	7.15	700	7.17	700	7.19
800	8.16	800	8.18	800	8.20	800	8.22
900	9.18	900	9.20	900	9.22	900	9.24
1000	10.20	1000	10.22	1000	10.25	1000	10.27
1100	11.22	1100	11.24	1100	11.27	1100	11.30
1200	12.24	1200	12.27	1200	12.30	1200	12.33
1300	13.26	1300	13.29	1300	13.32	1300	13.35
1400	14.28	1400	14.31	1400	14.35	1400	14.38
1500	15.30	1500	15.33	1500	15.37	1500	15.41
1600	16.32	1600	16.36	1600	16.40	1600	16.44
1700	17.34	1700	17.38	1700	17.42	1700	17.46
1800	18.36	1800	18.40	1800	18.45	1800	18.49
1900	19.38	1900	19.42	1900	19.47	1900	19.52
2000	20.40	2000	20.45	2000	20.50	2000	20.55
2100	21.42	2100	21.47	2100	21.52	2100	21.57
2200	22.44	2200	22.49	2200	22.55	2200	22.60
2300	23.46	2300	23.51	2300	23.57	2300	23.63
2400	24.48	2400	24.54	2400	24.60	2400	24.66
2500	25.50	2500	25.56	2500	25.62	2500	25.68
2600	26.52	2600	26.58	2600	26.65	2600	26.71
2700	27.54	2700	27.60	2700	27.67	2700	27.74
2800	28.56	2800	28.63	2800	28.70	2800	28.77
2900	29.58	2900	29.65	2900	29.72	2900	29.79
3000	30.60	3000	30.67	3000	30.75	3000	30.82
3100	31.62	3100	31.69	3100	31.77	3100	31.85
3200	32.64	3200	32.72	3200	32.80	3200	32.88
3300	33.66	3300	33.74	3300	33.82	3300	33.90
3400	34.68	3400	34.76	3400	34.85	3400	34.93
3500	35.70	3500	35.78	3500	35.87	3500	35.96
3600	36.72	3600	36.81	3600	36.90	3600	36.99
3700	37.74	3700	37.83	3700	37.92	3700	38.01
3800	38.76	3800	38.85	3800	38.95	3800	39.04
3900	39.78	3900	39.87	3900	39.97	3900	40.07
4000	40.80	4000	40.90	4000	41.00	4000	41.10

\$1.03		\$1.03¼		\$1.03½		\$1.03¾	
Lbs.	Amt.	Lbs.	Amt.	Lbs.	Amt.	Lbs.	Amt.
1	\$ .01	1	\$ .01	1	\$ .01	1	\$ .01
2	.02	2	.02	2	.02	2	.02
3	.03	3	.03	3	.03	3	.03
4	.04	4	.04	4	.04	4	.04
5	.05	5	.05	5	.05	5	.05
6	.06	6	.06	6	.06	6	.06
7	.07	7	.07	7	.07	7	.07
8	.08	8	.08	8	.08	8	.08
9	.09	9	.09	9	.09	9	.09
10	.10	10	.10	10	.10	10	.10
20	.20	20	.20	20	.20	20	.20
30	.30	30	.30	30	.31	30	.31
40	.41	40	.41	40	.41	40	.41
50	.51	50	.51	50	.51	50	.51
60	.61	60	.61	60	.62	60	.62
70	.72	70	.72	70	.72	70	.72
80	.82	80	.82	80	.82	80	.83
90	.92	90	.92	90	.93	90	.93
100	1.03	100	1.03	100	1.03	100	1.03
200	2.06	200	2.06	200	2.07	200	2.07
300	3.09	300	3.09	300	3.10	300	3.11
400	4.12	400	4.13	400	4.14	400	4.15
500	5.15	500	5.16	500	5.17	500	5.18
600	6.18	600	6.19	600	6.21	600	6.22
700	7.21	700	7.22	700	7.24	700	7.26
800	8.24	800	8.26	800	8.28	800	8.30
900	9.27	900	9.29	900	9.31	900	9.33
1000	10.30	1000	10.32	1000	10.35	1000	10.37
1100	11.33	1100	11.35	1100	11.38	1100	11.41
1200	12.36	1200	12.39	1200	12.42	1200	12.45
1300	13.39	1300	13.42	1300	13.45	1300	13.48
1400	14.42	1400	14.45	1400	14.49	1400	14.52
1500	15.45	1500	15.48	1500	15.52	1500	15.56
1600	16.48	1600	16.52	1600	16.56	1600	16.60
1700	17.51	1700	17.55	1700	17.59	1700	17.63
1800	18.54	1800	18.58	1800	18.63	1800	18.67
1900	19.57	1900	19.61	1900	19.66	1900	19.71
2000	20.60	2000	20.65	2000	20.70	2000	20.75
2100	21.63	2100	21.68	2100	21.73	2100	21.78
2200	22.66	2200	22.71	2200	22.77	2200	22.82
2300	23.69	2300	23.74	2300	23.80	2300	23.86
2400	24.72	2400	24.78	2400	24.84	2400	24.90
2500	25.75	2500	25.81	2500	25.87	2500	25.93
2600	26.78	2600	26.84	2600	26.91	2600	26.97
2700	27.81	2700	27.87	2700	27.94	2700	28.01
2800	28.84	2800	28.91	2800	28.98	2800	29.05
2900	29.87	2900	29.94	2900	30.01	2900	30.08
3000	30.90	3000	30.97	3000	31.05	3000	31.12
3100	31.93	3100	32.00	3100	32.08	3100	32.16
3200	32.96	3200	33.04	3200	33.12	3200	33.20
3300	33.99	3300	34.07	3300	34.15	3300	34.23
3400	35.02	3400	35.10	3400	35.19	3400	35.27
3500	36.05	3500	36.13	3500	36.22	3500	36.31
3600	37.08	3600	37.17	3600	37.26	3600	37.35
3700	38.11	3700	38.20	3700	38.29	3700	38.38
3800	39.14	3800	39.23	3800	39.33	3800	39.42
3900	40.17	3900	40.26	3900	40.36	3900	40.46
4000	41.20	4000	41.30	4000	41.40	4000	41.50

\$1.04		\$1.04¼		\$1.04½		\$1.04¾	
Lbs.	Amt.	Lbs.	Amt.	Lbs.	Amt.	Lbs.	Amt.
1	\$ .01	1	\$ .01	1	\$ .01	1	\$ .01
2	.02	2	.02	2	.02	2	.02
3	.03	3	.03	3	.03	3	.03
4	.04	4	.04	4	.04	4	.04
5	.05	5	.05	5	.05	5	.05
6	.06	6	.06	6	.06	6	.06
7	.07	7	.07	7	.07	7	.07
8	.08	8	.08	8	.08	8	.08
9	.09	9	.09	9	.09	9	.09
10	.10	10	.10	10	.10	10	.10
20	.20	20	.20	20	.20	20	.20
30	.31	30	.31	30	.31	30	.31
40	.41	40	.41	40	.41	40	.41
50	.52	50	.52	50	.52	50	.52
60	.62	60	.62	60	.62	60	.62
70	.72	70	.72	70	.73	70	.73
80	.83	80	.83	80	.83	80	.83
90	.93	90	.93	90	.94	90	.94
100	1.04	100	1.04	100	1.04	100	1.04
200	2.08	200	2.08	200	2.09	200	2.09
300	3.12	300	3.12	300	3.13	300	3.14
400	4.16	400	4.17	400	4.18	400	4.19
500	5.20	500	5.21	500	5.22	500	5.23
600	6.24	600	6.25	600	6.27	600	6.28
700	7.28	700	7.29	700	7.31	700	7.33
800	8.32	800	8.34	800	8.36	800	8.38
900	9.36	900	9.38	900	9.40	900	9.42
1000	10.40	1000	10.42	1000	10.45	1000	10.47
1100	11.44	1100	11.46	1100	11.49	1100	11.52
1200	12.48	1200	12.51	1200	12.54	1200	12.57
1300	13.52	1300	13.55	1300	13.58	1300	13.61
1400	14.56	1400	14.59	1400	14.63	1400	14.66
1500	15.60	1500	15.63	1500	15.67	1500	15.71
1600	16.64	1600	16.68	1600	16.71	1600	16.76
1700	17.68	1700	17.72	1700	17.76	1700	17.80
1800	18.72	1800	18.76	1800	18.81	1800	18.85
1900	19.76	1900	19.80	1900	19.85	1900	19.90
2000	20.80	2000	20.85	2000	20.90	2000	20.95
2100	21.84	2100	21.89	2100	21.94	2100	21.99
2200	22.88	2200	22.93	2200	22.99	2200	23.04
2300	23.92	2300	23.97	2300	24.03	2300	24.09
2400	24.96	2400	25.02	2400	25.08	2400	25.14
2500	26.00	2500	26.06	2500	26.12	2500	26.18
2600	27.04	2600	27.10	2600	27.17	2600	27.23
2700	28.08	2700	28.14	2700	28.21	2700	28.28
2800	29.12	2800	29.19	2800	29.26	2800	29.33
2900	30.16	2900	30.23	2900	30.30	2900	30.37
3000	31.20	3000	31.27	3000	31.35	3000	31.42
3100	32.24	3100	32.31	3100	32.39	3100	32.47
3200	33.28	3200	33.36	3200	33.44	3200	33.52
3300	34.32	3300	34.40	3300	34.48	3300	34.56
3400	35.36	3400	35.44	3400	35.53	3400	35.61
3500	36.40	3500	36.48	3500	36.57	3500	36.66
3600	37.44	3600	37.53	3600	37.62	3600	37.71
3700	38.48	3700	38.57	3700	38.66	3700	38.75
3800	39.52	3800	39.61	3800	39.71	3800	39.80
3900	40.56	3900	40.65	3900	40.75	3900	40.85
4000	41.60	4000	41.70	4000	41.80	4000	41.90

\$1.05		\$1.05¼		\$1.05½		\$1.05¾	
Lbs.	Amt.	Lbs.	Amt.	Lbs.	Amt.	Lbs.	Amt.
1	\$ .01	1	\$ .01	1	\$ .01	1	\$ .01
2	.02	2	.02	2	.02	2	.02
3	.03	3	.03	3	.03	3	.03
4	.04	4	.04	4	.04	4	.04
5	.05	5	.05	5	.05	5	.05
6	.06	6	.06	6	.06	6	.06
7	.07	7	.07	7	.07	7	.07
8	.08	8	.08	8	.08	8	.08
9	.09	9	.09	9	.09	9	.09
10	.10	10	.10	10	.10	10	.10
20	.21	20	.21	20	.21	20	.21
30	.31	30	.31	30	.31	30	.31
40	.42	40	.42	40	.42	40	.42
50	.52	50	.52	50	.52	50	.52
60	.63	60	.63	60	.63	60	.63
70	.73	70	.73	70	.73	70	.74
80	.84	80	.84	80	.84	80	.84
90	.94	90	.94	90	.94	90	.95
100	1.05	100	1.05	100	1.05	100	1.05
200	2.10	200	2.10	200	2.11	200	2.11
300	3.15	300	3.15	300	3.16	300	3.17
400	4.20	400	4.21	400	4.22	400	4.23
500	5.25	500	5.26	500	5.27	500	5.28
600	6.30	600	6.31	600	6.33	600	6.34
700	7.35	700	7.36	700	7.38	700	7.40
800	8.40	800	8.42	800	8.44	800	8.46
900	9.45	900	9.47	900	9.49	900	9.51
1000	10.50	1000	10.52	1000	10.55	1000	10.57
1100	11.55	1100	11.57	1100	11.60	1100	11.63
1200	12.60	1200	12.63	1200	12.66	1200	12.69
1300	13.65	1300	13.68	1300	13.71	1300	13.74
1400	14.70	1400	14.73	1400	14.77	1400	14.80
1500	15.75	1500	15.78	1500	15.82	1500	15.86
1600	16.80	1600	16.84	1600	16.88	1600	16.92
1700	17.85	1700	17.89	1700	17.93	1700	17.97
1800	18.90	1800	18.94	1800	18.99	1800	19.03
1900	19.95	1900	19.99	1900	20.04	1900	20.09
2000	21.00	2000	21.05	2000	21.10	2000	21.15
2100	22.05	2100	22.10	2100	22.15	2100	22.20
2200	23.10	2200	23.15	2200	23.21	2200	23.26
2300	24.15	2300	24.20	2300	24.26	2300	24.32
2400	25.20	2400	25.26	2400	25.32	2400	25.38
2500	26.25	2500	26.31	2500	26.37	2500	26.43
2600	27.30	2600	27.36	2600	27.43	2600	27.49
2700	28.35	2700	28.41	2700	28.48	2700	28.55
2800	29.40	2800	29.47	2800	29.54	2800	29.61
2900	30.45	2900	30.52	2900	30.59	2900	30.66
3000	31.50	3000	31.57	3000	31.65	3000	31.72
3100	32.55	3100	32.62	3100	32.70	3100	32.78
3200	33.60	3200	33.68	3200	33.76	3200	33.84
3300	34.65	3300	34.73	3300	34.81	3300	34.89
3400	35.70	3400	35.78	3400	35.87	3400	35.95
3500	36.75	3500	36.83	3500	36.92	3500	37.01
3600	37.80	3600	37.89	3600	37.98	3600	38.07
3700	38.85	3700	38.94	3700	39.03	3700	39.12
3800	39.90	3800	39.99	3800	40.09	3800	40.18
3900	40.95	3900	41.04	3900	41.14	3900	41.24
4000	42.00	4000	42.10	4000	42.20	4000	42.30

$1.06		$1.06¼		$1.06½		$1.06¾	
Lbs.	Amt.	Lbs.	Amt.	Lbs.	Amt.	Lbs.	Amt.
1	$ .01	1	$ .01	1	$ .01	1	$ .01
2	.02	2	.02	2	.02	2	.02
3	.03	3	.03	3	.03	3	.03
4	.04	4	.04	4	.04	4	.04
5	.05	5	.05	5	.05	5	.05
6	.06	6	.06	6	.06	6	.06
7	.07	7	.07	7	.07	7	.07
8	.08	8	.08	8	.08	8	.08
9	.09	9	.09	9	.09	9	.09
10	.10	10	.10	10	.10	10	.10
20	.21	20	.21	20	.21	20	.21
30	.31	30	.31	30	.31	30	.32
40	.42	40	.42	40	.42	40	.42
50	.53	50	.53	50	.53	50	.53
60	.63	60	.63	60	.63	60	.64
70	.74	70	.74	70	.74	70	.74
80	.84	80	.85	80	.85	80	.85
90	.95	90	.95	90	.95	90	.95
100	1.06	100	1.06	100	1.06	100	1.06
200	2.12	200	2.12	200	2.13	200	2.13
300	3.18	300	3.18	300	3.19	300	3.20
400	4.24	400	4.25	400	4.26	400	4.27
500	5.30	500	5.31	500	5.32	500	5.33
600	6.36	600	6.37	600	6.39	600	6.40
700	7.42	700	7.43	700	7.45	700	7.47
800	8.48	800	8.50	800	8.52	800	8.54
900	9.54	900	9.56	900	9.58	900	9.60
1000	10.60	1000	10.62	1000	10.65	1000	10.67
1100	11.66	1100	11.68	1100	11.71	1100	11.74
1200	12.72	1200	12.75	1200	12.78	1200	12.81
1300	13.78	1300	13.81	1300	13.84	1300	13.87
1400	14.84	1400	14.87	1400	14.91	1400	14.94
1500	15.90	1500	15.93	1500	15.97	1500	16.01
1600	16.96	1600	17.00	1600	17.04	1600	17.08
1700	18.02	1700	18.06	1700	18.10	1700	18.14
1800	19.08	1800	19.12	1800	19.17	1800	19.21
1900	20.14	1900	20.18	1900	20.23	1900	20.28
2000	21.20	2000	21.25	2000	21.30	2000	21.35
2100	22.26	2100	22.31	2100	22.36	2100	22.41
2200	23.32	2200	23.37	2200	23.43	2200	23.48
2300	24.38	2300	24.43	2300	24.49	2300	24.55
2400	25.44	2400	25.50	2400	25.56	2400	25.62
2500	26.50	2500	26.56	2500	26.62	2500	26.68
2600	27.56	2600	27.62	2600	27.69	2600	27.75
2700	28.62	2700	28.68	2700	28.75	2700	28.82
2800	29.68	2800	29.75	2800	29.82	2800	29.89
2900	30.74	2900	30.81	2900	30.88	2900	30.95
3000	31.80	3000	31.87	3000	31.95	3000	32.02
3100	32.86	3100	32.93	3100	33.01	3100	33.09
3200	33.92	3200	34.00	3200	34.08	3200	34.16
3300	34.98	3300	35.06	3300	35.14	3300	35.22
3400	36.04	3400	36.12	3400	36.21	3400	36.29
3500	37.10	3500	37.18	3500	37.27	3500	37.36
3600	38.16	3600	38.25	3600	38.34	3600	38.43
3700	39.22	3700	39.31	3700	39.40	3700	39.49
3800	40.28	3800	40.37	3800	40.47	3800	40.56
3900	41.34	3900	41.43	3900	41.53	3900	41.63
4000	42.40	4000	42.50	4000	42.60	4000	42.70

\$1.07		\$1.07¼		\$1.07½		\$1.07¾	
Lbs.	Amt.	Lbs.	Amt.	Lbs.	Amt.	Lbs.	Amt.
1	\$ .01	1	\$ .01	1	\$ .01	1	\$ .01
2	.02	2	.02	2	.02	2	.02
3	.03	3	.03	3	.03	3	.03
4	.04	4	.04	4	.04	4	.04
5	.05	5	.05	5	.05	5	.05
6	.06	6	.06	6	.06	6	.06
7	.07	7	.07	7	.07	7	.07
8	.08	8	.08	8	.08	8	.08
9	.09	9	.09	9	.09	9	.09
10	.10	10	.10	10	.10	10	.10
20	.21	20	.21	20	.21	20	.21
30	.32	30	.32	30	.32	30	.32
40	.42	40	.42	40	.43	40	.43
50	.53	50	.53	50	.53	50	.53
60	.64	60	.64	60	.64	60	.64
70	.74	70	.75	70	.75	70	.75
80	.85	80	.85	80	.86	80	.86
90	.96	90	.96	90	.96	90	.96
100	1.07	100	1.07	100	1.07	100	1.07
200	2.14	200	2.14	200	2.15	200	2.15
300	3.21	300	3.21	300	3.22	300	3.23
400	4.28	400	4.29	400	4.30	400	4.31
500	5.35	500	5.36	500	5.37	500	5.38
600	6.42	600	6.43	600	6.45	600	6.46
700	7.49	700	7.50	700	7.52	700	7.54
800	8.56	800	8.58	800	8.60	800	8.62
900	9.63	900	9.65	900	9.67	900	9.69
1000	10.70	1000	10.72	1000	10.75	1000	10.77
1100	11.77	1100	11.79	1100	11.82	1100	11.85
1200	12.84	1200	12.87	1200	12.90	1200	12.93
1300	13.91	1300	13.94	1300	13.97	1300	14.00
1400	14.98	1400	15.01	1400	15.05	1400	15.08
1500	16.05	1500	16.08	1500	16.12	1500	16.16
1600	17.12	1600	17.16	1600	17.20	1600	17.24
1700	18.19	1700	18.23	1700	18.27	1700	18.31
1800	19.26	1800	19.30	1800	19.35	1800	19.39
1900	20.33	1900	20.37	1900	20.42	1900	20.47
2000	21.40	2000	21.45	2000	21.50	2000	21.55
2100	22.47	2100	22.52	2100	22.57	2100	22.62
2200	23.54	2200	23.59	2200	23.65	2200	23.70
2300	24.61	2300	24.66	2300	24.72	2300	24.78
2400	25.68	2400	25.74	2400	25.80	2400	25.86
2500	26.75	2500	26.81	2500	26.87	2500	26.93
2600	27.82	2600	27.88	2600	27.95	2600	28.01
2700	28.89	2700	28.95	2700	29.02	2700	29.09
2800	29.96	2800	30.03	2800	30.10	2800	30.17
2900	31.03	2900	31.10	2900	31.17	2900	31.24
3000	32.10	3000	32.17	3000	32.25	3000	32.32
3100	33.17	3100	33.24	3100	33.32	3100	33.40
3200	34.24	3200	34.32	3200	34.40	3200	34.48
3300	35.31	3300	35.39	3300	35.47	3300	35.55
3400	36.38	3400	36.46	3400	36.55	3400	36.63
3500	37.45	3500	37.53	3500	37.62	3500	37.71
3600	38.52	3600	38.61	3600	38.70	3600	38.79
3700	39.59	3700	39.68	3700	39.77	3700	39.86
3800	40.66	3800	40.75	3800	40.85	3800	40.94
3900	41.73	3900	41.82	3900	41.92	3900	42.02
4000	42.80	4000	42.90	4000	43.00	4000	43.10

\$1.08		\$1.08¼		\$1.08½		\$1 08¾	
Lbs.	Amt.	Lbs.	Amt.	Lbs.	Amt.	Lbs,	Amt.
1	\$ .01	1	\$ .01	1	\$ .01	1	\$ .01
2	.02	2	.02	2	.02	2	.02
3	.03	3	.03	3	.03	3	.03
4	.04	4	.04	4	.04	4	.04
5	.05	5	.05	5	.05	5	.05
6	.06	6	.06	6	.06	6	.06
7	.07	7	.07	7	.07	7	.07
8	.08	8	.08	8	.08	8	.08
9	.09	9	.09	9	.09	9	.09
10	.10	10	.10	10	.10	10	.10
20	.21	20	.21	20	.21	20	.21
30	.32	30	.32	30	.32	30	.32
40	.43	40	.43	40	.43	40	.43
50	.54	50	.54	50	.54	50	.54
60	.64	60	.64	60	.65	60	.65
70	.75	70	.75	70	.75	70	.76
80	.86	80	.86	80	.86	80	.87
90	.97	90	.97	90	.97	90	.97
100	1.08	100	1.08	100	1.08	100	1.08
200	2.16	200	2.16	200	2.17	200	2.17
300	3.24	300	3.24	300	3.25	300	3.26
400	4.32	400	4.33	400	4.34	400	4.35
500	5.40	500	5.41	500	5.42	500	5.43
600	6.48	600	6.49	600	6.51	600	6.52
700	7.56	700	7.57	700	7.59	700	7.61
800	8.64	800	8.66	800	8.68	800	8.70
900	9.72	900	9.74	900	9.76	900	9.78
1000	10.80	1000	10.82	1000	10.85	1000	10.87
1100	11.88	1100	11.90	1100	11.93	1100	11.96
1200	12.96	1200	12.99	1200	13.02	1200	13.05
1300	14.04	1300	14.07	1300	14.10	1300	14.13
1400	15.12	1400	15.15	1400	15.19	1400	15.22
1500	16.20	1500	16.23	1500	16.27	1500	16.31
1600	17.28	1600	17.32	1600	17.36	1600	17.40
1700	18.36	1700	18.40	1700	18.44	1700	18.48
1800	19.44	1800	19.48	1800	19.53	1800	19.57
1900	20.52	1900	20.56	1900	20.61	1900	20.66
2000	21.60	2000	21.65	2000	21.70	2000	21.75
2100	22.68	2100	22.73	2100	22.78	2100	22.83
2200	23.76	2200	23.81	2200	23.87	2200	23.92
2300	24.84	2300	24.89	2300	24.95	2300	25.01
2400	25.92	2400	25.98	2400	26.04	2400	26.10
2500	27.00	2500	27.06	2500	27.12	2500	27.18
2600	28.08	2600	28.14	2600	28.21	2600	28.27
2700	29.16	2700	29.22	2700	29.29	2700	29.36
2800	30.24	2800	30.31	2800	30.38	2800	30.45
2900	31.32	2900	31.39	2900	31.46	2900	31.52
3000	32.40	3000	32.47	3000	32.55	3000	32.62
3100	33.48	3100	33.55	3100	33.63	3100	33.71
3200	34.56	3200	34.64	3200	34.72	3200	34.80
3300	35.64	3300	35.72	3300	35.80	3300	35.88
3400	36.72	3400	36.80	3400	36.89	3400	36.97
3500	37.80	3500	37.88	3500	37.97	3500	38.06
3600	38.88	3600	38.97	3600	39.06	3600	39.15
3700	39.96	3700	40.05	3700	40.14	3700	40.23
3800	41.04	3800	41.13	3800	41.23	3800	41.32
3900	42.12	3900	42.21	3900	42.31	3900	42.41
4000	43.20	4000	43.30	4000	43.40	4000	43.50

\$1.09		\$1.09¼		\$1.09½		\$1.09¾	
Lbs.	Amt.	Lbs.	Amt.	Lbs.	Amt.	Lbs.	Amt.
1	\$ .01	1	\$ .01	1	\$ .01	1	\$ .01
2	.02	2	.02	2	.02	2	.02
3	.03	3	.03	3	.03	3	.03
4	.04	4	.04	4	.04	4	.04
5	.05	5	.05	5	.05	5	.05
6	.06	6	.06	6	.06	6	.06
7	.07	7	.07	7	.07	7	.07
8	.08	8	.08	8	.08	8	.08
9	.09	9	.09	9	.09	9	.09
10	.10	10	.10	10	.10	10	.10
20	.21	20	.21	20	.21	20	.21
30	.32	30	.32	30	.32	30	.32
40	.43	40	.43	40	.43	40	.43
50	.54	50	.54	50	.54	50	.54
60	.65	60	.65	60	.65	60	.65
70	.76	70	.76	70	.76	70	.76
80	.87	80	.87	80	.87	80	.87
90	.98	90	.98	90	.98	90	.98
100	1.09	100	1.09	100	1.09	100	1.09
200	2.18	200	2.18	200	2.19	200	2.19
300	3.27	300	3.27	300	3.28	300	3.29
400	4.36	400	4.37	400	4.38	400	4.39
500	5.45	500	5.46	500	5.47	500	5.48
600	6.54	600	6.55	600	6.57	600	6.58
700	7.63	700	7.64	700	7.66	700	7.68
800	8.72	800	8.74	800	8.76	800	8.78
900	9.81	900	9.83	900	9.85	900	9.87
1000	10.90	1000	10.92	1000	10.95	1000	10.97
1100	11.99	1100	12.01	1100	12.04	1100	12.07
1200	13.08	1200	13.11	1200	13.14	1200	13.17
1300	14.17	1300	14.20	1300	14.23	1300	14.26
1400	15.26	1400	15.29	1400	15.33	1400	15.36
1500	16.35	1500	16.38	1500	16.42	1500	16.46
1600	17.44	1600	17.48	1600	17.52	1600	17.56
1700	18.53	1700	18.57	1700	18.61	1700	18.65
1800	19.62	1800	19.66	1800	19.71	1800	19.75
1900	20.71	1900	20.75	1900	20.80	1900	20.85
2000	21.80	2000	21.85	2000	21.90	2000	21.95
2100	22.89	2100	22.94	2100	22.99	2100	23.04
2200	23.98	2200	24.03	2200	24.09	2200	24.14
2300	25.07	2300	25.12	2300	25.18	2300	25.24
2400	26.16	2400	26.22	2400	26.28	2400	26.34
2500	27.25	2500	27.31	2500	27.37	2500	27.43
2600	28.34	2600	28.40	2600	28.47	2600	28.53
2700	29.43	2700	29.49	2700	29.56	2700	29.63
2800	30.52	2800	30.59	2800	30.66	2800	30.73
2900	31.61	2900	31.68	2900	31.75	2900	31.82
3000	32.70	3000	32.77	3000	32.85	3000	32.92
3100	33.79	3100	33.86	3100	33.94	3100	34.02
3200	34.88	3200	34.96	3200	35.04	3200	35.12
3300	35.97	3300	36.05	3300	36.13	3300	36.21
3400	37.06	3400	37.14	3400	37.23	3400	37.31
3500	38.15	3500	38.23	3500	38.32	3500	38.41
3600	39.24	3600	39.33	3600	39.42	3600	39.51
3700	40.33	3700	40.42	3700	40.51	3700	40.60
3800	41.42	3800	41.51	3800	41.61	3800	41.70
3900	42.51	3900	42.60	3900	42.70	3900	42.80
4000	43.60	4000	43.70	4000	43.80	4000	43 90

\$1.10		\$1.10¼		\$1.10½		\$1.10¾	
Lbs.	Amt.	Lbs.	Amt.	Lbs.	Amt.	Lbs.	Amt.
1	\$ .01	1	\$ .01	1	\$ .01	1	\$ .01
2	.02	2	.02	2	.02	2	.02
3	.03	3	.03	3	.03	3	.03
4	.04	4	.04	4	.04	4	.04
5	.05	5	.05	5	.05	5	.05
6	.06	6	.06	6	.06	6	.06
7	.07	7	.07	7	.07	7	.07
8	.08	8	.08	8	.08	8	.08
9	.09	9	.09	9	.09	9	.09
10	.11	10	.11	10	.11	10	.11
20	.22	20	.22	20	.22	20	.22
30	.33	30	.33	30	.33	30	.33
40	.44	40	.44	40	.44	40	.44
50	.55	50	.55	50	.55	50	.55
60	.66	60	.66	60	.66	60	.66
70	.77	70	.77	70	.77	70	.77
80	.88	80	.88	80	.88	80	.88
90	.99	90	.99	90	.99	90	.99
100	1.10	100	1.10	100	1.10	100	1.10
200	2.20	200	2.20	200	2.21	200	2.21
300	3.30	300	3.30	300	3.31	300	3.32
400	4.40	400	4.41	400	4.42	400	4.43
500	5.50	500	5.51	500	5.52	500	5.53
600	6.60	600	6.61	600	6.63	600	6.64
700	7.70	700	7.71	700	7.73	700	7.75
800	8.80	800	8.82	800	8.84	800	8.86
900	9.90	900	9.92	900	9.94	900	9.96
1000	11.00	1000	11.02	1000	11.05	1000	11.07
1100	12.10	1100	12.12	1100	12.15	1100	12.18
1200	13.20	1200	13.23	1200	13.26	1200	13.29
1300	14.30	1300	14.33	1300	14.36	1300	14.39
1400	15.40	1400	15.43	1400	15.47	1400	15.50
1500	16.50	1500	16.53	1500	16.57	1500	16.61
1600	17.60	1600	17.64	1600	17.68	1600	17.72
1700	18.70	1700	18.74	1700	18.78	1700	18.82
1800	19.80	1800	19.84	1800	19.89	1800	19.93
1900	20.90	1900	20.94	1900	20.99	1900	21.04
2000	22.00	2000	22.05	2000	22.10	2000	22.15
2100	23.10	2100	23.15	2100	23.20	2100	23.25
2200	24.20	2200	24.25	2200	24.31	2200	24.36
2300	25.30	2300	25.35	2300	25.41	2300	25.47
2400	26.40	2400	26.46	2400	26.52	2400	26.58
2500	27.50	2500	27.56	2500	27.62	2500	27.68
2600	28.60	2600	28.66	2600	28.73	2600	28.79
2700	29.70	2700	29.76	2700	29.83	2700	29.90
2800	30.80	2800	30.87	2800	30.94	2800	31.01
2900	31.90	2900	31.97	2900	32.04	2900	32.11
3000	33.00	3000	33.07	3000	33.15	3000	33.22
3100	34.10	3100	34.17	3100	34.25	3100	34.33
3200	35.20	3200	35.28	3200	35.36	3200	35.44
3300	36.30	3300	36.38	3300	36.46	3300	36.54
3400	37.40	3400	37.48	3400	37.57	3400	37.65
3500	38.50	3500	38.58	3500	38.67	3500	38.76
3600	39.60	3600	39.69	3600	39.78	3600	39.87
3700	40.70	3700	40.79	3700	40.88	3700	40.97
3800	41.80	3800	41.89	3800	41.99	3800	42.08
3900	42.90	3900	42.99	3900	43.09	3900	43.19
4000	44.00	4000	44.10	4000	44.20	4000	44.30

$1.11		$1.11¼		$1.11½		1.11¾	
Lbs.	Amt.	Lbs.	Amt.	Lbs.	Amt.	Lbs.	Amt.
1	$ .01	1	$ .01	1	$ .01	1	$ .01
2	.02	2	.02	2	.02	2	.02
3	.03	3	.03	3	.03	3	.03
4	.04	4	.04	4	.04	4	.04
5	.05	5	.05	5	.05	5	.05
6	.06	6	.06	6	.06	6	.06
7	.07	7	.07	7	.07	7	.07
8	.08	8	.08	8	.08	8	.08
9	.09	9	.10	9	.10	9	.10
10	.11	10	.11	10	.11	10	.11
20	.22	20	.22	20	.22	20	.22
30	.33	30	.33	30	.33	30	.33
40	.44	40	.44	40	.44	40	.44
50	.55	50	.55	50	.55	50	.55
60	.66	60	.66	60	.66	60	.67
70	.77	70	.77	70	.78	70	.78
80	.88	80	.89	80	.89	80	.89
90	.99	90	1.00	90	1.00	90	1.00
100	1.11	100	1.11	100	1.11	100	1.11
200	2.22	200	2.22	200	2.23	200	2.23
300	3.33	300	3.33	300	3.34	300	3.35
400	4.44	400	4.45	400	4.46	400	4.47
500	5.55	500	5.56	500	5.57	500	5.58
600	6.66	600	6.67	600	6.69	600	6.70
700	7.77	700	7.78	700	7.80	700	7.82
800	8.88	800	8.90	800	8.92	800	8.94
900	9.99	900	10.01	900	10.03	900	10.05
1000	11.10	1000	11.12	1000	11.15	1000	11.17
1100	12.21	1100	12.23	1100	12.26	1100	12.29
1200	13.32	1200	13.35	1200	13.38	1200	13.41
1300	14.43	1300	14.46	1300	14.49	1300	14.52
1400	15.54	1400	15.57	1400	15.61	1400	15.64
1500	16.65	1500	16.68	1500	16.72	1500	16.76
1600	17.76	1600	17.80	1600	17.84	1600	17.88
1700	18.87	1700	18.91	1700	18.95	1700	18.99
1800	19.98	1800	20.02	1800	20.07	1800	20.11
1900	21.09	1900	21.13	1900	21.18	1900	21.23
2000	22.20	2000	22.25	2000	22.30	2000	22.35
2100	23.31	2100	23.36	2100	23.41	2100	23.46
2200	24.42	2200	24.47	2200	24.53	2200	24.58
2300	25.53	2300	25.58	2300	25.64	2300	25.70
2400	26.64	2400	26.70	2400	26.76	2400	26.82
2500	27.75	2500	27.81	2500	27.87	2500	27.93
2600	28.86	2600	28.92	2600	28.99	2600	29.05
2700	29.97	2700	30.03	2700	30.10	2700	30.17
2800	31.08	2800	31.15	2800	31.22	2800	31.29
2900	32.19	2900	32.26	2900	32.33	2900	32.40
3000	33.30	3000	33.37	3000	33.45	3000	33.52
3100	34.41	3100	34.48	3100	34.56	3100	34.64
3200	35.52	3200	35.60	3200	35.68	3200	35.76
3300	36.63	3300	36.71	3300	36.79	3300	36.87
3400	37.74	3400	37.82	3400	37.91	3400	37.99
3500	38.85	3500	38.93	3500	39.02	3500	39.11
3600	39.96	3600	40.05	3600	40.14	3600	40.23
3700	41.07	3700	41.16	3700	41.25	3700	41.34
3800	42.18	3800	42.27	3800	42.37	3800	42.46
3900	43.29	3900	43.38	3900	43.48	3900	43.58
4000	44.40	4000	44.50	4000	44.60	4000	44.70

$1.12		$1.12¼		$1.12½		1.12¾	
Lbs.	Amt.	Lbs.	Amt.	Lbs.	Amt.	Lbs.	Amt.
1	$ .01	1	$ .01	1	$ .01	1	$ .01
2	.02	2	.02	2	.02	2	.02
3	.03	3	.03	3	.03	3	.03
4	.04	4	.04	4	.04	4	.04
5	.05	5	.05	5	.05	5	.05
6	.06	6	.06	6	.06	6	.06
7	.07	7	.07	7	.07	7	.07
8	.08	8	.09	8	.09	8	.09
9	.10	9	.10	9	.10	9	.10
10	.11	10	.11	10	.11	10	.11
20	.22	20	.22	20	.22	20	.22
30	.33	30	.33	30	.33	30	.33
40	.44	40	.44	40	.45	40	.45
50	.56	50	.56	50	.56	50	.56
60	.67	60	.67	60	.67	60	.67
70	.78	70	.78	70	.78	70	.78
80	.89	80	.89	80	.90	80	.90
90	1.00	90	1.01	90	1.01	90	1.01
100	1.12	100	1.12	100	1.12	100	1.12
200	2.24	200	2.24	200	2.25	200	2.25
300	3.36	300	3.36	300	3.37	300	3.38
400	4.48	400	4.49	400	4.50	400	4.51
500	5.60	500	5.61	500	5.62	500	5.63
600	6.72	600	6.73	600	6.75	600	6.76
700	7.84	700	7.85	700	7.87	700	7.89
800	8.96	800	8.98	800	9.00	800	9.02
900	10.08	900	10.10	900	10.12	900	10.14
1000	11.20	1000	11.22	1000	11.25	1000	11.27
1100	12.32	1100	12.34	1100	12.37	1100	12.40
1200	13.44	1200	13.47	1200	13.50	1200	13.53
1300	14.56	1300	14.59	1300	14.62	1300	14.65
1400	15.68	1400	15.71	1400	15.75	1400	15.78
1500	16.80	1500	16.83	1500	16.87	1500	16.91
1600	17.92	1600	17.96	1600	18.00	1600	18.04
1700	19.04	1700	19.08	1700	19.12	1700	19.16
1800	20.16	1800	20.20	1800	20.25	1800	20.29
1900	21.28	1900	21.32	1900	21.37	1900	21.42
2000	22.40	2000	22.45	2000	22.50	2000	22.55
2100	23.52	2100	23.57	2100	23.62	2100	23.67
2200	24.64	2200	24.69	2200	24.75	2200	24.80
2300	25.76	2300	25.81	2300	25.87	2300	25.93
2400	26.88	2400	26.94	2400	27.00	2400	27.06
2500	28.00	2500	28.06	2500	28.12	2500	28.18
2600	29.12	2600	29.18	2600	29.25	2600	29.31
2700	30.24	2700	30.30	2700	30.37	2700	30.44
2800	31.36	2800	31.43	2800	31.50	2800	31.57
2900	32.48	2900	32.55	2900	32.62	2900	32.69
3000	33.60	3000	33.67	3000	33.75	3000	33.82
3100	34.72	3100	34.79	3100	34.87	3100	34.95
3200	35.84	3200	35.92	3200	36.00	3200	36.08
3300	36.96	3300	37.04	3300	37.12	3300	37.20
3400	38.08	3400	38.16	3400	38.25	3400	38.33
3500	39.20	3500	39.28	3500	39.37	3500	39.46
3600	40.32	3600	40.41	3600	40.50	3600	40.59
3700	41.44	3700	41.53	3700	41.62	3700	41.71
3800	42.56	3800	42.65	3800	42.75	3800	42.84
3900	43.68	3900	43.77	3900	43.87	3900	43.97
4000	44.80	4000	44.90	4000	45.00	4000	45.10

$1.13		$1.13¼		$1.13½		1.13¾	
Lbs.	Amt.	Lbs.	Amt.	Lbs.	Amt.	Lbs.	Amt.
1	$ .01	1	$ .01	1	$ .01	1	$ .01
2	.02	2	.02	2	.02	2	.02
3	.03	3	.03	3	.03	3	.03
4	.04	4	.04	4	.04	4	.04
5	.05	5	.05	5	.05	5	.05
6	.06	6	.06	6	.06	6	.06
7	.07	7	.07	7	.07	7	.07
8	.09	8	.09	8	.09	8	.09
9	.10	9	.10	9	.10	9	.10
10	.11	10	.11	10	.11	10	.11
20	.22	20	.22	20	.22	20	.22
30	.33	30	.33	30	.34	30	.34
40	.45	40	.45	40	.45	40	.45
50	.56	50	.56	50	.56	50	.56
60	.67	60	.67	60	.68	60	.68
70	.79	70	.79	70	.79	70	.79
80	.90	80	.90	80	.90	80	.90
90	1.01	90	1.01	90	1.02	90	1.02
100	1.13	100	1.13	100	1.13	100	1.13
200	2.26	200	2.26	200	2.27	200	2.27
300	3.39	300	3.39	300	3.40	300	3.41
400	4.52	400	4.53	400	4.54	400	4.55
500	5.65	500	5.66	500	5.67	500	5.68
600	6.78	600	6.79	600	6.81	600	6.82
700	7.91	700	7.92	700	7.94	700	7.96
800	9.04	800	9.05	800	9.08	800	9.10
900	10.17	900	10.19	900	10.21	900	10.23
1000	11.30	1000	11.32	1000	11.35	1000	11.37
1100	12.43	1100	12.45	1100	12.48	1100	12.51
1200	13.56	1200	13.59	1200	13.62	1200	13.65
1300	14.69	1300	14.72	1300	14.75	1300	14.78
1400	15.82	1400	15.85	1400	15.89	1400	15.92
1500	16.95	1500	16.98	1500	17.02	1500	17.06
1600	18.08	1600	18.12	1600	18.16	1600	18.20
1700	19.21	1700	19.25	1700	19.29	1700	19.33
1800	20.34	1800	20.38	1800	20.43	1800	20.47
1900	21.47	1900	21.51	1900	21.56	1900	21.61
2000	22.60	2000	22.65	2000	22.70	2000	22.75
2100	23.73	2100	23.78	2100	23.83	2100	23.88
2200	24.86	2200	24.91	2200	24.97	2200	25.02
2300	25.99	2300	26.04	2300	26.10	2300	26.16
2400	27.12	2400	27.18	2400	27.24	2400	27.30
2500	28.25	2500	28.31	2500	28.37	2500	28.43
2600	29.38	2600	29.44	2600	29.51	2600	29.57
2700	30.51	2700	30.57	2700	30.64	2700	30.71
2800	31.64	2800	31.71	2800	31.78	2800	31.85
2900	32.77	2900	32.84	2900	32.91	2900	32.98
3000	33.90	3000	33.97	3000	34.05	3000	34.12
3100	35.03	3100	35.10	3100	35.18	3100	35.26
3200	36.16	3200	36.24	3200	36.32	3200	36.40
3300	37.29	3300	37.37	3300	37.45	3300	37.53
3400	38.42	3400	38.50	3400	38.59	3400	38.67
3500	39.55	3500	39.63	3500	39.72	3500	39.81
3600	40.68	3600	40.77	3600	40.86	3600	40.95
3700	41.81	3700	41.90	3700	41.99	3700	42.08
3800	42.94	3800	43.03	3800	43.13	3800	43.22
3900	44.07	3900	44.16	3900	44.26	3900	44.36
4000	45.20	4000	45.30	4000	45.40	4000	45.50

$1.14		$1.14¼		$1.14½		1.14¾	
Lbs.	Amt.	Lbs	Amt.	Lbs.	Amt.	Lbs.	Amt.
1	$ .01	1	$ .01	1	$ .01	1	$ .01
2	.02	2	.02	2	.02	2	.02
3	.03	3	.03	3	.03	3	.03
4	.04	4	.04	4	.04	4	.04
5	.05	5	.05	5	.05	5	.05
6	.06	6	.06	6	.06	6	.06
7	.07	7	.07	7	.08	7	.08
8	.09	8	.09	8	.09	8	.09
9	.10	9	.10	9	.10	9	.10
10	.11	10	.11	10	.11	10	.11
20	.22	20	.22	20	.22	20	.22
30	.34	30	.34	30	.34	30	.34
40	.45	40	.45	40	.45	40	.45
50	.57	50	.57	50	.57	50	.57
60	.68	60	.68	60	.68	60	.68
70	.79	70	.79	70	.80	70	.80
80	.91	80	.91	80	.91	80	.91
90	1.02	90	1.02	90	1.03	90	1.03
100	1.14	100	1.14	100	1.14	100	1 14
200	2.28	200	2.28	200	2.29	200	2.29
300	3.42	300	3.42	300	3.43	300	3.44
400	4.56	400	4.57	400	4.58	400	4.59
500	5.70	500	5.71	500	5.72	500	5.73
600	6.84	600	6.85	600	6.87	600	6.88
700	7.98	700	7.99	700	8.01	700	8.03
800	9.12	800	9.14	800	9.16	800	9.18
900	10.26	900	10.28	900	10.30	900	10.32
1000	11.40	1000	11.42	1000	11.45	1000	11.47
1100	12.54	1100	12.56	1100	12.59	1100	12.62
1200	13.68	1200	13.71	1200	13.74	1200	13.77
1300	14.82	1300	14.85	1300	14.88	1300	14.91
1400	15.96	1400	15.99	1400	16.03	1400	16.06
1500	17.10	1500	17.13	1500	17.17	1500	17.21
1600	18.24	1600	18.28	1600	18.32	1600	18.36
1700	19.38	1700	19.42	1700	19.46	1700	19.50
1800	20.52	1800	20.56	1800	20.61	1800	20.65
1900	21.66	1900	21.70	1900	21.75	1900	21.80
2000	22.80	2000	22.85	2000	22.90	2000	22.95
2100	23.94	2100	23.99	2100	24.04	2100	24.09
2200	25.08	2200	25.13	2200	25.19	2200	25.24
2300	26.22	2300	26.27	2300	26.33	2300	26.39
2400	27.36	2400	27.42	2400	27.48	2400	27.54
2500	28.50	2500	28.56	2500	28.62	2500	28.68
2600	29.64	2600	29.70	2600	29.77	2600	29.83
2700	30.78	2700	30.84	2700	30.91	2700	30.98
2800	31.92	2800	31.97	2800	32.04	2800	32.11
2900	33.06	2900	33.13	2900	33.20	2900	33.27
3000	34.20	3000	34.27	3000	34.35	3000	34.42
3100	35.34	3100	35.41	3100	35.49	3100	35.57
3200	36.48	3200	36.56	3200	36.64	3200	36.72
3300	37.62	3300	37.70	3300	37.78	3300	37.86
3400	38.76	3400	38.84	3400	38.93	3400	39.01
3500	39.90	3500	39.98	3500	40.07	3500	40.16
3600	41.04	3600	41.13	3600	41.22	3600	41.31
3700	42.18	3700	42.27	3700	42.36	3700	42.45
3800	43.32	3800	43.41	3800	43.51	3800	43.60
3900	44.46	3900	44.55	3900	44.65	3900	44.75
4000	45.60	4000	45.70	4000	45.80	4000	45.90

\$1.15		\$1.15¼		\$1.15½		1.15¾	
Lbs.	Amt.	Lbs.	Amt.	Lbs.	Amt.	Lbs.	Amt.
1	\$ .01	1	\$ .01	1	\$ .01	1	\$ .01
2	.02	2	.02	2	.02	2	.02
3	.03	3	.03	3	.03	3	.03
4	.04	4	.04	4	.04	4	.04
5	.05	5	.05	5	.05	5	.05
6	.06	6	.06	6	.06	6	.06
7	.08	7	.08	7	.08	7	.08
8	.09	8	.09	8	.09	8	.09
9	.10	9	.10	9	.10	9	.10
10	.11	10	.11	10	.11	10	.11
20	.23	20	.23	20	.23	20	.23
30	.34	30	.34	30	.34	30	.34
40	.46	40	.46	40	.46	40	.46
50	.57	50	.57	50	.57	50	.57
60	.69	60	.69	60	.69	60	.69
70	.80	70	.80	70	.80	70	.81
80	.92	80	.92	80	.92	80	.92
90	1.03	90	1.03	90	1.03	90	1.04
100	1.15	100	1.15	100	1.15	100	1.15
200	2.30	200	2.30	200	2.31	200	2.31
300	3.45	300	3.45	300	3.46	300	3.47
400	4.60	400	4.61	400	4.62	400	4.63
500	5.75	500	5.76	500	5.77	500	5.78
600	6.90	600	6.91	600	6.93	600	6.94
700	8.05	700	8.06	700	8.08	700	8.10
800	9.20	800	9.22	800	9.24	800	9.26
900	10.35	900	10.37	900	10.39	900	10.41
1000	11.50	1000	11.52	1000	11.55	1000	11.57
1100	12.65	1100	12.67	1100	12.70	1100	12.73
1200	13.80	1200	13.83	1200	13.86	1200	13.89
1300	14.95	1300	14.98	1300	15.01	1300	15.04
1400	15.10	1400	16.13	1400	16.17	1400	16.20
1500	17.25	1500	17.28	1500	17.32	1500	17.36
1600	18.40	1600	18.44	1600	18.48	1600	18.52
1700	19.55	1700	19.59	1700	19.63	1700	19.67
1800	20.70	1800	20.74	1800	20.79	1800	20.83
1900	21.85	1900	21.89	1900	21.94	1900	21.99
2000	23.00	2000	23.05	2000	23.10	2000	23.15
2100	24.15	2100	24.20	2100	24.25	2100	24.30
2200	25.30	2200	25.35	2200	25.41	2200	25.46
2300	26.45	2300	26.50	2300	26.56	2300	26.62
2400	27.60	2400	27.66	2400	27.72	2400	27.78
2500	28.75	2500	28.81	2500	28.87	2500	28.93
2600	29.90	2600	29.96	2600	30.03	2600	30.09
2700	31.05	2700	31.11	2700	31.18	2700	31.25
2800	32.20	2800	32.27	2800	32.34	2800	32.41
2900	33.35	2900	33.42	2900	33.49	2900	33.56
3000	34.50	3000	34.57	3000	34.65	3000	34.72
3100	35.65	3100	35.72	3100	35.80	3100	35.88
3200	36.80	3200	36.88	3200	36.96	3200	37.04
3300	37.95	3300	38.03	3300	38.11	3300	38.19
3400	39.10	3400	39.18	3400	39.27	3400	39.35
3500	40.25	3500	40.33	3500	40.42	3500	40.51
3600	41.40	3600	41.49	3600	41.58	3600	41.67
3700	42.55	3700	42.64	3700	42.73	3700	42.82
3800	43.70	3800	43.79	3800	43.89	3800	43.98
3900	44.85	3900	44.94	3900	45.04	3900	45.14
4000	46.00	4000	46.10	4000	46.20	4000	46.30

$1.16		$1.16¼		$1.16½		1.16¾	
Lbs.	Amt.	Lbs.	Amt.	Lbs.	Amt.	Lbs.	Amt.
1	$ .01	1	$ .01	1	$ .01	1	$ .01
2	.02	2	.02	2	.02	2	.02
3	.03	3	.03	3	.03	3	.03
4	.04	4	.04	4	.04	4	.04
5	.05	5	.05	5	.05	5	.05
6	.06	6	.06	6	.06	6	.07
7	.08	7	.08	7	.08	7	.08
8	.09	8	.09	8	.09	8	.09
9	.10	9	.10	9	.10	9	.10
10	.11	10	.11	10	.11	10	.11
20	.23	20	.23	20	.23	20	.23
30	.34	30	.34	30	.34	30	.35
40	.46	40	.46	40	.46	40	.46
50	.58	50	.58	50	.58	50	.58
60	.69	60	.69	60	.69	60	.70
70	.81	70	.81	70	.81	70	.81
80	.92	80	.93	80	.93	80	.93
90	1.04	90	1.04	90	1.04	90	1.05
100	1.16	100	1.16	100	1.16	100	1.16
200	2.32	200	2.32	200	2.33	200	2.34
300	3.48	300	3.48	300	3.49	300	3.50
400	4.64	400	4.65	400	4.66	400	4.67
500	5.80	500	5.81	500	5.82	500	5.83
600	6.96	600	6.97	600	6.99	600	7.00
700	8.12	700	8.13	700	8.15	700	8.17
800	9.28	800	9.30	800	9.32	800	9.34
900	10.44	900	10.46	900	10.48	900	10.50
1000	11.60	1000	11.62	1000	11.65	1000	11.67
1100	12.76	1100	12.78	1100	12.81	1100	12.84
1200	13.92	1200	13.95	1200	13.98	1200	14.01
1300	15.08	1300	15.11	1300	15.14	1300	15.17
1400	16.24	1400	16.27	1400	16.31	1400	16.34
1500	17.40	1500	17.43	1500	17.47	1500	17.51
1600	18.56	1600	18.60	1600	18.64	1600	18.68
1700	19.72	1700	19.76	1700	19.80	1700	19.84
1800	20.88	1800	20.92	1800	20.97	1800	21.01
1900	22.04	1900	22.08	1900	22.13	1900	22.18
2000	23.20	2000	23.25	2000	23.30	2000	23.35
2100	24.36	2100	24.41	2100	24.46	2100	24.51
2200	25.52	2200	25.57	2200	25.63	2200	25.68
2300	26.68	2300	26.73	2300	26.79	2300	26.85
2400	27.84	2400	27.90	2400	27.96	2400	28.02
2500	29.00	2500	29.06	2500	29.12	2500	29.18
2600	30.16	2600	30.22	2600	30.29	2600	30.35
2700	31.32	2700	31.38	2700	31.45	2700	31.52
2800	32.48	2800	32.55	2800	32.62	2800	32.69
2900	33.64	2900	33.71	2900	33.78	2900	33.85
3000	34.80	3000	34.87	3000	34.95	3000	35.02
3100	35.96	3100	36.03	3100	36.11	3100	36.19
3200	37.12	3200	37.20	3200	37.28	3200	37.36
3300	38.28	3300	38.36	3300	38.44	3300	38.52
3400	39.44	3400	39.52	3400	39.61	3400	39.69
3500	40.60	3500	40.68	3500	40.77	3500	40.86
3600	41.76	3600	41.85	3600	41.94	3600	42.03
3700	42.92	3700	43.01	3700	43.10	3700	43.19
3800	44.08	3800	44.17	3800	44.27	3800	44.36
3900	45.24	3900	45.33	3900	45.43	3900	45.53
4000	46.40	4000	46.50	4000	46.60	4000	46.70

$1.17		$1.17¼		$1.17½		1.17¾	
Lbs.	Amt.	Lbs.	Amt.	Lbs.	Amt.	Lbs.	Amt.
1	$ .01	1	$ .01	1	$ .01	1	$ .01
2	.02	2	.02	2	.02	2	.02
3	.03	3	.03	3	.03	3	.03
4	.04	4	.04	4	.04	4	.04
5	.05	5	.05	5	.05	5	.05
6	.07	6	.07	6	.07	6	.07
7	.08	7	.08	7	.08	7	.08
8	.09	8	.09	8	.09	8	.09
9	.10	9	.10	9	.10	9	.10
10	.11	10	.11	10	.11	10	.11
20	.23	20	.23	20	.23	20	.23
30	.35	30	.35	30	.35	30	.35
40	.46	40	.46	40	.47	40	.47
50	.58	50	.58	50	.58	50	.58
60	.70	60	.70	60	.70	60	.70
70	.81	70	.82	70	.82	70	.82
80	.93	80	.93	80	.94	80	.94
90	1.05	90	1.05	90	1.05	90	1.05
100	1.17	100	1.17	100	1.17	100	1.17
200	2.34	200	2.34	200	2.35	200	2.35
300	3.51	300	3.51	300	3.52	300	3.53
400	4.68	400	4.69	400	4.70	400	4.71
500	5.85	500	5.86	500	5.87	500	5.88
600	7.02	600	7.03	600	7.05	600	7.06
700	8.19	700	8.20	700	8.22	700	8.24
800	9.36	800	9.38	800	9.40	800	9.42
900	10.53	900	10.55	900	10.57	900	10.59
1000	11.70	1000	11.72	1000	11.75	1000	11.77
1100	12.87	1100	12.89	1100	12.92	1100	12.95
1200	14.04	1200	14.07	1200	14.10	1200	14.13
1300	15.21	1300	15.24	1300	15.27	1300	15.30
1400	16.38	1400	16.41	1400	16.45	1400	16.48
1500	17.55	1500	17.58	1500	17.62	1500	17.66
1600	18.72	1600	18.76	1600	18.80	1600	18.84
1700	19.89	1700	19.93	1700	19.97	1700	20.01
1800	21.06	1800	21.10	1800	21.15	1800	21.19
1900	22.23	1900	22.27	1900	22.32	1900	22.37
2000	23.40	2000	23.45	2000	23.50	2000	23.55
2100	24.57	2100	24.62	2100	24.67	2100	24.72
2200	25.74	2200	25.79	2200	25.85	2200	25.90
2300	26.91	2300	26.96	2300	27.02	2300	27.08
2400	28.08	2400	28.14	2400	28.20	2400	28.26
2500	29.25	2500	29.31	2500	29.37	2500	29.43
2600	30.42	2600	30.48	2600	30.55	2600	30.61
2700	31.59	2700	31.65	2700	31.72	2700	31.79
2800	32.76	2800	32.83	2800	32.90	2800	32.97
2900	33.93	2900	34.00	2900	34.07	2900	34.14
3000	35.10	3000	35.17	3000	35.25	3000	35.32
3100	36.27	3100	36.34	3100	36.42	3100	36.50
3200	37.44	3200	37.52	3200	37.60	3200	37.68
3300	38.61	3300	38.69	3300	38.77	3300	38.85
3400	39.78	3400	39.86	3400	39.95	3400	40.03
3500	40.95	3500	41.03	3500	41.12	3500	41.21
3600	42.12	3600	42.21	3600	42.30	3600	42.39
3700	43.29	3700	43.38	3700	43.47	3700	43.56
3800	44.46	3800	44.55	3800	44.65	3800	44.74
3900	45.63	3900	45.72	3900	45.82	3900	45.92
4000	46.80	4000	46.90	4000	47.00	4000	47.10

\$1.18		\$1.18¼		\$1.18½		1.18¾	
Lbs.	Amt.	Lbs.	Amt.	Lbs.	Amt.	Lbs.	Amt.
1	\$ .01	1	\$ .01	1	\$ .01	1	\$ .01
2	.02	2	.02	2	.02	2	.02
3	.03	3	.03	3	.03	3	.03
4	.04	4	.04	4	.04	4	.04
5	.05	5	.05	5	.05	5	.05
6	.07	6	.07	6	.07	6	.07
7	.08	7	.08	7	.08	7	.08
8	.09	8	.09	8	.09	8	.09
9	.10	9	.10	9	.10	9	.10
10	.11	10	.11	10	.11	10	.11
20	.23	20	.23	20	.23	20	.23
30	.35	30	.35	30	.35	30	.35
40	.47	40	.47	40	.47	40	.47
50	.59	50	.59	50	.59	50	.59
60	.70	60	.70	60	.71	60	.71
70	.82	70	.82	70	.82	70	.83
80	.94	80	.94	80	.94	80	.95
90	1.06	90	1.06	90	1.06	90	1.06
100	1.18	100	1.18	100	1.18	100	1.18
200	2.36	200	2.36	200	2.37	200	2.37
300	3.54	300	3.54	300	3.55	300	3.56
400	4.72	400	4.73	400	4.74	400	4.75
500	5.90	500	5.91	500	5.92	500	5.93
600	7.08	600	7.09	600	7.11	600	7.12
700	8.26	700	8.27	700	8.29	700	8.31
800	9.44	800	9.46	800	9.48	800	9.50
900	10.62	900	10.64	900	10.66	900	10.68
1000	11.80	1000	11.82	1000	11.85	1000	11.87
1100	12.98	1100	13.00	1100	13.03	1100	13.06
1200	14.16	1200	14.19	1200	14.22	1200	14.25
1300	15.34	1300	15.37	1300	15.40	1300	15.43
1400	16.52	1400	16.55	1400	16.59	1400	16.62
1500	17.70	1500	17.73	1500	17.77	1500	17.81
1600	18.88	1600	18.92	1600	18.96	1600	19.00
1700	20.06	1700	20.10	1700	20.14	1700	20.18
1800	21.24	1800	21.28	1800	21.33	1800	21.37
1900	22.42	1900	22.46	1900	22.51	1900	22.56
2000	23.60	2000	23.65	2000	23.70	2000	23.75
2100	24.78	2100	24.83	2100	24.88	2100	24.93
2200	25.96	2200	26.01	2200	26.07	2200	26.12
2300	27.14	2300	27.19	2300	27.25	2300	27.31
2400	28.32	2400	28.38	2400	28.44	2400	28.50
2500	29.50	2500	29.56	2500	29.62	2500	29.68
2600	30.68	2600	30.74	2600	30.81	2600	30.87
2700	31.86	2700	31.92	2700	31.99	2700	32.06
2800	33.04	2800	33.11	2800	33.18	2800	33.25
2900	34.22	2900	34.29	2900	34.36	2900	34.43
3000	35.40	3000	35.47	3000	35.55	3000	35.62
3100	36.58	3100	36.65	3100	36.73	3100	36.81
3200	37.76	3200	37.84	3200	37.92	3200	38.00
3300	38.94	3300	39.02	3300	39.10	3300	39.18
3400	40.12	3400	40.20	3400	40.29	3400	40.37
3500	41.30	3500	41.38	3500	41.47	3500	41.56
3600	42.48	3600	42.57	3600	42.66	3600	42.75
3700	43.66	3700	43.75	3700	43.84	3700	43.93
3800	44.84	3800	44.93	3800	45.03	3800	45.12
3900	46.02	3900	46.11	3900	46.21	3900	46.31
4000	47.20	4000	47.30	4000	47.40	4000	47.50

$1.19		$1.19¼		$1.19½		1.19¾	
Lbs.	Amt.	Lbs.	Amt.	Lbs.	Amt.	Lbs.	Amt.
1	$ .01	1	$ .01	1	$ .01	1	$ .01
2	.02	2	.02	2	.02	2	.02
3	.03	3	.03	3	.03	3	.03
4	.04	4	.04	4	.04	4	.04
5	.05	5	.05	5	.05	5	.05
6	.07	6	.07	6	.07	6	.07
7	.08	7	.08	7	.08	7	.08
8	.09	8	.09	8	.09	8	.09
9	.10	9	.10	9	.10	9	.10
10	.11	10	.11	10	.11	10	.11
20	.23	20	.23	20	.23	20	.23
30	.35	30	.35	30	.35	30	.35
40	.47	40	.47	40	.47	40	.47
50	.59	50	.59	50	.59	50	.59
60	.71	60	.71	60	.71	60	.71
70	.83	70	.83	70	.83	70	.83
80	.95	80	.95	80	.95	80	.95
90	1.07	90	1.07	90	1.07	90	1.07
100	1.19	100	1.19	100	1.19	100	1.19
200	2.38	200	2.38	200	2.39	200	2.39
300	3.57	300	3.57	300	3.58	300	3.59
400	4.76	400	4.77	400	4.78	400	4.79
500	5.95	500	5.96	500	5.97	500	5.98
600	7.14	600	7.15	600	7.17	600	7.18
700	8.33	700	8.34	700	8.36	700	8.38
800	9.52	800	9.54	800	9.56	800	9.58
900	10.71	900	10.73	900	10.75	900	10.77
1000	11.90	1000	11.92	1000	11.95	1000	11.97
1100	13.09	1100	13.11	1100	13.14	1100	13.17
1200	14.28	1200	14.31	1200	14.34	1200	14.37
1300	15.47	1300	15.50	1300	15.53	1300	15.56
1400	16.66	1400	16.69	1400	16.73	1400	16.76
1500	17.85	1500	17.88	1500	17.92	1500	17.96
1600	19.04	1600	19.08	1600	19.12	1600	19.16
1700	20.23	1700	20.27	1700	20.31	1700	20.35
1800	21.42	1800	21.46	1800	21.51	1800	21.55
1900	22.61	1900	22.65	1900	22.70	1900	22.75
2000	23.80	2000	23.85	2000	23.90	2000	23.95
2100	24.99	2100	25.04	2100	25.09	2100	25.14
2200	26.18	2200	26.23	2200	26.29	2200	26.34
2300	27.37	2300	27.42	2300	27.48	2300	27.54
2400	28.56	2400	28.62	2400	28.68	2400	28.74
2500	29.75	2500	29.81	2500	29.87	2500	29.93
2600	30.94	2600	31.00	2600	31.07	2600	31.13
2700	32.13	2700	32.19	2700	32.26	2700	32.33
2800	33.32	2800	33.39	2800	33.46	2800	33.53
2900	34.51	2900	34.58	2900	34.65	2900	34.72
3000	35.70	3000	35.77	3000	35.85	3000	35.92
3100	36.89	3100	36.96	3100	37.04	3100	37.12
3200	38.08	3200	38.16	3200	38.24	3200	38.32
3300	39.27	3300	39.35	3300	39.43	3300	39.51
3400	40.46	3400	40.54	3400	40.63	3400	40.71
3500	41.65	3500	41.73	3500	41.82	3500	41.91
3600	42.84	3600	42.93	3600	43.02	3600	43.11
3700	44.03	3700	44.12	3700	44.21	3700	44.30
3800	45.22	3800	45.31	3800	45.41	3800	45.50
3900	46.41	3900	46.50	3900	46.60	3900	46.70
4000	47.60	4000	47.70	4000	47.80	4000	47.90

$1.20		$1.20¼		$1.20½		1.20¾	
Lbs.	Amt.	Lbs.	Amt.	Lbs.	Amt.	Lbs.	Amt.
1	$ .01	1	$ .01	1	$ .01	1	$ .01
2	.02	2	.02	2	.02	2	.02
3	.03	3	.03	3	.03	3	.03
4	.04	4	.04	4	.04	4	.04
5	.06	5	.06	5	.06	5	.06
6	.07	6	.07	6	.07	6	.07
7	.08	7	.08	7	.08	7	.08
8	.09	8	.09	8	.09	8	.09
9	.10	9	.10	9	.10	9	.10
10	.12	10	.12	10	.12	10	.12
20	.24	20	.24	20	.24	20	.24
30	.36	30	.36	30	.36	30	.36
40	.48	40	.48	40	.48	40	.48
50	.60	50	.60	50	.60	50	.60
60	.72	60	.72	60	.72	60	.72
70	.84	70	.84	70	.84	70	.84
80	.96	80	.96	80	.96	80	.96
90	1.08	90	1.08	90	1.08	90	1.08
100	1.20	100	1.20	100	1.20	100	1.20
200	2.40	200	2.40	200	2.41	200	2.41
300	3.60	300	3.60	300	3.61	300	3.62
400	4.80	400	4.81	400	4.82	400	4.83
500	6.00	500	6.01	500	6.02	500	6.03
600	7.20	600	7.21	600	7.23	600	7.24
700	8.40	700	8.41	700	8.43	700	8.45
800	9.60	800	9.62	800	9.64	800	9.66
900	10.80	900	10.82	900	10.84	900	10.86
1000	12.00	1000	12.02	1000	12.05	1000	12.07
1100	13.20	1100	13.22	1100	13.25	1100	13.28
1200	14.40	1200	14.43	1200	14.46	1200	14.49
1300	15.60	1300	15.63	1300	15.66	1300	15.69
1400	16.80	1400	16.83	1400	16.87	1400	16.90
1500	18.00	1500	18.03	1500	18.07	1500	18.11
1600	19.20	1600	19.24	1600	19.28	1600	19.32
1700	20.40	1700	20.44	1700	20.48	1700	20.52
1800	21.60	1800	21.64	1800	21.69	1800	21.73
1900	22.80	1900	22.84	1900	22.89	1900	22.94
2000	24.00	2000	24.05	2000	24.10	2000	24.15
2100	25.20	2100	25.25	2100	25.30	2100	25.35
2200	26.40	2200	26.45	2200	26.51	2200	26.56
2300	27.60	2300	27.65	2300	27.71	2300	27.77
2400	28.80	2400	28.86	2400	28.92	2400	28.98
2500	30.00	2500	30.06	2500	30.12	2500	30.18
2600	31.20	2600	31.26	2600	31.33	2600	31.39
2700	32.40	2700	32.46	2700	32.53	2700	32.60
2800	33.60	2800	33.67	2800	33.74	2800	33.81
2900	34.80	2900	34.87	2900	34.94	2900	35.01
3000	36.00	3000	36.07	3000	36.15	3000	36.22
3100	37.20	3100	37.27	3100	37.35	3100	37.43
3200	38.40	3200	38.48	3200	38.56	3200	38.64
3300	39.60	3300	39.68	3300	39.76	3300	39.84
3400	40.80	3400	40.88	3400	40.97	3400	41.05
3500	42.00	3500	42.08	3500	42.17	3500	42.26
3600	43.20	3600	43.29	3600	43.38	3600	43.47
3700	44.40	3700	44.49	3700	44.58	3700	44.67
3800	45.60	3800	45.69	3800	45.79	3800	45.88
3900	46.80	3900	46.89	3900	46.99	3900	47.09
4000	48.00	4000	48.10	4000	48.20	4000	48.30

\$1.21		\$1.21¼		\$1.21½		1.21¾	
Lbs.	Amt.	Lbs.	Amt.	Lbs.	Amt.	Lbs.	Amt.
1	\$ .01	1	\$ .01	1	\$ .01	1	\$ .01
2	.02	2	.02	2	.02	2	.02
3	.03	3	.03	3	.03	3	.03
4	.04	4	.04	4	.04	4	.04
5	.06	5	.06	5	.06	5	.06
6	.07	6	.07	6	.07	6	.07
7	.08	7	.08	7	.08	7	.08
8	.09	8	.09	8	.09	8	.09
9	.10	9	.10	9	.10	9	.10
10	.12	10	.12	10	.12	10	.12
20	.24	20	.24	20	.24	20	.24
30	.36	30	.36	30	.36	30	.36
40	.48	40	.48	40	.48	40	.48
50	.60	50	.60	50	.60	50	.60
60	.72	60	.72	60	.72	60	.73
70	.84	70	.84	70	.85	70	.85
80	.96	80	.97	80	.97	80	.97
90	1.08	90	1 09	90	1.09	90	1.09
100	1.21	100	1.21	100	1.21	100	1.21
200	2.42	200	2.42	200	2.43	200	2.43
300	3.63	300	3.63	300	3.64	300	3.65
400	4.84	400	4.85	400	4.86	400	4.87
500	6.05	500	6.06	500	6.07	500	6.08
600	7.26	600	7.27	600	7.29	600	7.30
700	8.47	700	8.48	700	8.50	700	8.52
800	9.68	800	9.70	800	9.72	800	9.74
900	10.89	900	10.91	900	10.93	900	10.95
1000	12.10	1000	12.12	1000	12.15	1000	12.17
1100	13.31	1100	13.33	1100	13.36	1100	13.39
1200	14.52	1200	14.55	1200	14.58	1200	14.61
1300	15.73	1300	15.76	1300	15.79	1300	15.82
1400	16.94	1400	16.97	1400	17.01	1400	17.04
1500	18.15	1500	18.18	1500	18.22	1500	18.26
1600	19.36	1600	19.40	1600	19.44	1600	19.48
1700	20.57	1700	20.61	1700	20.65	1700	20.69
1800	21.78	1800	21.82	1800	21.87	1800	21.91
1900	22.99	1900	23.03	1900	23.08	1900	23.13
2000	24.20	2000	24.25	2000	24.30	2000	24.35
2100	25.41	2100	25.46	2100	25.51	2100	25.56
2200	26.62	2200	26.67	2200	26.73	2200	26.78
2300	27.83	2300	27.88	2300	27.94	2300	28.00
2400	29.04	2400	29.10	2400	29.16	2400	29.22
2500	30.25	2500	30.31	2500	30.37	2500	30.43
2600	31.46	2600	31.52	2600	31.59	2600	31.65
2700	32.67	2700	32.73	2700	32.80	2700	32.87
2800	33.88	2800	33.95	2800	34.02	2800	34.09
2900	35.09	2900	35.16	2900	35.23	2900	35.30
3000	36.30	3000	36.37	3000	36.45	3000	36.52
3100	37.51	3100	37.58	3100	37.66	3100	37.74
3200	38.72	3200	38.80	3200	38.88	3200	38.96
3300	39.93	3300	40.01	3300	40.09	3300	40.17
3400	41.14	3400	41.22	3400	41.31	3400	41.39
3500	42.35	3500	42.43	3500	42.52	3500	42.61
3600	43.56	3600	43.65	3600	43.74	3600	43.83
3700	44.77	3700	44.86	3700	44.95	3700	45.04
3800	45.98	3800	46.07	3800	46.17	3800	46.26
3900	47.19	3900	47.28	3900	47.38	3900	47.48
4000	48.40	4000	48.50	4000	48.60	4000	48.70

$1.22		$1.22¼		$1.22½		1.22¾	
Lbs.	Amt.	Lbs.	Amt.	Lbs.	Amt.	Lbs.	Amt.
1	$ .01	1	$ .01	1	$ .01	1	$ .01
2	.02	2	.02	2	.02	2	.02
3	.03	3	.03	3	.03	3	.03
4	.04	4	.04	4	.04	4	.04
5	.06	5	.06	5	.06	5	.06
6	.07	6	.07	6	.07	6	.07
7	.08	7	.08	7	.08	7	.08
8	.09	8	.09	8	.09	8	.09
9	.10	9	.11	9	.11	9	.11
10	.12	10	.12	10	.12	10	.12
20	.24	20	.24	20	.24	20	.24
30	.36	30	.36	30	.36	30	.36
40	.48	40	.48	40	.49	40	.49
50	.61	50	.61	50	.61	50	.61
60	.73	60	.73	60	.73	60	.73
70	.85	70	.85	70	.85	70	.85
80	.97	80	.97	80	.98	80	.98
90	1 09	90	1.10	90	1.10	90	1.10
100	1.22	100	1.22	100	1.22	100	1.22
200	2.44	200	2.44	200	2.45	200	2.45
300	3.66	300	3.66	300	3.67	300	3.68
400	4.88	400	4.89	400	4.90	400	4.91
500	6.10	500	6.11	500	6.12	500	6.13
600	7.32	600	7.33	600	7.35	600	7.36
700	8.54	700	8.55	700	8.57	700	8.59
800	9.76	800	9.78	800	9.80	800	9.82
900	10.98	900	11.00	900	11.02	900	11.04
1000	12.20	1000	12.22	1000	12.25	1000	12.27
1100	13.42	1100	13.44	1100	13.47	1100	13.50
1200	14.64	1200	14.67	1200	14.70	1200	14.73
1300	15.86	1300	15.89	1300	15.92	1300	15.95
1400	17.08	1400	17.11	1400	17.15	1400	17.18
1500	18.30	1500	18.33	1500	18.37	1500	18.41
1600	19.52	1600	19.56	1600	19.60	1600	19.64
1700	20.74	1700	20.78	1700	20.82	1700	20.86
1800	21.96	1800	22.00	1800	22.05	1800	22.09
1900	23.18	1900	23.22	1900	23.27	1900	23.32
2000	24.40	2000	24.45	2000	24.50	2000	24.55
2100	25.62	2100	25.67	2100	25.72	2100	25.77
2200	26.84	2200	26.89	2200	26.95	2200	27.00
2300	28.06	2300	28.11	2300	28.17	2300	28.23
2400	29.28	2400	29.34	2400	29.40	2400	29.46
2500	30.50	2500	30.56	2500	30.62	2500	30.68
2600	31.72	2600	31.78	2600	31.85	2600	31.91
2700	32.94	2700	33.00	2700	33.07	2700	33.14
2800	34.16	2800	34.23	2800	34.30	2800	34.37
2900	35.38	2900	35.45	2900	35.52	2900	35.59
3000	36.60	3000	36.67	3000	36.75	3000	36.82
3100	37.82	3100	37.89	3100	37.97	3100	38.05
3200	39.04	3200	39.12	3200	39.20	3200	39.28
3300	40.26	3300	40.34	3300	40.42	3300	40.50
3400	41.48	3400	41.56	3400	41.65	3400	41.73
3500	42.70	3500	42.78	3500	42.87	3500	42.96
3600	43.92	3600	44.01	3600	44.10	3600	44.19
3700	45.14	3700	45.23	3700	45.32	3700	45.41
3800	46.36	3800	46.45	3800	46.55	3800	46.64
3900	47.58	3900	47.67	3900	47.77	3900	47.87
4000	48.80	4000	48.90	4000	49.00	4000	49.10

\$1.23		\$1.23¼		\$1.23½		1.23¾	
Lbs.	Amt.	Lbs.	Amt.	Lbs.	Amt.	Lbs.	Amt.
1	\$ .01	1	\$ .01	1	\$ .01	1	\$ .01
2	.02	2	.02	2	.02	2	.02
3	.03	3	.03	3	.03	3	.03
4	.04	4	.04	4	.04	4	.04
5	.06	5	.06	5	.06	5	.06
6	.07	6	.07	6	.07	6	.07
7	.08	7	.08	7	.08	7	.08
8	.09	8	.09	8	.09	8	.09
9	.11	9	.11	9	.11	9	.11
10	.12	10	.12	10	.12	10	.12
20	.24	20	.24	20	.24	20	.24
30	.36	30	.36	30	.37	30	.37
40	.49	40	.49	40	.49	40	.49
50	.61	50	.61	50	.61	50	.61
60	.73	60	.73	60	.74	60	.74
70	.86	70	.86	70	.86	70	.86
80	.98	80	.98	80	.98	80	.99
90	1.10	90	1.10	90	1.11	90	1.11
100	1.23	100	1.23	100	1.23	100	1.23
200	2.46	200	2.46	200	2.47	200	2.47
300	3.69	300	3.69	300	3.70	300	3.71
400	4.92	400	4.93	400	4.94	400	4.95
500	6.15	500	6.16	500	6.17	500	6.18
600	7.38	600	7.39	600	7.41	600	7.42
700	8.61	700	8.62	700	8.64	700	8.66
800	9.84	800	9.86	800	9.88	800	9.90
900	11.07	900	11.09	900	11.11	900	11.13
1000	12.30	1000	12.32	1000	12.35	1000	12.37
1100	13.53	1100	13.55	1100	13.58	1100	13.61
1200	14.76	1200	14.79	1200	14.82	1200	14.85
1300	15.99	1300	16.02	1300	16.05	1300	16.08
1400	17.22	1400	17.25	1400	17.29	1400	17.32
1500	18.45	1500	18.48	1500	18.52	1500	18.56
1600	19.68	1600	19.72	1600	19.76	1600	19.80
1700	20.91	1700	20.95	1700	20.99	1700	21.03
1800	22.14	1800	22.18	1800	22.23	1800	22.27
1900	23.37	1900	23.41	1900	23.46	1900	23.51
2000	24.60	2000	24.65	2000	24.70	2000	24.75
2100	25.83	2100	25.88	2100	25.93	2100	25.98
2200	27.06	2200	27.11	2200	27.17	2200	27.22
2300	28.29	2300	28.34	2300	28.40	2300	28.46
2400	29.52	2400	29.58	2400	29.64	2400	29.70
2500	30.75	2500	30.81	2500	30.87	2500	30.93
2600	31.98	2600	32.04	2600	32.11	2600	32.17
2700	33.21	2700	33.27	2700	33.34	2700	33.41
2800	34.44	2800	34.51	2800	34.58	2800	34.65
2900	35.67	2900	35.74	2900	35.81	2900	35.88
3000	36.90	3000	36.97	3000	37.05	3000	37.12
3100	38.13	3100	38.20	3100	38.28	3100	38.36
3200	39.36	3200	39.44	3200	39.52	3200	39.60
3300	40.59	3300	40.67	3300	40.75	3300	40.83
3400	41.82	3400	41.90	3400	41.99	3400	42.07
3500	43.05	3500	43.13	3500	43.22	3500	43.31
3600	44.28	3600	44.37	3600	44.46	3600	44.55
3700	45.51	3700	45.60	3700	45.69	3700	45.78
3800	46.74	3800	46.83	3800	46.93	3800	47.02
3900	47.97	3900	48.06	3900	48.16	3900	48.26
4000	49.20	4000	49.30	4000	49.40	4000	49.50

\$1.24		\$1.24¼		\$1.24½		1.24¾	
Lbs.	Amt.	Lbs.	Amt.	Lbs.	Amt.	Lbs.	Amt.
1	\$ .01	1	\$ .01	1	\$ .01	1	\$ .01
2	.02	2	.02	2	.02	2	.02
3	.03	3	.03	3	.03	3	.03
4	.04	4	.04	4	.04	4	.04
5	.06	5	.06	5	.06	5	.06
6	.07	6	.07	6	.07	6	.07
7	.08	7	.08	7	.08	7	.08
8	.09	8	.09	8	.09	8	.09
9	.11	9	.11	9	.11	9	.11
10	.12	10	.12	10	.12	10	.12
20	.24	20	.24	20	.24	20	.24
30	.37	30	.37	30	.37	30	.37
40	.49	40	.49	40	.49	40	.49
50	.62	50	.62	50	.62	50	.62
60	.74	60	.74	60	.74	60	.74
70	.86	70	.86	70	.87	70	.87
80	.99	80	.99	80	.99	80	.99
90	1.11	90	1.11	90	1.11	90	1.12
100	1.24	100	1.24	100	1.24	100	1.24
200	2.48	200	2.48	200	2.49	200	2.49
300	3.72	300	3.72	300	3.73	300	3.74
400	4.96	400	4.97	400	4.98	400	4.98
500	6.20	500	6.21	500	6.22	500	6.23
600	7.44	600	7.45	600	7.47	600	7.48
700	8.68	700	8.69	700	8.71	700	8.73
800	9.92	800	9.94	800	9.96	800	9.98
900	11.16	900	11.18	900	11.20	900	11.22
1000	12.40	1000	12.42	1000	12.45	1000	12.47
1100	13.64	1100	13.66	1100	13.69	1100	13.72
1200	14.88	1200	14.91	1200	14.94	1200	14.97
1300	16.12	1300	16.15	1300	16.18	1300	16.21
1400	17.36	1400	17.39	1400	17.43	1400	17.46
1500	18.60	1500	18.63	1500	18.67	1500	18.71
1600	19.84	1600	19.88	1600	19.92	1600	19.96
1700	21.08	1700	21.12	1700	21.16	1700	21.20
1800	22.32	1800	22.36	1800	22.41	1800	22.45
1900	23.56	1900	23.60	1900	23.65	1900	23.70
2000	24.80	2000	24.85	2000	24.90	2000	24.95
2100	26.04	2100	26.09	2100	26.14	2100	26.19
2200	27.28	2200	27.33	2200	27.39	2200	27.44
2300	28.52	2300	28.57	2300	28.63	2300	28.69
2400	29.76	2400	29.82	2400	29.88	2400	29.94
2500	31.00	2500	31.06	2500	31.12	2500	31.18
2600	32.24	2600	32.30	2600	32.37	2600	32.43
2700	33.48	2700	33.54	2700	33.61	2700	33.68
2800	34.72	2800	34.79	2800	34.86	2800	34.93
2900	35.96	2900	36.03	2900	36.10	2900	36.17
3000	37.20	3000	37.27	3000	37.35	3000	37.42
3100	38.44	3100	38.51	3100	38.59	3100	38.67
3200	39.68	3200	39.76	3200	39.84	3200	39.92
3300	40.92	3300	41.00	3300	41.08	3300	41.16
3400	42.16	3400	42.24	3400	42.33	3400	42.41
3500	43.40	3500	43.48	3500	43.57	3500	43.66
3600	44.64	3600	44.73	3600	44.82	3600	44.91
3700	45.88	3700	45.97	3700	46.06	3700	46.15
3800	47.12	3800	47.21	3800	47.31	3800	47.40
3900	48.36	3900	48.45	3900	48.55	3900	48.65
4000	49.60	4000	49.70	4000	49.80	4000	49.90

$1.25		$1.25¼		$1.25½		1.25¾	
Lbs.	Amt.	Lbs.	Amt.	Lbs.	Amt.	Lbs.	Amt.
1	$ .01	1	$ .01	1	$ .01	1	$ .01
2	.02	2	.02	2	.02	2	.02
3	.03	3	.03	3	.03	3	.03
4	.05	4	.05	4	.05	4	.05
5	.06	5	.06	5	.06	5	.06
6	.07	6	.07	6	.07	6	.07
7	.08	7	.08	7	.08	7	.08
8	.10	8	.10	8	.10	8	.10
9	.11	9	.11	9	.11	9	.11
10	.12	10	.12	10	.12	10	.12
20	.25	20	.25	20	.25	20	.25
30	.37	30	.37	30	.37	30	.37
40	.50	40	.50	40	.50	40	.50
50	.62	50	.62	50	.62	50	.62
60	.75	60	.75	60	.75	60	.75
70	.87	70	.87	70	.87	70	.88
80	1.00	80	1.00	80	1.00	80	1.00
90	1.12	90	1.12	90	1.12	90	1.13
100	1.25	100	1.25	100	1.25	100	1.25
200	2.50	200	2.50	200	2.51	200	2.51
300	3.75	300	3.75	300	3.76	300	3.77
400	5.00	400	5.01	400	5.02	400	5.03
500	6.25	500	6.26	500	6.27	500	6.28
600	7.50	600	7.51	600	7.53	600	7.54
700	8.75	700	8.76	700	8.78	700	8.80
800	10.00	800	10.02	800	10.04	800	10.06
900	11.25	900	11.27	900	11.29	900	11.31
1000	12.50	1000	12.52	1000	12.55	1000	12.57
1100	13.75	1100	13.77	1100	13.80	1100	13.83
1200	15.00	1200	15.03	1200	15.06	1200	15.09
1300	16.25	1300	16.28	1300	16.31	1300	16.34
1400	17.50	1400	17.53	1400	17.57	1400	17.60
1500	18.75	1500	18.78	1500	18.82	1500	18.86
1600	20.00	1600	20.04	1600	20.08	1600	20.12
1700	21.25	1700	21.29	1700	21.33	1700	21.37
1800	22.50	1800	22.54	1800	22.59	1800	22.63
1900	23.75	1900	23.79	1900	23.84	1900	23.89
2000	25.00	2000	25.05	2000	25.10	2000	25.15
2100	26.25	2100	26.30	2100	26.35	2100	26.40
2200	27.50	2200	27.55	2200	27.61	2200	27.66
2300	28.75	2300	28.80	2300	28.86	2300	28.92
2400	30.00	2400	30.06	2400	30.12	2400	30.18
2500	31.25	2500	31.31	2500	31.37	2500	31.43
2600	32.50	2600	32.56	2600	32.63	2600	32.69
2700	33.75	2700	33.81	2700	33.88	2700	33.95
2800	35.00	2800	35.07	2800	35.14	2800	35.21
2900	36.25	2900	36.32	2900	36.39	2900	36.46
3000	37.50	3000	37.57	3000	37.65	3000	37.72
3100	38.75	3100	38.82	3100	38.90	3100	38.98
3200	40.00	3200	40.08	3200	40.16	3200	40.24
3300	41.25	3300	41.33	3300	41.41	3300	41.49
3400	42.50	3400	42.58	3400	42.67	3400	42.75
3500	43.75	3500	43.83	3500	43.92	3500	44.01
3600	45.00	3600	45.09	3600	45.18	3600	45.27
3700	46.25	3700	46.34	3700	46.43	3700	46.52
3800	47.50	3800	47.59	3800	47.69	3800	47.78
3900	48.75	3900	48.84	3900	48.94	3900	49.04
4000	50.00	4000	50.10	4000	50.20	4000	50.30

\$1.26		\$1.26¼		\$1.26½		1.26¾	
Lbs.	Amt.	Lbs.	Amt.	Lbs.	Amt.	Lbs.	Amt.
1	\$ .01	1	\$ .01	1	\$ .01	1	\$ .01
2	.02	2	.02	2	.02	2	.02
3	.03	3	.03	3	.03	3	.03
4	.05	4	.05	4	.05	4	.05
5	.06	5	.06	5	.06	5	.06
6	.07	6	.07	6	.07	6	.07
7	.08	7	.08	7	.08	7	.08
8	.10	8	.10	8	.10	8	.10
9	.11	9	.11	9	.11	9	.11
10	.12	10	.12	10	.12	10	.12
20	.25	20	.25	20	.25	20	.25
30	.37	30	.37	30	.37	30	.38
40	.50	40	.50	40	.50	40	.50
50	.63	50	.63	50	.63	50	.63
60	.75	60	.75	60	.75	60	.76
70	.88	70	.88	70	.88	70	.88
80	1.00	80	1.01	80	1.01	80	1.01
90	1.13	90	1.13	90	1.13	90	1.14
100	1.26	100	1.26	100	1.26	100	1.26
200	2.52	200	2.52	200	2.53	200	2.53
300	3.78	300	3.78	300	3.79	300	3.80
400	5.04	400	5.05	400	5.06	400	5.07
500	6.30	500	6.31	500	6.32	500	6.33
600	7.56	600	7.57	600	7.59	600	7.60
700	8.82	700	8.83	700	8.85	700	8.87
800	10.08	800	10.10	800	10.12	800	10.14
900	11.34	900	11.36	900	11.38	900	11.40
1000	12.60	1000	12.62	1000	12.65	1000	12.67
1100	13.86	1100	13.88	1100	13.91	1100	13.94
1200	15.12	1200	15.15	1200	15.18	1200	15.21
1300	16.38	1300	16.41	1300	16.44	1300	16.47
1400	17.64	1400	17.67	1400	17.71	1400	17.74
1500	18.90	1500	18.93	1500	18.97	1500	19.01
1600	20.16	1600	20.20	1600	20.24	1600	20.28
1700	21.42	1700	21.46	1700	21.50	1700	21.54
1800	22.68	1800	22.72	1800	22.77	1800	22.81
1900	23.94	1900	23.98	1900	24.03	1900	24.08
2000	25.20	2000	25.25	2000	25.30	2000	25.35
2100	26.46	2100	26.51	2100	26.56	2100	26.61
2200	27.72	2200	27.77	2200	27.83	2200	27.88
2300	28.98	2300	29.03	2300	29.09	2300	29.15
2400	30.24	2400	30.30	2400	30.36	2400	30.42
2500	31.50	2500	31.56	2500	31.62	2500	31.68
2600	32.76	2600	32.82	2600	32.89	2600	32.95
2700	34.02	2700	34.08	2700	34.15	2700	34.22
2800	35.28	2800	35.35	2800	35.42	2800	35.49
2900	36.54	2900	36.61	2900	36.68	2900	36.75
3000	37.80	3000	37.87	3000	37.95	3000	38.02
3100	39.06	3100	39.13	3100	39.21	3100	39.29
3200	40.32	3200	40.40	3200	40.48	3200	40.56
3300	41.58	3300	41.66	3300	41.74	3300	41.82
3400	42.84	3400	42.92	3400	43.01	3400	43.09
3500	44.10	3500	44.18	3500	44.27	3500	44.36
3600	45.36	3600	45.45	3600	45.54	3600	45.63
3700	46.62	3700	46.71	3700	46.80	3700	46.89
3800	47.88	3800	47.97	3800	48.07	3800	48.16
3900	49.14	3900	49.23	3900	49.23	3900	49.33
4000	50.40	4000	50.50	4000	50.60	4000	50.70

\$1.27		\$1.27¼		\$1.27½		1.27¾	
Lbs.	Amt.	Lbs.	Amt.	Lbs.	Amt.	Lbs.	Amt.
1	\$ .01	1	\$ .01	1	\$ .01	1	\$ .01
2	.02	2	.02	2	.02	2	.02
3	.03	3	.03	3	.03	3	.03
4	.05	4	.05	4	.05	4	.05
5	.06	5	.06	5	.06	5	.06
6	.07	6	.07	6	.07	6	.07
7	.08	7	.08	7	.08	7	.08
8	.10	8	.10	8	.10	8	.10
9	.11	9	.11	9	.11	9	.11
10	.12	10	.12	10	.12	10	.12
20	.25	20	.25	20	.25	20	.25
30	.38	30	.38	30	.38	30	.38
40	.50	40	.50	40	.51	40	.51
50	.63	50	.63	50	.63	50	.63
60	.76	60	.76	60	.76	60	.76
70	.88	70	.89	70	.89	70	.89
80	1.01	80	1.01	80	1.02	80	1.02
90	1.14	90	1.14	90	1.14	90	1.14
100	1.27	100	1.27	100	1.27	100	1.27
200	2.54	200	2.54	200	2.55	200	2.55
300	3.81	300	3.81	300	3.82	300	3.83
400	5.08	400	5.09	400	5.10	400	5.11
500	6.35	500	6.36	500	6.37	500	6.38
600	7.62	600	7.63	600	7.65	600	7.66
700	8.89	700	8.90	700	8.92	700	8.94
800	10.16	800	10.18	800	10.20	800	10.22
900	11.43	900	11.45	900	11.47	900	11.49
1000	12.70	1000	12.72	1000	12.75	1000	12.77
1100	13.97	1100	13.99	1100	14.02	1100	14.05
1200	15.24	1200	15.27	1200	15.30	1200	15.33
1300	16.51	1300	16.54	1300	16.57	1300	16.60
1400	17.78	1400	17.81	1400	17.85	1400	17.88
1500	19.05	1500	19.08	1500	19.12	1500	19.16
1600	20.32	1600	20.36	1600	20.40	1600	20.44
1700	21.59	1700	21.63	1700	21.67	1700	21.71
1800	22.86	1800	22.90	1800	22.95	1800	22.99
1900	24.13	1900	24.17	1900	24.22	1900	24.27
2000	25.40	2000	25.45	2000	25.50	2000	25.55
2100	26.67	2100	26.72	2100	26.77	2100	26.82
2200	27.94	2200	27.99	2200	28.05	2200	28.10
2300	29.21	2300	29.26	2300	29.32	2300	29.38
2400	30.48	2400	30.54	2400	30.60	2400	30.66
2500	31.75	2500	31.81	2500	31.87	2500	31.93
2600	33.02	2600	33.08	2600	33.15	2600	33.21
2700	34.29	2700	34.35	2700	34.42	2700	34.49
2800	35.56	2800	35.63	2800	35.70	2800	35.77
2900	36.83	2900	36.90	2900	36.97	2900	37.04
3000	38.10	3000	38.18	3000	38.26	3000	38.33
3100	39.37	3100	39.44	3100	39.52	3100	39.60
3200	40.64	3200	40.72	3200	40.80	3200	40.88
3300	41.91	3300	41.99	3300	42.07	3300	42.15
3400	43.18	3400	43.26	3400	43.35	3400	43.43
3500	44.45	3500	44.53	3500	44.62	3500	44.71
3600	45.72	3600	45.81	3600	45.90	3600	45.99
3700	46.99	3700	47.08	3700	47.17	3700	47.26
3800	48.26	3800	48.35	3800	48.45	3800	48.54
3900	49.53	3900	49.62	3900	49.72	3900	49.82
4000	50.80	4000	50.90	4000	51.00	4000	51.10

$1.28		$1.28¼		$1.28½		1.28¾	
Lbs.	Amt.	Lbs.	Amt.	Lbs.	Amt.	Lbs.	Amt.
1	$ .01	1	$ .01	1	$ .01	1	$ .01
2	.02	2	.02	2	.02	2	.02
3	.03	3	.03	3	.03	3	.03
4	.05	4	.05	4	.05	4	.05
5	.06	5	.06	5	.06	5	.06
6	.07	6	.07	6	.07	6	.07
7	.08	7	.08	7	.08	7	.09
8	.10	8	.10	8	.10	8	.10
9	.11	9	.11	9	.11	9	.11
10	.12	10	.12	10	.12	10	.12
20	.25	20	.25	20	.25	20	.25
30	.38	30	.38	30	.38	30	.38
40	.51	40	.51	40	.51	40	.51
50	.64	50	.64	50	.64	50	.64
60	.76	60	.76	60	.77	60	.77
70	.89	70	.89	70	.89	70	.90
80	1.02	80	1.02	80	1.02	80	1.03
90	1.15	90	1.15	90	1.15	90	1.16
100	1.28	100	1.28	100	1.28	100	1.28
200	2.56	200	2.56	200	2.57	200	2.57
300	3.84	300	3.84	300	3.85	300	3.86
400	5.12	400	5.13	400	5.14	400	5.15
500	6.40	500	6.41	500	6.42	500	6.43
600	7.68	600	7.69	600	7.71	600	7.72
700	8.96	700	8.97	700	8.99	700	9.01
800	10.24	800	10.26	800	10.28	800	10.30
900	11.52	900	11.54	900	11.56	900	11.58
1000	12.80	1000	12.82	1000	12.85	1000	12.87
1100	14.08	1100	14.10	1100	14.13	1100	14.16
1200	15.36	1200	15.39	1200	15.42	1200	15.45
1300	16.64	1300	16.67	1300	16.70	1300	16.73
1400	17.92	1400	17.95	1400	17.99	1400	18.02
1500	19.20	1500	19.23	1500	19.27	1500	19.31
1600	20.48	1600	20.52	1600	20.56	1600	20.60
1700	21.76	1700	21.80	1700	21.84	1700	21.88
1800	23.04	1800	23.08	1800	23.13	1800	23.17
1900	24.32	1900	24.36	1900	24.41	1900	24.46
2000	25.60	2000	25.65	2000	25.70	2000	25.75
2100	26.88	2100	26.93	2100	26.98	2100	27.03
2200	28.16	2200	28.21	2200	28.27	2200	28.32
2300	29.44	2300	29.49	2300	29.55	2300	29.61
2400	30.72	2400	30.78	2400	30.84	2400	30.90
2500	32.00	2500	32.06	2500	32.12	2500	32.18
2600	33.28	2600	33.34	2600	33.41	2600	33.47
2700	34.56	2700	34.62	2700	34.69	2700	34.76
2800	35.84	2800	35.91	2800	35.98	2800	36.05
2900	37.12	2900	37.19	2900	37.26	2900	37.33
3000	38.40	3000	38.47	3000	38.55	3000	38.62
3100	39.68	3100	39.75	3100	39.83	3100	39.91
3200	40.96	3200	41.04	3200	41.12	3200	41.20
3300	42.24	3300	42.32	3300	42.40	3300	42.48
3400	43.52	3400	43.60	3400	43.69	3400	43.77
3500	44.80	3500	44.88	3500	44.97	3500	45.06
3600	46.08	3600	46.17	3600	46.26	3600	46.35
3700	47.36	3700	47.45	3700	47.54	3700	47.63
3800	48.64	3800	48.73	3800	48.83	3800	48.92
3900	49.92	3900	50.01	3900	50.11	3900	50.21
4000	51.20	4000	51.30	4000	51.40	4000	51.50

$1.29		$1.29¼		$1.29½		1.29¾	
Lbs.	Amt.	Lbs.	Amt.	Lbs.	Amt.	Lbs.	Amt.
1	$ .01	1	$ .01	1	$ .01	1	$ .01
2	.02	2	.02	2	.02	2	.02
3	.03	3	.03	3	.03	3	.03
4	.05	4	.05	4	.05	4	.05
5	.06	5	.06	5	.06	5	.06
6	.07	6	.07	6	.07	6	.07
7	.09	7	.09	7	.09	7	.09
8	.10	8	.10	8	.10	8	.10
9	.11	9	.11	9	.11	9	.11
10	.12	10	.12	10	.12	10	.12
20	.25	20	.25	20	.25	20	.25
30	.38	30	.38	30	.38	30	.38
40	.51	40	.51	40	.51	40	.51
50	.64	50	.64	50	.64	50	.64
60	.77	60	.77	60	.77	60	.77
70	.90	70	.90	70	.90	70	.90
80	1.03	80	1.03	80	1.03	80	1.03
90	1.16	90	1.16	90	1.16	90	1.16
100	1.29	100	1.29	100	1.29	100	1.29
200	2.58	200	2.58	200	2.59	200	2.59
300	3.87	300	3.87	300	3.88	300	3.89
400	5.16	400	5.17	400	5.18	400	5.19
500	6.45	500	6.46	500	6.47	500	6.48
600	7.74	600	7.75	600	7.77	600	7.78
700	9.03	700	9.04	700	9.06	700	9.08
800	10.32	800	10.34	800	10.36	800	10.38
900	11.61	900	11.63	900	11.65	900	11.67
1000	12.90	1000	12.92	1000	12.95	1000	12.97
1100	14.19	1100	14.21	1100	14.24	1100	14.27
1200	15.48	1200	15.51	1200	15.54	1200	15.57
1300	16.77	1300	16.80	1300	16.83	1300	16.86
1400	18.06	1400	18.09	1400	18.13	1400	18.16
1500	19.35	1500	19.38	1500	19.42	1500	19.46
1600	20.64	1600	20.68	1600	20.72	1600	20.76
1700	21.93	1700	21.97	1700	22.01	1700	22.05
1800	23.22	1800	23.26	1800	23.31	1800	23.35
1900	24.51	1900	24.55	1900	24.60	1900	24.65
2000	25.80	2000	25.85	2000	25.90	2000	25.95
2100	27.09	2100	27.14	2100	27.19	2100	27.24
2200	28.38	2200	28.43	2200	28.49	2200	28.34
2300	29.67	2300	29.72	2300	29.78	2300	29.84
2400	30.96	2400	31.02	2400	31.08	2400	31.14
2500	32.25	2500	32.31	2500	32.37	2500	32.43
2600	33.54	2600	33.60	2600	33.67	2600	33.73
2700	34.83	2700	34.89	2700	34.96	2700	35.03
2800	36.12	2800	36.19	2800	36.26	2800	36.33
2900	37.41	2900	37.48	2900	37.55	2900	37.62
3000	38.70	3000	38.77	3000	38.85	3000	38.92
3100	39.99	3100	40.06	3100	40.14	3100	40.22
3200	41.28	3200	41.36	3200	41.44	3200	41.52
3300	42.57	3300	42.65	3300	42.73	3300	42.81
3400	43.86	3400	43.94	3400	44.03	3400	44.11
3500	45.15	3500	45.23	3500	45.32	3500	45.41
3600	46.44	3600	46.53	3600	46.62	3600	46.71
3700	47.73	3700	47.82	3700	47.91	3700	48.00
3800	49.02	3800	49.11	3800	49.21	3800	49.30
3900	50.31	3900	50.40	3900	50.50	3900	50.60
4000	51.60	4000	51.70	4000	51.80	4000	51.90

$1.30		$1.30¼		$1.30½		1.30¾	
Lbs.	Amt.	Lbs.	Amt.	Lbs.	Amt.	Lbs.	Amt.
1	$ .01	1	$ .01	1	$ .01	1	$ .01
2	.02	2	.02	2	.02	2	.02
3	.03	3	.03	3	.03	3	.03
4	.05	4	.05	4	.05	4	.05
5	.06	5	.06	5	.06	5	.06
6	.07	6	.07	6	.07	6	.07
7	.09	7	.09	7	.09	7	.09
8	.10	8	.10	8	.10	8	.10
9	.11	9	.11	9	.11	9	.11
10	.13	10	.13	10	.13	10	.13
20	.26	20	.26	20	.26	20	.26
30	.39	30	.39	30	.39	30	.39
40	.52	40	.52	40	.52	40	.52
50	.65	50	.65	50	.65	50	.65
60	.78	60	.78	60	.78	60	.78
70	.91	70	.91	70	.91	70	.91
80	1.04	80	1.04	80	1.04	80	1.04
90	1.17	90	1.17	90	1.17	90	1.17
100	1.30	100	1.30	100	1.30	100	1.30
200	2.60	200	2.60	200	2.61	200	2.61
300	3.90	300	3.90	300	3.91	300	3.92
400	5.20	400	5.21	400	5.22	400	5.23
500	6.50	500	6.51	500	6.52	500	6.53
600	7.80	600	7.81	600	7.83	600	7.84
700	9.10	700	9.11	700	9.13	700	9.15
800	10.40	800	10.42	800	10.44	800	10.46
900	11.70	900	11.72	900	11.74	900	11.76
1000	13.00	1000	13.02	1000	13.05	1000	13.07
1100	14.30	1100	14.32	1100	14.35	1100	14.38
1200	15.60	1200	15.63	1200	15.66	1200	15.69
1300	16.90	1300	16.93	1300	16.96	1300	16.99
1400	18.20	1400	18.23	1400	18.27	1400	18.30
1500	19.50	1500	19.53	1500	19.57	1500	19.61
1600	20.80	1600	20.84	1600	20.88	1600	20.92
1700	22.10	1700	22.14	1700	22.18	1700	22.22
1800	23.40	1800	23.44	1800	23.49	1800	23.53
1900	24.70	1900	24.74	1900	24.79	1900	24.84
2000	26.00	2000	26.05	2000	26.10	2000	26.15
2100	27.30	2100	27.35	2100	27.40	2100	27.45
2200	28.60	2200	28.65	2200	28.71	2200	28.76
2300	29.90	2300	29.95	2300	30.01	2300	30.07
2400	31.20	2400	31.26	2400	31.32	2400	31.38
2500	32.50	2500	32.56	2500	32.62	2500	32.68
2600	33.80	2600	33.86	2600	33.93	2600	33.99
2700	35.10	2700	35.16	2700	35.23	2700	35.30
2800	36.40	2800	36.47	2800	36.54	2800	36.61
2900	37.70	2900	37.77	2900	37.84	2900	37.91
3000	39.00	3000	39.07	3000	39.15	3000	39.22
3100	40.30	3100	40.37	3100	40.45	3100	40.53
3200	41.60	3200	41.68	3200	41.76	3200	41.84
3300	42.90	3300	42.98	3300	43.06	3300	43.14
3400	44.20	3400	44.28	3400	44.37	3400	44.45
3500	45.50	3500	45.58	3500	45.67	3500	45.76
3600	46.80	3600	46.89	3600	46.98	3600	47.07
3700	48.10	3700	48.19	3700	48.28	3700	48.37
3800	49.40	3800	49.49	3800	49.59	3800	49.68
3900	50.70	3900	50.79	3900	50.89	3900	50.99
4000	52.00	4000	52.10	4000	52.20	4000	52.30

CPSIA information can be obtained at www.ICGtesting.com
Printed in the USA
BVOW09s1430290615

406617BV00016B/145/P